Living
Water

Living *Water*

a creative resource for the Liturgy

Complete Resource Book
YEAR C

Susan Sayers

with Father Andrew Moore

Kevin Mayhew

First published in 2000 by
KEVIN MAYHEW LTD
Buxhall
Stowmarket
Suffolk IP14 3BW

0 1 2 3 4 5 6 7 8 9

ISBN 1 84003 513 7
Catalogue No. 1500340

The other titles in the *Living Water* series are		
Prayer of the Faithful	ISBN 1 84003 553 6	Cat. No. 1500355
Treasure Seekers	ISBN 1 84003 516 1	Cat. No. 1500341
Pearl Divers	ISBN 1 84003 515 3	Cat. No. 1500342
Gold Panners	ISBN 1 84003 514 5	Cat. No. 1500343

Cover photographs:
Family group – courtesy of SuperStock Photo Library
Background – courtesy of Images Colour Library Limited, London
Cover design by Jaquetta Sergeant
Edited by Katherine Laidler
Typesetting by Louise Selfe
Illustrations by Arthur Baker
Printed in Great Britain

FOREWORD

Living Water is designed to help you make the most of the possibilities of the three-year lectionary, particularly in parishes which are concerned to meet the needs of all ages and stages.

My aim is to spark ideas and start you off. The demands on those leading worship and preparing teaching are enormous, and I hope you will find here materials and suggestions which help take the strain and free you to enjoy the work of enabling people's faith to grow and of deepening their relationship with the living God.

As I was writing, I tried to keep these principles in mind:

- All-age worship needs to be just that, and not children's worship at which adults happen to be present.

- Different age groups need some teaching suited to their particular stage of development, but all benefit from studying the same passages of scripture on the same day. The whole parish is then able to grow together and share insights and discoveries.

- Separate children's ministry for part of the service is there to develop the children's faith now, and also to prepare them for taking a full part in your church's Sunday worship when they are older. Their age-appropriate worship and activities should aim to ease them gradually into full participation with the adults in church, rather than creating a completely separate culture which makes the transition difficult.

- We sell our children and young people short if we only teach them facts about our faith; what they need is to be introduced to a real relationship with God, in which the foundations are laid for life-long habits of prayer, study of the Bible and an openness to God's Spirit.

- We journey into faith, so all our worship and teaching must respect the diversity of stages reached, and the emotional and cultural luggage brought along. Any resource material should therefore be flexible, easily adapted, and accessible at a number of different levels.

- The cerebral and the academic approaches cherished by many in positions of leadership are not the only, nor necessarily the most effective ways to explore and express our faith! Unless we also make use of the senses and the emotions, we shall be shutting doors through which our God could reach the people he loves.

Let us worship the Lord in the beauty of holiness.

SUSAN SAYERS
with Father Andrew Moore

This book is dedicated to my family and friends,
whose encouraging support has been wonderful,
and to all those whose good ideas are included here for others to share.

ACKNOWLEDGEMENTS

The publishers wish to express their gratitude to the following for permission to reproduce their copyright material in this publication:

CopyCare, PO Box 77, Hailsham, East Sussex, BN27 3EF, for the text of *Open our eyes, Lord* © 1976 Maranatha! Music.

Make Way Music, PO Box 263, Croydon, CR9 5AP, UK, for *Lord, the light of your love (Shine, Jesus, Jesus, Shine)*.

Kingsway's Thankyou Music, PO Box 75, Eastbourne, East Sussex, BN23 6NW, for the text and music of *Waiting for your Spirit*.

All other material contained in this publication is © Kevin Mayhew Ltd.

CONTENTS

Complete programmes for the following special feasts, covering Years A, B and C, may be found in the *Living Water* Complete Resource Book for Year A. (Worksheets for the children and young people are included in the Treasure Seekers, Pearl Divers and Gold Panners books for Year A.)

Mary, Mother of God – 1 January
The Presentation of the Lord (Candlemas) – 2 February
Saint John the Baptist – 24 June
Saints Peter and Paul – 29 June
The Transfiguration of the Lord – 6 August
The Assumption – 15 August
The Triumph of the Holy Cross – 14 September
All Saints – 1 November
Feasts of the Dedication of a Church

How to use
this book

PLANNING

You can select from the week's material as much as you find useful for your particular needs on any one week, as all the ideas are independent of one another, although they are all linked to the weekly readings.

All-age worship is not about the entertainment business, nor is it child-centred worship, or 'watered-down' worship. Neither need it be noisy and extra-hassle worship. There are usually many other age groups represented in our churches as well as children and our aim must be to provide for the middle-aged and elderly as well as for the young, for the stranger as well as the regulars.

Since God is in a far better position to know the needs of your congregation than anyone, it is naturally essential to prepare for Sunday worship in prayer. I don't mean asking God to bless what we have already planned, but to spend time discerning God's priorities and listening, since he is tuned in to the needs of those who will be there. Think about gathering a group of all ages to commit themselves to this each week, either together in church or separately at an agreed time. All the ideas in this book and other resource books are only secondary to this prayerful preparation.

Each week is set out as follows:

Thought for the day

Use this on the weekly handout, or as an initial focus when starting your planning.

Reflection on the readings

There are ideas here for getting your mind going when sermon preparation jams. Or the reflection can be used for individual and group Bible study.

Discussion starters

These are provided for adult group work and could sometimes be used for adults in the sermon slot while toddlers, children and young people follow their own programmes. Small group work within a service is rarely contemplated, but it can be a valuable way of involving everyone, avoiding the automatic pilot syndrome, and bringing the readings to life.

Some churches have parents present during the children's liturgy; consider providing a parents' class within that programme for a short time as a way of reaching those who are wary of actually 'going to church'.

All-stage talk

In my experience the difference in faith stages is more important than the age differences, so these talks aim to present the teaching in ways that people of all ages and stages can relate to. There are so many ordinary experiences which are common to all of us and these can be used and enjoyed without anyone being excluded. Abstract thinking and reading skills are not necessarily common to all, but deep and abstract concepts can often be grasped if explained through concrete images, like three-dimensional parables.

In all these talks I want to encourage adaptation, so that the talks come across as fresh and owned by you, rather than another person's jacket, stiffly worn. Get the ideas, and then enjoy yourself!

All-age ideas

I have suggested particular worship ideas for each week, but here are some more general guidelines to use to get your own ideas flowing.

Dramatised readings

Having read and prayed the readings, I find it helps to imagine myself sitting in the congregation, seeing and hearing the readings creatively expressed. If I imagine I am a child, a young adult, an elderly person and so on, I am more likely to pick up on what *won't* be helpful, and what *will* really make me think.

- Have a narrator to read, and simply mime what is read. Anyone not involved in the action at any one time freezes in his/her last position, like 'statues'.

- Give individuals their words to say. During the narration the characters act their parts and speak their own words.

- Have one or two instruments (guitar and flute, for instance, or organ) to play quietly as a background to the reading.

- Use a few materials as props and costumes. They need not be elaborate, just enough to aid imagination.

- Use live or taped music and depict not only the actions, but also the atmosphere, through mime or dance. Keep it natural, simple and controlled, and do make sure all types and ages are involved.

- There may be times, not just Palm Sunday, for involving the whole congregation in the telling of a story, either by writing their words on the weekly sheet, or by displaying their words, noises and actions at appropriate places in the narration.

Acts of worship

Sometimes something very simple will speak deeply to people. As you prepare try to give the cerebral a break for a while, and listen to what the readings make you feel. Then translate this into some music, communal action (or stillness), which will help people respond to God with their hearts as well as their minds.

Church decoration

The church building speaks. Our churches are visited and admired by many, and it is important that visitors see evidence of the living church of today as well as the beauty of the past. During services the mind and heart can be steered quietly towards the message of the day by means of a particular flower arrangement, exhibition of pictures, display or banner.

If those who arrange the flowers so faithfully, week by week, have access to the *Thought for the day* and the *Reflection on the readings*, they will be able to express these themes in an arrangement.

Prayer of the Faithful

The main aim of those who lead the people's intercessions is to provide a climate for prayer, so that the congregation are not just listening passively, but are actively involved in the work of prayer. I suggest times of silence at each section, rather than pauses, so as to allow for this, and you could have music playing quietly during these times, open prayer or prayer clusters as well as individuals praying fervently together in the stillness of their Father's company.

During this time the young children can be praying through pictures, following a prayer trail, praying in pairs with an adult, or singing some quiet worship songs.

Music

Music, played or sung well, drawn from a range of traditions, always sensitive to the liturgy of the day or season and appropriate to the resources available, can provide a 'landscape for worship' in which people are helped to focus their attention on God, and lift their hearts to him.

Both recorded and live music can be used in worship to help people settle to an inner stillness, give them space for reflection, and provide the environment for spiritual attentiveness. Use whatever gifts your congregation offers; organ music is lovely but need not be used exclusively. Consider a small ensemble of string and wind instruments with piano; a single instrument such as recorder, flute or trumpet; or a selection of percussion instruments such as shakers, triangles and bells. Many churches develop a music group of voices and instruments to provide a different sound for certain services each month. Welcome and involve young people and children, not necessarily as a separate group.

Choose recorded music from a wide range of traditions and styles, bearing in mind the people who are likely to be present. Keep a notebook handy to record titles of suitable pieces that you hear, and ask members of the congregation for their ideas.

There is now such a richness of material available that an attempt at an exhaustive list would be foolish and impractical. Whatever books you use at your parish, make the most of the choice they provide.

Treasure Seekers
3-5 year olds

I have included suggestions for a programme which picks up on some of the important truths of the weekly readings which form a foundation to build on. For the youngest children this teaching can slot into a general play session, where the care, good humour and friendliness of those in charge of the children will continue to help them realise how much God loves them, and enable them to develop trust – the beginning of faith.

Parents are encouraged to pray with their children during the week, using the worksheet prayers.

Pearl Divers
6-10 year olds

When planning for children's work it is advisable to read through the Bible passages prayerfully, followed by the *Reflection on the readings*. You are then in a better position to see how the programme relates to the readings, enabling you to supplement and vary the programme as a result of your own insights and the specific needs of your group.

You may prefer to split your Pearl Divers group into two age groups, adapting the suggestions and worksheets accordingly.

The children are encouraged to pray during the week, using the suggestions on their worksheet. These can be built into a collection of prayers and made into a personal prayer book.

A few general ideas about story-telling:

- Tell the story from the viewpoint of a character in the situation. To create the time-machine effect, avoid eye contact as you slowly put on the appropriate cloth or cloak, and then make eye contact as you greet the children in character.

- Have an object with you which leads into the story – a water jug, or a lunch box, for instance.

- Walk the whole group through the story, so that they are physically moving from one place to another; and use all kinds of places, such as broom cupboards, under the stairs, outside under the trees, and so on.

- Collect some carpet tiles – blue and green – so that at story time the children can sit round the edge of this and help you place on the cut-outs for the story.

Gold Panners

11 years and over

Many churches are concerned about this age group feeling too old for children's liturgy but not able to relate to what the adults are doing in church. We have a wonderful resource here which we tend to ignore: many young people are happy to be involved with a music or drama group, and are excellent at preparing role-play material with a wit and challenge that is good for everyone; others are skilled at using technology in worship.

As they move towards owned faith, it is vital that the church provides plenty of opportunity for questions and discussion, in an atmosphere which is accepting and willing to listen. Although many will be very valuable on the children's liturgy teams, I am convinced that they need feeding at their own level as well.

The factfiles on each week's worksheet can be collected into a book so that the course becomes a reference manual.

The Gold Panners material provides a transitional course from separate ministry for children to full participation in the service with adults.

RECOMMENDED BIBLES

It is often a good idea to look at a passage in several different versions before deciding which to use for a particular occasion, especially if you plan to involve several people in the reading. As far as children are concerned, separate Bible stories, such as those published by Palm Tree Press and Lion, are a good introduction for the very young. Once children are reading, a very helpful version is the *International Children's Bible* (New Century version) published by Word Publishing. Here children have a translation based on experienced scholarship, using language structure suitable for young readers, with short sentences and appropriate vocabulary. There is a helpful dictionary, and clear maps and pictures are provided.

For young people the New Century version is called *The Youth Bible*, and the layout includes various anecdotes and Bible studies which are inviting and challenging. A vivid version of the New Testament and parts of the Old Testament in contemporary language is Eugene Peterson's *The Message*. This catches the imagination and aids understanding. It is particularly good for reading aloud.

ADVENT

FIRST SUNDAY OF ADVENT

Thought for the day

The gathered hopes of generations remind us to get ourselves ready, so that Christ's return will be a day of excitement and great joy.

Reflection on the readings

Jeremiah 33:14-16
Psalm 24
1 Thessalonians 3:12-4:2
Luke 21:25-28, 34-36

Today is filled with a sense of expectancy. It's rather like knowing that when you come of age you'll inherit a fortune, or that in another few years your ISA account will mature. Only this is rather more mind-blowing than mere financial hope. The promise is there and stands secure, and God, being faithful, will keep that promise. Eventually, when the time is ripe, he will gather up all the goodness and honour and patience and long-suffering that has been grown throughout the ages, and bring things to completion.

This week's readings speak to the deep-seated longings of humanity for right and justice to triumph. They speak to our yearning for a final end to all the cruelty and misery of our world, some of which we all know from first-hand experience. Of course, it is serious and sombre stuff to be considering the winding-up of all the created universe as we know it, and it is very necessary to be reminded of our need to be ready by the lives we are leading.

Yet running through the readings is a clear, bright shaft of strong and exhilarating hope, which we can catch and make our own. God is familiar with our world. He too hears the cry, generation by generation, of those who find faith in a good God impossible because they are overwhelmed by the sorrows and tragedies screaming at them. But ultimately, as Christ has already shown us on the cross, and in his risen life, it is good that triumphs, and God's harvesting at the end of time will be a glorious celebration of all that is just, right and loving. This is not wishful thinking but hope, in all its integrity.

Discussion starters

1. On what is your hope of the second coming founded?

2. How does our foreknowledge of the second coming affect our own lives, and also our attitude to evangelisation, mission and witness?

All-stage talk

Have ready a good supply of inflated balloons on strings. These will be needed later.

Bring out three sweets or apples and explain that three people are going to get them. Give them out completely randomly and then ask if that was fair. Agree with them that it wasn't fair, and often life seems unfair to us. (This is something that all ages know about.) Explain how our world is full of injustice and sometimes cruel and terrible things happen which don't make sense.

Now ask anyone who would like a balloon to raise a hand. Invite these people to come and collect a balloon and return to their seats. You will need them to gather with their balloons later on, when you beckon them.

As Christians we don't have to pretend the bad things aren't there, or try to work out easy answers that don't make sense. God knows there are sad and bad things happening in our world as well. They happened just the same when Jesus was walking around in Galilee. A tower fell on some people and killed them. The people asked Jesus to explain it, but he didn't. He felt very, very sorry for anyone who was ill or whose child had died, and, instead of explaining why, he set about comforting them and doing everything he could to make things better. So that's what we need to do as well while we are alive.

But Jesus did tell us that life wouldn't always be unjust. One day, he said, everything as we know it will finish, and on that day everything you, and everyone else, have ever done which is good or kind, or helpful, friendly or honest will be gathered in, like harvest, and kept. (As you say this, gather all those with balloons together in the centre.) It will be an exciting and very beautiful harvest!

Let's make sure that we grow plenty of love and thoughtfulness and honesty and integrity in our lives, however old or young we are, so that whenever that last day comes, we'll be helping to make it a bumper harvest.

All-age ideas

- If you have a set of advent candles, have the candles lit each week by representatives of different age groups, so that by the fourth Sunday in Advent there is a child, a teenager, a working-age adult and a senior citizen.

- Ask a few people to write these words on large posters for the walls or pillars: 'Heaven and earth will pass away but my words will never pass away.'

Prayer of the Faithful

Celebrant
As we think about the fulfilment of all things today,
let us speak with the God of our making.

Reader
We pray that we will all be ready
to meet God face to face,
whenever and however that will be.

Silence

Lord, show us how to live:
and give us the courage to go forward.

We pray that all who lead and advise
may be led and advised by the Spirit,
so that our decisions are in line
with the Father's compassionate will.

Silence

Lord, show us how to live:
and give us the courage to go forward.

We pray that our families and neighbours
may be brought into contact
with the one true, living God
and know his affection for them.

Silence

Lord, show us how to live:
and give us the courage to go forward.

We ask that, through our prayers and our actions,
those hurt by injustice may know support,
the frail, encouragement,
and the timid, reassurance.

Silence

Lord, show us how to live:
and give us the courage to go forward.

We pray that those moving into eternity
through the gate of death
may be welcomed,
and their grieving loved ones comforted.

Silence

Lord, show us how to live:
and give us the courage to go forward.

As we prepare to celebrate Christmas,
let us join our prayers with those of Mary:
Hail, Mary . . .

In the silence of God's stillness
we name any we know
who specially need our prayer.

Silence

Celebrant
Father, you came to show us the true way to life.
Help us progress along that way in your strength.
Through Jesus Christ, our Lord.
Amen.

TREASURE SEEKERS

Aim: To help them understand getting ready for Christmas in terms of getting ready to meet Jesus in person.

Starter

Stop . . . Get ready . . . Go! Starting always from standing still in a space on their own, on the word 'Go!' the children do whatever the leader calls out (e.g. hop like rabbits, swim around like fish, slither like snakes). When the leader calls 'Stop!' the children stop and at 'Get ready!' they go to the starting position again.

Teaching

Draw their attention to the way they had to get ready for the game each time. Christmas is coming – whose birthday is it at Christmas? How are we going to get ready for Christmas?

Jesus told us that one day he would come back. We will be able to see him, either then or when we die, whichever happens first.

How can we get ready to meet Jesus? What would he like to see us doing?

During the discussion, make simple drawings of the way they think Jesus would like to see them living.

Praying

The children find a space on their own again. Taking the ideas they have come up with, lead the children to pray: 'Jesus, we want to be ready to meet you. Please help us to . . . (share our toys/forgive each other/be kind to our brothers and sisters, etc.)', and everyone mimes the activity. Then call out 'Stop!' and the children go back to their space for the next prayer.

Activities

Use the worksheet to reinforce the idea of getting ready for Christmas being linked with getting ready to meet Jesus.

PEARL DIVERS

Aim: To help them understand that at Christmas we also look ahead to the second coming.

Starter

Split the group in two (or four if numbers are larger) and give the members of each group short strands of wool in their group's colour. All the children now drop or hide their wool all around the room. Now ask each group to find and collect a different colour. (First group back wins, if you want to add some competition.)

Teaching

Remind the children of how, when they were gathering up the wool, they were looking out for a particular type of wool, and only collecting that. We'll come back to this later.

They will all be aware that Christmas is approaching, and that we celebrate Jesus coming to live on earth as a human baby at that time. Enjoy the thought of Christmas coming.

Explain that while he was on earth, Jesus told us he would come back again one day and we will all be able to see him then. Make it quite clear that we have not been told when this will happen, and read Luke 21:25-28; 34-36, asking them to listen out for the signs to notice. Readers will find it helpful to follow the words using the worksheet.

Have a short 'Any questions?' slot at this point.

Now back to the wool gathering. At this second coming, all that is or has been good, honest, generous, kind, forgiving and loving will be gathered up, or 'harvested', and last for ever. Jesus suggests that we make sure we are ready for this, so we can enjoy being part of the harvest.

Praying

Using the sprinter's 'Take your marks . . . get set . . . go!' actions, the children line up and crouch down,

Take me as I am, Lord Jesus,
  (raise themselves to the 'get set' position)
make me more loving / forgiving / honest,
  (and run to the opposite wall)
and use me for good!

Activities

Use the worksheet to work on ways to get ready and prepare for the time when all things will be fulfilled.

GOLD PANNERS

Aim: To explore what we know and don't know about the second coming.

Starter

A quick fitness training circuit – running on the spot, skipping, stepping and press-ups, perhaps.

Teaching and activities

First read the Jeremiah passage, helping them to see how and when this prophecy was fulfilled. Have a flipchart headed 'He will come again in glory'. Point out that we say this in the Creed, and we know it hasn't happened yet.

At intervals down the page have these headings: When? Where? How? Why? What will happen? How do we know?

Give pairs of young people a heading to have in mind as they read the passages from 1 Thessalonians and Luke. As they find any information relevant to their heading they can write it in.

Look together at the completed chart and any gaps. Talk over what we do and don't know, and emphasise the need to be fit and ready spiritually.

Praying

Use the Thessalonians passage to see how Paul was praying in this context, and pray along these lines for one another.

SECOND SUNDAY OF ADVENT

Thought for the day

It had been prophesied that there would be a messenger to prepare the way for the coming of the Messiah. Now John the Baptist appears with his urgent message of repentance.

Reflection on the readings

Baruch 5:1-9
Psalm 125
Philippians 1:3-6, 8-11
Luke 3:1-6

Today we read one example of many references from the prophets to a messenger who will prepare people for the coming of the anointed one, the long-awaited Messiah or Christ. It is typical of God's provision for his people. All teachers and builders know the necessity for thorough preparation and the way this so often involves chipping back to the solid foundations and making good. Anyone in advertising knows that people may need telling the same thing several times before they are likely to do anything about changing their favourite product.

So God, knowing human nature affectionately and realistically, tells us beforehand what he will do, and then provides John who himself points towards someone else. Hopefully there will be those who, having heard the prophecies, will already be waiting expectantly, ready to latch on to what the messenger is saying. There will be those who, through John's urgent message, will be sorting their lives out so that when Jesus' ministry begins, their hearts will already be attuned to receive what he has to say and eventually to recognise who he is.

And what about us? Paul's prayer, similar to that in the letter to the Thessalonians last week, is rather like the image of carrying a very full mug of tea from the kitchen back to bed, carefully holding it so that nothing spills and nothing is lost on the way. We are in the privileged position of having read the prophecies, seen them fulfilled in John the Baptist, and having met Jesus through the Gospels and his living presence. So in a sense we are like the full mug of tea. What we now have to do is make the journey to death and the second coming without losing a drop of what we have been given.

At another level is the recognition that it isn't enough to hear John's message once. It does us all good to use each Advent as a fresh chance to look at our lives and habits, and sort them out; to be ruthless about anything which is impairing our walk with God.

Discussion starters

1. Luke wants to place John firmly in the historical context. How does he do this, and why?

2. 'Repentance for the forgiveness of sins.' Why was John told to preach this particular message at this particular time?

All-stage talk

Beforehand arrange for a local builder/decorator to be interviewed, preferably in working clothes and carrying his tools.

Introduce the guest, and ask his advice about a structural problem (either real or imagined). When the builder talks about the importance of all the 'making good', suggest that surely he could just smear some more plaster over the top, and wouldn't that be as good? Or put on thick wallpaper to hide the cracks? Let the builder explain what will eventually happen if the real problem isn't sorted out.

Thank the guest builder and have a couple of the children bring him a mug of tea as it's time for his tea break.

While the builder drinks his tea, explain how what is true for walls and windows is true for us as well. If we have been mean or a pain, or lazy, or if we've been telling lies or living lies, or if there is anything at all in the way we behave which is not right, loving and honest, then we are like a building with bad cracks and damp. As the builder told us, the only way to put it right is to have the wrong things cleared away, and then be built up soundly again.

God can do that in us if we want. He will help us put our lives right, however bad a state they are in. Tell him you are sorry you tell lies, and want to be more honest. He will help you become an honest person who others can trust. Tell God your sister/father-in-law/colleague winds you up and you hate all the rows and want to be more able to cope. God will help you improve those relationships. Tell God you find it hard to share your toys or your money, and want to be more generous. He will help you do it.

But we can't put anything right until we see that there is a problem. It was only when the damp and cracks were noticed that the builder was called in.

John the Baptist spoke about 'repentance'. That means he is saying to us: 'Look at your lives; see those cracks and damp patches; and get them sorted out.'

All-age ideas

• Instead of a flower arrangement or as a separate display, have an arrangement of an open DIY manual, and various tools and materials, with a title: 'Get your life sorted out!' This can be done by someone doing their own property up at the moment, or a student on a building course.

• Give everyone a small paper house shape. Ask everyone to look at their house as their life, and listen to what God is saying needs putting in order or sorting out. Then the houses are collected up and placed in front of the cross (or people can bring them up to the cross). At the end they can be given out for people to take home and remind them of what they and God are going to tackle together.

Prayer of the Faithful

Celebrant
We know that God is here with us,
and hears what is in our thoughts and in our hearts.

Reader
So we pray for all who claim to be Christians
all over the world.
We ask for a real longing for God in our lives;
a longing that is not satisfied by anything else.

Silence

Holy God:
we want to know you better.

We pray for the different countries
and those with power and influence.
We pray for honesty, justice and integrity.

Silence

Holy God:
we want to know you better.

We pray for those we love
and those we find it hard to relate to.
We pray for a deeper, and a loving forgiveness.

Silence

Holy God:
we want to know you better.

We pray for those in pain
and those imprisoned by addiction.
We pray for healing, wholeness and freedom.

Silence

Holy God:
we want to know you better.

We pray for those who have died
and now see God face to face.
We pray for those who miss them here.

Silence

Holy God:
we want to know you better.

Mindful of Mary's quiet
and prayerful acceptance of God's will,
we join our prayers with hers:
Hail, Mary . . .

As we get ready for the coming of his Son,
let us bring to God our Father
our own particular concerns.

Silence

Celebrant
Father, accept these prayers:
as you prepared humanity
for your coming in Bethlehem,
prepare us to receive you in our hearts.
We ask this through Christ our Lord.
Amen.

TREASURE SEEKERS

Aim: To understand that John was the messenger helping people get ready for Jesus.

Starter

Call and change. Sit round in a circle. One person calls someone else's name and these two change places. The one who was called becomes the next caller. This game helps build the group together, and is an acting-out of what John the Baptist was doing.

Teaching

Find out if any of the children have cousins, and what their names are. Point out that they may not live with you but they are members of your family.

Tell them that one of Jesus' cousins was John. And God had a job he needed John to do. When John was grown up God asked him to go and get people ready for Jesus.

How could he do that? First he went off on his own to pray. Then he started talking to the people. He said to them, 'Listen, I've got a message for you!'

'A message for us?' asked the people. 'What message have you got for us?'

'Well,' said John, 'we all need to get ready. Soon God will be coming to us, and we aren't ready for him yet.'

'How exciting!' said the people. 'You are right, we must be ready to welcome him. But what can we do?'

John said, 'God will want to find that we are kind and loving and being fair to one another.'

'Oh dear!' said the people. 'I'm afraid we're not always like that. Some of us have bad tempers and some of us are greedy and some of us want our own way all the time. But we do want to be ready. Please help us get ready.'

'All you have to do,' said John, 'is to be sorry about those things and want to put them right.'

'We are sorry,' said the people. 'We don't want to be bad tempered and greedy and wanting our own way all the time. We want to make God happy when he comes.'

'In that case,' said John, 'I will wash you in the river as a sign that your bad temper and greediness and wanting your own way all the time are washed away and you are forgiven.'

The people felt happy and free. They went back home to enjoy loving and sharing and being fair. It would not be easy, but they were determined to do their best.

Praying

Ask the children to sit with their hands closed up as if they are hiding something inside. Imagine that one hand holds something for which you want to thank God that you are good at. As you open that hand, think of showing the thing you are good at to God. Everyone says, 'Thank you, God, for making me good at this.' Imagine that in the other hand you are holding something you would like to be better at (telling the truth/being a good friend/helping at home). As you open this hand, think of showing God and say, 'Please, God, help me to be better at this.'

Activities

Use the worksheet to continue getting the crib ready for Christmas – today is the manger – and reinforce the teaching about John the Baptist.

PEARL DIVERS

Aim: To understand that John was the prophesied forerunner to prepare the people for the Messiah.

Starter

Advance notice. Have a selection of posters and flyers for local events (the local press usually drops several on your floor as you open the paper each week). Have some with pictures to help non-readers. Have the posters at different places on the walls and give the children a minute to walk round and look at them. Then have everyone in the centre. Call out: 'Did you know there was going to be a circus next Saturday?' The children run to the appropriate poster.

Teaching

Beforehand prepare a poster that says: 'Good news – don't miss it! The Messiah is coming!' and a sign with a string attached saying 'John the Baptist'.

Explain that for thousands of years people had known that one day God would come among his people on earth in a very close way. The people of Israel were waiting for the day when the Messiah would appear on earth. (Display the poster.) Everyone can shout the message together. The name 'Messiah' means 'the chosen one' or 'the Christ'. But God didn't rely on posters: he went for a better idea. He went for a personal messenger.

At this point one of the leaders interrupts to say that she wants to give advance notice of a children's Christmas party / carol singing (or whatever exciting event you have planned for Christmas). The excitement generated by this will enable you to show how effective it is to have a personal messenger. Explain that the name of the personal messenger God chose was John, known as John the Baptist. (Hang the notice round the messenger's neck.)

What was John's message?

God told John to tell the people that to get ready for the coming Messiah, they needed to put their crooked lives straight. Their lives needed to be like clear firm roads. That meant sorting out all lying and cheating, all cruel and unkind behaviour, all mean and selfish living. The people wanted to get ready for the Messiah, so they wanted to sort their lives out. This turning away from sin is called 'repentance'. As a sign that their sins had been forgiven, John baptised the people in the water of the River Jordan. The people felt happy and free. It feels good to be forgiven.

Praying

Have everyone standing in a space facing the same direction. Whenever the leader says *Turn us round* the children turn around and continue with the prayer.

Father, whenever we are wanting our own way,
    Turn us round to think of other people.

Whenever we know we are not being honest,
    Turn us round to speak the truth.

Whenever we find ourselves being greedy,
    Turn us round to share with others.

Thanks for helping, Lord.
Amen.

Activities

Use the worksheet to reinforce today's teaching and express the message of John in poster form for the rest of the congregation.

GOLD PANNERS

Aim: To explore the nature of repentance and forgiveness as necessary preparation for welcoming Jesus into our lives.

Starter

Sketch to be read by different members of the group.

Patient 1   Doctor, doctor, I feel like a pair of curtains.

Doctor   Well, pull yourself together! Next patient, please.

Patient 2   Doctor, doctor, I can't get to sleep at night.

Doctor	Well, lie on the edge of the bed and you'll soon drop off. Next patient, please.
Patient 3	Doctor, doctor, everyone ignores me as if I'm not there.
Doctor	Next patient, please.
Patient 4	Doctor, doctor, I demand to change my doctor!
Doctor	Oh really? Why?
Patient 4	Your jokes are making me ill!

Teaching

When people find their bodies are not working properly they usually go to a doctor (hopefully one with better jokes!) because they want their bodies sorted out. Often the way to recovery means doing something differently – having more rest, giving up smoking, taking medicine or more exercise, perhaps.

When John told the people that they needed to sort their lives out, it made them look at the way they were behaving. They could see that they were not actually living in the best way. They asked John to help them put things right, and John told them to repent so they could be forgiven.

To repent means to change direction and turn round. That is sometimes quite easy (deciding to give up swearing), and sometimes very difficult (forgiving someone who has hurt you a lot). But it is only when we recognise what is wrong in our lives, and really want to change direction, that we can know the relief and freeing that comes from God's forgiveness.

God knows that, and offers us all we need to be able to put things right. If we go to a doctor and the doctor offers us help, we'd be foolish not to accept. Yet often people will worry secretly about a sin they know they have a problem with, and not take up God's offer to help. People can change. You can change. And repenting and being forgiven opens life up again and feels very, very good.

Praying

Using the suggestions on the worksheet, give everyone time to decide one area in their own lives which needs changing for the better in some way. Play some music (suggestions given above) while the group offers these areas in silence or aloud, for God to work on.

Activities

Begin to build up the fact sheet file based on this week's worksheet, and try the interview with John the Baptist in pairs or in the full group.

THIRD SUNDAY OF ADVENT

Thought for the day

Our period of preparation shifts from repentance and forgiveness to the freed exhilaration of hope, as the momentous truth of God's immanence begins to dawn on us.

Reflection on the readings

Zephaniah 3:14-18
Canticle: Isaiah 12:2-6
Philippians 4:4-7
Luke 3:10-18

Over the first two weeks in Advent we have been focusing our attention on putting our lives straight, and this may well have been a very challenging and painful task. We may still be wrestling with its implications.

The shaft of hope has always been present in all this. But now it is as if the forgiveness we are receiving, resulting from real repentance, has enabled that shaft of hope to flood us with unexpected light and joy. From the viewpoint of forgiveness, the coming of Christ, both as we look back to Bethlehem and forward to the last day, is not something to fear, but to anticipate with great delight and enthusiasm.

There is Zephaniah's image of light-hearted and liberated singing and dancing, with something of the flavour of the street parties which celebrate peace after war. And there is Paul's signing-off message as he draws to a close his letter to the Christians at Philippi, the sense of God's closeness throbbing through the words. Everything is going to be all right; they can rejoice and go on rejoicing, whatever the immediate sufferings, because God has them ultimately safe.

And the people are enthusiastically taking up John the Baptist's challenge, and throwing themselves into giving up the behaviour they'd probably always known was wrong, but which they had never had the desire to address before.

In the gathering momentum some of them get over-enthusiastic, and how easily John could have been tempted to go along with their misguided assumptions.

Thankfully his own rigorous self-awareness keeps him humble, and he is able to use their questions to point their expectations in the right direction – towards the Christ.

Discussion starters

1. What changes have you noticed in your own life as a result of repentance and forgiveness?

2. It is difficult to keep a sense of immediacy when days turn into centuries and millennia. How does the season of Advent help us in this?

All-stage talk

Bring with you a sealed envelope containing an invitation to a very special party or wedding. The date for the celebration needs to say 'to be arranged'.

Tell everyone how you have received this letter, and it looked so exciting that you thought you'd bring it to church and open it there. Invite someone to come and help you open the envelope, and someone a bit older to read it out. Show your excitement and start planning what to give as a present, and what to wear, getting suggestions from people and scribbling it all down on a list. Such a lot to think about!

Then stop as you ask to check the date of the celebration. Realise that it only says 'Date to be arranged'. *Date to be arranged!* That means you have no idea when to get ready. It might be ages to wait. It might be next week! Suppose it's next week!

Come to the conclusion that the only way you can be sure to be ready is to get ready straightaway.

Put the invitation down and pick up a Bible. As you flick through the pages talk about how you are sure there is an invitation to a party somewhere in here as well. Find the Zephaniah reading and discover that it's the one we heard this morning, with all the dancing and singing in it.

It's going to be quite a day, and we'll need to make sure we're ready for it. But what was the date again? Look and find it's another case of 'Date to be arranged'. Only God knows the actual date. That means it could be a long time ahead or it could be very close, so the best thing to do is to get ready straightaway.

What kind of presents would be in order for this party?

Collect ideas like loving kindness, peacemaking, compassion, forgiveness, goodness and self-control. If we start now, we can grow those in our lives.

What kind of clothes would be suitable?

Clean clothes and good habits like honesty, faithfulness, humility, just or fair behaviour, and thoughtfulness. If we haven't got any yet, we can go to God's wardrobe and he'll make them to fit us perfectly. And if we have got them, but haven't worn them lately, now is the time to get them out and put them on again. These clothes get more and more beautiful as you wear them.

The second coming will be a wonderful celebration, and whether we are alive here or the other side of death, we will all be able to see it and take part.

All-age ideas

- Continue lighting the Advent candles with representatives from different age groups.

- Have the Luke passage read by a group of voices as appropriate.

Prayer of the Faithful

Celebrant
God is here with us now.
Let us pray.

Reader
We want to be ready to receive the Lord.
May he take us as we are and cultivate in us
a heart that longs for and worships the God of love
above and beyond everything else.

Silence

Come, O come:
Emmanuel, God with us.

We open to the Father's love
the spiritual journeys of all who walk the way of Christ;
may they be protected from evil
and kept steadfast in faith.

Silence

Come, O come:
Emmanuel, God with us.

We pray for those who give us support,
and encourage us and listen to us,
and make us laugh and share our sorrows.
May their lives be blessed and filled with joy.

Silence

Come, O come:
Emmanuel, God with us.

We remember in God's presence
those whose memories are painful,
and those whose bitter resentment
cramps and distorts present relationships.
We ask for the healing only God can give.

Silence

Come, O come:
Emmanuel, God with us.

We call to mind those we know who have died,
and any who are close to death at the moment.
As they meet the one true God
may their hearts be opened to receive his love,
mercy and forgiveness.

Silence

Come, O come:
Emmanuel, God with us.

We make our prayer with Mary,
who mothered the Son of God:
Hail, Mary . . .

As the love of God our Father fills our hearts,
we pray for any needs
known to us personally.

Silence

Celebrant
Father, we ask these things
through Jesus Christ our Lord.
Amen.

TREASURE SEEKERS

Aim: To celebrate looking forward to Christmas as a time of God's love being shown to us.

Starter

I'm thinking of someone . . . Everyone sits in a circle and tries to guess who you are thinking of. Start with something that could refer to lots of children (he's a boy / wearing a sweater) and gradually get more specific (his shoes have green dinosaurs on the bottom) until lots of children know who you mean. Everyone says, 'God made Jack and God loves Jack.'

Teaching

Beforehand, get a good quality picture of the nativity (from a Christmas card) and put it in a box. Wrap the box in Christmas paper. We will use this during the teaching.

Get out some wrapping paper and scissors, and let the children guess what they are used for. Talk about why we give each other presents at Christmas, and establish that it isn't because we want something back but because we love the people and want them to see that we love them.

Now remind them of the starter activity and how God knows and loves each of us. Explain that at the first Christmas he gave the world the best Christmas present ever, not because he wanted anything back, but just because he loves us so much. Show the Christmas present. What was God's Christmas present to the world, to show he loves us? Open the present and let the children see that it is Jesus.

Praying

As you hold the Christmas present and then open it and hold up the picture, say this prayer together:

Thank you God
for loving the world so much
that you gave us Jesus
to be with us for ever. Amen.

Activities

Use the worksheet to continue getting ready for Christmas by making the crib – this week it's Mary, Joseph and Jesus. The present-wrapping activity will need a variety of small pieces of Christmas paper.

PEARL DIVERS

Aim: To develop their understanding from last week about the importance of John as the forerunner to Christ.

Starter

Name and throw. Stand in a circle with a beach ball. Call out the name of someone else in the circle and then throw the ball to them. Remind them beforehand to see if they can make sure that everyone has at least one go. This activity helps build community, includes new children, and picks up on the fact that being chosen and called gets you ready to receive.

Teaching

Get the children to help recap the teaching from last week about who John was and why he was called the Baptist.

Have two leaders discussing what had gone on by the River Jordan when they were there in the crowd. One is a soldier and one a tax collector. To be able to do this effectively they will need to be very familiar with the Luke text and practise beforehand so that the conversation sounds natural and interesting while bringing out a) the teaching that John has given and b) their excitement about waiting for this other person John has told them to look out for.

Following the conversation, draw out the main points from the children, noting them on a flipchart, board or OHP.

Praying

Have this leader / response prayer shout, written up so everyone can join in:

Leader   What do we want?

All	We want to be ready!
Leader	When do we want it?
All	Now!
Leader	Who can help us?
All	God can help us
Leader	When can he help us?
All	Now!

Activities

Today's worksheet helps the children consolidate their understanding of the events at the River Jordan, placing them in their historical context. They can also make a stand-up model.

GOLD PANNERS

Aim: To understand the freedom and joy that result from repentance and forgiveness.

Starter

Tell them calmly and seriously something you know will really make them panic (their group have to sing on their own when they get back into church this morning / do all the washing up for the old people's dinner today). Allow a short time of apoplexy and then let them know you were only joking and they haven't really got to do it at all.

Teaching

Talk over the sense of relief everyone felt when they had been 'set free' from doing something they dreaded. It's a bit like the way your arms almost float up to the sky when you stop carrying a really heavy suitcase. Whenever we think, say or do something we know is wrong, unkind or dishonest, it stays with us, weighing us down like a heavy case. Sometimes (usually) we try to squash the feeling of shame and guilt away at first. (The worksheet gives some examples of how we do this.)

If we do this often enough, our conscience will get less sensitive, and we won't notice its nudging so easily. But neither will we enjoy that carefree joy that comes when we are right with our Creator.

So we have the choice. Either we can go on blunting our conscience, or we can put down our luggage and run free again.

At this point read the Luke passage, with different people taking different speaking parts.

What John was doing to the crowds was sharpening their consciences again so that they realised

their need to put down the shame and guilt and be forgiven and set free. It wasn't so much one or two terrible things they had done wrong; it was more like a build-up of habits like grumbling, being discontented, cheating and fiddling accounts, not noticing others' needs and so on.

As we use this Advent to sort our lives out, it may mean sharpening our consciences again, and using them to help us. The freedom that repentance and forgiveness give is well worth it.

Read the passage from Zephaniah which expresses this joy.

Praying

While music is played, think over the week and notice any areas which have been helped by last week's prayer time. Thank God for what is already being done in each of us, and ask him to continue and deepen the process during the coming week. Read the Zephaniah passage again to affirm, reassure and encourage.

Activities

Working with the Luke passage the group are linking the individuals in the crowd at the Jordan to our own society and the areas we need to tackle both as individuals and as a community. Do any ideas arise for local action?

FOURTH SUNDAY OF ADVENT

Thought for the day

When we co-operate with God amazing things happen.

Reflection on the readings

Micah 5:1-4
Psalm 79
Hebrews 10:5-10
Luke 1:39-44

It is not only Mary and Elizabeth who are pregnant in today's readings. The whole atmosphere this week is full of expectancy and the sense that what we are looking forward to has already begun to be fulfilled. It may be hidden but it leaps within us.

The prophet Micah speaks of events far greater

than he imagines, and we, with our knowledge of the Gospel, can pick up on the image of a shepherd saviour being brought to birth and establishing a reign of peace. The writer of the letter to the Hebrews reminds us not just of Christ's birth but also of his death. As an unborn child already has the DNA pattern for the potential adult, so we are given here a kind of spiritual antenatal scan of Jesus, stretching back into the longing and forward to the sacrificial giving which secures our future.

There is enormous strength in the capacity to set aside something precious to you in order that a greater good may be enabled to happen. We marvel at Jesus laying aside his glory; laying aside his garments to wash the disciples' feet; laying aside the law – all in obedience and out of love. It is a hallmark of true Godliness.

So when we find human beings like Mary willing to lay aside so much in obedience and out of love, we are watching the most real and beautiful of human nature; God and humanity co-operating together for the good of the world.

Today we are given the chance to press the pause button as Mary and Elizabeth meet, with their unborn children within them, and wonder at what can happen when we allow God to work in us and with us for the good of the world.

Discussion starters

1. What are some of the thoughts and feelings that Mary and Elizabeth might have had at this meeting?

2. Is our desire to co-operate with God as individuals and as a church blurred and hazy or sharply in focus?

All-stage talk

Try a kind of Mexican wave, first with one side of the church and then the other. The side not involved can enjoy the effect. Row by row, starting with the front row, everyone stands together and then sits together. The row behind gets up as soon as the row in front of them has sat down. Point out that for this to work they all needed to co-operate with one another and also with you, in agreeing to try it in the first place. Today we are watching what can happen when people are willing to co-operate with God.

Last week we found John the Baptist challenging people to sort out their lives and giving them some practical advice. Those who went away and did as John suggested found that once they had started to co-operate with God their lives took on a new sparkle and freshness many had lost. Those of us who took last week's teaching to heart and started looking seriously at what needed changing in our lives will also be here this morning with a new lightness in our step and a more positive sparkle in our lives because co-operating with God is very exhilarating and liberating. Working together with God sets us free. (And if we haven't yet got round to that there is still time for us to shake ourselves awake and use Advent profitably.)

Mary was one of those people who had decided to work together with God. And that meant that God could use her. So he did. It was through Mary co-operating with God that Jesus could come into the world.

Mary and Elizabeth are both pregnant. Mary is expecting Jesus, and her cousin Elizabeth is expecting John the Baptist. It's the same John the Baptist we met last week when he was grown up, teaching people by the River Jordan. Today we have a flashback to before he was born. Any mothers here will know that exciting feeling when the baby you are carrying first moves. Luke tells us that the unborn baby John was so excited at sensing the unborn Jesus, brought along in Mary, that he leapt about in his mother's womb!

Never before had God come among his people so closely. And now his birth into the world was less than a year away. No wonder Elizabeth and Mary were so excited. Having agreed to co-operate with God they found themselves being used for such an extraordinary and important job that they could hardly believe it. And they weren't even rich or powerful! They probably weren't even that well educated!

When anyone (and that includes you and me) says to God, 'I want to spend my life working together with you', God takes us up on our offer. If we don't opt out as soon as he asks of us things we may not want to give, he will be able to work with us in our lives to do amazing things. Imagine if everyone here in church decided to work with God. He could get us making waves in our community which would completely transform people's lives.

All-age ideas

• Continue the lighting of the Advent candles using representatives from different age groups. Or you could have a child dressed as Mary lighting today's candle.

• The meeting of Mary and Elizabeth in Luke's Gospel can be mimed while it is being read, using nativity costumes if you have them. It always seems a pity to have these packed away for most of the year when they are such a useful resource.

• If you have a member of the congregation who is pregnant, it would be valuable to have her lead the intercessions, or take part in a short interview about the way the baby moves, as she will be able to add insights which will help our understanding.

Prayer of the Faithful

Celebrant
As we share in Mary and Elizabeth's joy
at the coming of our Saviour,
let us quieten and still ourselves
in the presence of God.

Reader
We can only marvel at the way
the heavenly Father is happy to work with us.
We want him to know
that we are willing to be used.

Silence

Let it be to me:
according to your will.

We call to mind those
whom we would love to know the Lord
and we ask that their hearts
may be prepared to recognise him.

Silence

Let it be to me:
according to your will.

We pray for reassurance and encouragement
in this parish,
and for insight to the real needs
and what the Lord would have us do.

Silence

Let it be to me:
according to your will.

We ask for the courage
to continue working with and for the Lord,
even during the dark and dangerous times.

Silence

Let it be to me:
according to your will.

We call to mind those who are struggling
with poverty, illness or despair;
may the Lord comfort them,
and use us however he wants.

Silence

Let it be to me:
according to your will.

We remember those who have died
and give thanks for the good

that the Lord has worked in their lives.
May we, with them, share in the life
that lasts for ever.

Silence

Let it be to me:
according to your will.

With Mary, the bearer of God's Son,
we make our prayer:
Hail, Mary . . .

We pray to our loving Father,
in silence,
for everything we need.

Silence

Celebrant
In thankfulness we ask you, Father,
to hear our prayers,
through Christ our Lord.
Amen.

TREASURE SEEKERS

Aim: To understand that Mary was happy to work with God.

Starter

Working together. Ask the children to help you do various jobs as you get ready for the session. If you have access to a parachute, play some parachute games which need everyone to work together (such as 'mushroom', 'roll the ball' or tent making). Alternatively have everyone helping to make a 'Happy Christmas' frieze for the church.

Teaching

Point out how we all worked together in that activity. What jobs do they help with at home? Each time emphasise the co-operation that gets the job done well.

Use rag dolls or cut-out figures to tell the story.

God needed a very important job done. He needed someone to bring Jesus into our world and look after him. So he looked around and saw just the right person: Mary. He didn't choose her because she was rich or pretty or clever. He chose her because she was ready to work with God. She was already friends with him. She talked to him and listened to him in her prayers each day, and tried to live as God wanted her to. (How was that?)

So one day God told her he had chosen her to be the mother of Jesus. Mary was very surprised. It was such an important job, and she knew it would be a hard job to do well. What do you think – did she say yes or no?

Mary said 'Yes!' and went off to visit her cousin Elizabeth who lived in another town. Elizabeth was going to have a baby, too. You remember John the Baptist we met last week? Well, it was him, only he hadn't been born yet when Mary went to see his mother.

As soon as they met they hugged and kissed, and John started leaping about inside his mum because he was so excited! (Have you ever felt a baby moving about inside your mum? It's a funny feeling.)

Mary didn't need to tell Elizabeth her news. Elizabeth seemed to know already, and they sang and danced to praise God for being so wonderful.

Praying

Leader Dear God,
when you want us to be kind, help us to say

All Yes!

Leader When you want us to be honest, help us to say

All Yes!

Leader When you want us to help someone, help us to say

All Yes!

Activities

The worksheet helps the children to complete their Christmas crib today, so these can be blessed in church and taken home. They are also going over the main points of today's story.

PEARL DIVERS

Aim: To explore what it meant for Mary to say 'Yes'.

Starter

Either join with the younger children for parachute games, or have a team game which needs team members to co-operate (football is the obvious choice, or you could try French cricket or pass the balloon between the knees).

Teaching

Find out if anyone has ever been asked to play for the school team or orchestra, or sing in the choir. Have some pictures of well-known footballers and actors as well. Talk about how pleased and proud

you feel to be asked to do an important job, but bring out the point that you can't just go along to play in the match or act in the performance. What other things would you have to do? List both the up- and the down-sides of such a privilege. Looking at it as a whole, would they still want to take it on? (You could vote on it.)

Have another sheet with a picture of Mary in the middle. It is headed, 'Chosen to be Jesus' mother'.

Look at what Mary was chosen for, and on one side of the picture list all the good things about it. Then think over Jesus' life and see if you can think of any sad, painful or difficult things that might be part of the job. List these on the other side of the picture. How would they feel about taking on the job?

At the bottom write, 'Mary still said "Yes!".' It amazed her that God had chosen her, and it made her realise how wonderful and sensible and patient and courageous God was to set about saving the world in this way.

Mary went to visit her cousin Elizabeth, who was six months pregnant with John the Baptist at the time, and both Mary and Elizabeth (and John) were filled with excitement and delight at what God was up to.

Praying

Have some happy music on to dance to and while the music is still playing everyone claps a rhythm and shouts these words to it:

My soul glorifies the Lord
and my spirit rejoices in God my saviour.

Activities

Consolidate the teaching using the worksheet and follow the instructions on it to make a Christmas table decoration.

GOLD PANNERS

Aim: To explore the implications of Mary's willingness to co-operate with God.

Starter

A football game, with three minutes each way, or a short video clip of a recent game.

Teaching

Talk over the need for co-operation within the team, and how God calls us to co-operate with him. When we do, great things can happen. When we don't, great opportunities are missed.

Read the prophecy from Micah and use the

worksheet to give a brief background to it. Pick up on Micah's passionate longing for a new, fresh start which is free from all corruption and power-seeking.

Now look at the words of the Magnificat in which Mary poured out her excitement at what God was bringing to birth within her own body. Imagine a conversation between Micah and Mary: what would they both agree about? What do they both loathe in society? What values do they both share?

(If you are blessed with a man in the congregation who is familiar with the book of Micah, and a woman who is familiar with the Magnificat, you could ask them along to stage such a conversation.)

Read the first part of today's Gospel now, to see how Mary and Elizabeth reacted to this extraordinary event. Bear in mind that Elizabeth's husband, Zachariah, had been dumb ever since failing to believe what God's messenger had told him. Keep a record of the thoughts and feelings that are suggested, and draw out the darker side of Mary's commission as well as all the honour and excitement.

Praying

My soul praises the Lord.
My heart is happy because God is my saviour.
I am not important,
but God has shown his care for me, his servant girl.
From now on, all people will say that I am blessed,
because the Powerful One
has done great things for me.
His name is holy.
God will always give mercy
to those who worship him.
God's arm is strong.
He scatters the people who are proud
and think great things about themselves.
God brings down rulers from their thrones
and he raises up the humble.
God fills the hungry with good things
but he sends the rich away with nothing.
God has helped his people Israel who serve him.
He gave them his mercy.
God has done what he promised to our ancestors,
to Abraham and to his children for ever.

Activities

Using the worksheet and the list you have made together, fill in the suggested framework to create the character studies of Mary and Elizabeth.

CHRISTMAS

CHRISTMAS DAY

Thought for the day

Emmanuel – 'God with us' – is born at Bethlehem into the human family. Now we will be able to understand, in human terms, what God is really like.

Reflection on the readings

Note: These readings are for Midnight Mass. Reflections on the readings for the Day Mass are to be found in *Living Water* Year A, and for the Mass at Dawn in *Living Water* Year B.

Isaiah 9:2-7
Psalm 97
Titus 2:11-14
Luke 2:1-14 (15-20)

The rejoicing Isaiah speaks of is a deliriously abandoned relief. After years and generations of oppression and injustice, this coming day is filled with evocative images of the security of a good harvest, the elation of overcoming an enemy in battle, and the freedom of slavery yokes being triumphantly shattered.

Typically, God brings about this longed-for day amid all the noise and confusion of ordinary life, with the census crowds jostling for space in the Bethlehem streets, the usual mix of noble and base behaviour, and in the context of unsettling circumstances. It is as if God is proving a point by acting out his name 'Emmanuel'; as if he is emphasising beyond doubt that he is truly with us in the untidy and muddled world we really inhabit. Nothing special is expected to be laid on, because he is not coming to meet us on our best behaviour, but on our real behaviour.

It is only when we are ourselves before God that he can truly be born in us. And if that place is crowded and dusty, or insecure or dark or full of questions, then he will be feeling very much at home.

Discussion starters

1. Do all the traditional Christmas festivities and expectations enable us to rejoice over the real message of Christmas, or do they distract us from it?

2. How would you explain on a local radio interview what Christmas is really about?

All-stage talk

You will need to borrow a mobile phone (unless you have received one as a Christmas present!) and a helper who is expert at sorting out OHPs.

Begin by telling everyone you want to show them something on the OHP, and then find that you can't work the equipment properly. Before anyone rushes to your aid, produce the mobile phone, delighted that this is an opportunity to use it to get in touch with an expert. Pretend to use the phone to get through to the expert, and have a mock conversation with them about how to work the apparatus, during which the expert suggests coming to help in person.

Welcome the help and pretend to talk through their (speedy) journey, which can be from anywhere in the world. As you get to guiding the expert down the road and into the church your helper arrives in person, mobile phone to his/her ear. (They have been standing hidden somewhere at the back of the building.)

The expert is able to get the apparatus going, and you enthuse about how much more helpful it is to have them there in person. You can now show the OHP acetate, which says: 'EMMANUEL = God with us in person.' The helper can point out that you've just been saying that it's much more helpful having them there in person. Is that what Emmanuel means?

You can then draw out the similarities – that with Jesus being born into the world as one of us, we have God with us in person to help us live good lives, make good decisions and guide us in all the tricky places. It's not that things won't ever go wrong any more, but it does mean we can always be in touch with the one who can help us sort things out. And that is a truth well worth celebrating in style! Suggest that over the Christmas festivities we live out this truth to one another. It will mean being generous-hearted, thankful, available and willing to meet people where they are, whether that is a group of friends at a party, or relatives we find it less easy to relate to. Welcome God in person to your home this Christmas and enjoy yourselves in his company.

All-age ideas

- The Advent candles will all be lit today, together with a white one in the centre. Continue to use representatives from different age groups for this. Perhaps the centre candle can be lit during the singing of the Christmas Day verse of *O come, all ye faithful*.

- Have people dressed in costume to mime the Gospel. Have a narrator who is sensitive to the actors and is able to give them the cues they need if necessary.

• Have a nativity tableau during a carol and children standing round the altar with candles during the consecration.

Prayer of the Faithful

Celebrant
As we celebrate God's coming to us
as a human child,
we bring the needs of our world
before the God we can trust.

Reader
We pray for all those who worship God
in every country of our world.
We pray for the grace
to know and love God more deeply.

Silence

Emmanuel, God with us:
we welcome you!

We pray for those who are spending this Christmas
apart from those they love.
We pray for those whose celebrations
are tempered with sorrow or fear.

Silence

Emmanuel, God with us:
we welcome you!

We pray for peace in the Holy Land
and for all who now live in the city of Bethlehem.

Silence

Emmanuel, God with us:
we welcome you!

We pray for those working over Christmas,
for all women giving birth
and all babies being born today.
We pray for their homes and families.

Silence

Emmanuel, God with us:
we welcome you!

We pray for those being born into eternal life
through the gate of death,
and commend them to God's love and mercy.

Silence

Emmanuel, God with us:
we welcome you!

We join our prayers with those of Mary,
who shared her joy with the shepherds:
Hail, Mary . . .

We pray in silence, now,
for our own particular needs and concerns.

Silence

Celebrant
Heavenly Father, accept these prayers
and give us the strength and the will
to walk in love,
through Jesus Christ.
Amen.

TREASURE SEEKERS, PEARL DIVERS AND GOLD PANNERS

It is important that children, young people and adults are together for a festival such as Christmas. Involve all age groups in the singing and playing, welcoming, serving, collection of gifts and so on. Have nativity toys to play with in the toddlers' area such as knitted Mary, Joseph and Jesus, shepherds and sheep. Involve the young people in planning part of the service, and all ages in decorating the church.

FIRST SUNDAY OF CHRISTMAS: THE HOLY FAMILY

Thought for the day

Jesus' perception and understanding of his purpose and work begins to take shape throughout his childhood in the Holy Family.

Reflection on the readings

Ecclesiasticus 3:2-6, 12-14
Psalm 127
Colossians 3:12-21
Luke 2:41-52

In the reading from Colossians we are reminded of our calling to be Christians and the clothing that entails. It is a clothing with those qualities of good Christian living which are so often lacking in our world, and often dismissed or despised. Yet, as people sense things moving out of control, and the extent of violence and the breakdown of trust shock us into taking stock of our direction, there is also a yearning for the possibility of these qualities of compassion, kindness, humility, gentleness and patience.

As we celebrate the Incarnation it is important that we also have this picture of a gradually developing recognition in the child Jesus of his life's work and purpose. Throughout his early childhood Mary, Joseph and Jesus must have talked together about the events surrounding his birth. Now, at the annual Passover visit to Jerusalem, with Jesus come of age in the Jewish tradition, he is starting to see the prophecies and hints of scripture adding up, and the vision of his role and purpose sharpens into focus.

Mary, scolding him in her anxiety for his safety, points out that she and his father have been worried sick, searching for him. Jesus, with the enormity of his life's work flooding into consciousness, has spent the past few days beginning to grasp what it means to be God's son, and cannot understand why they should be searching for him when he is at home in his Father's house. Capital letters are not always audible! No wonder Mary and Joseph couldn't understand what he was saying to them – they hadn't been part of this emerging revelation taking place in the temple.

It is rather comforting to read that Jesus went back to live according to their rules, nursing his vision as Mary nursed her experiences, treasuring them but not imposing them on anyone. Not even sharing them until the time was right. God will always go with us at our own pace and in ways that we can cope with. That is all part of what Incarnation means.

Discussion starters

1. How does today's Gospel add to our understanding of what the Incarnation means?

2. Many carols speak of God being 'clothed in flesh'. We have been hearing about our need to be clothed. What does the clothing in flesh tell us about God?

All-stage talk

Beforehand, cut out two simple white cloth tunics like this, one to fit a three- or four-year-old and a larger one for a twelve-year-old.

Invite a couple of toddlers and their parents to the front and interview them about the coats or jackets the children are wearing. Admire them and ask where they were bought, and what size was needed compared with their last coat.

When God came to earth at Christmas as a baby, it was like him putting on the clothing of being human, and it was God's way of showing how much he loves us and is with us. It also helps us to see what God is like, because we cannot see God, but in Jesus we can see how God behaves. We can see that he enjoys people's company, wants to help them and shares their sadness and joy.

And Jesus didn't suddenly arrive on earth as a grown-up. He was born as a baby (draw attention to the size of someone very small in the congregation) and grew to be a toddler and a child (use other people of appropriate ages to demonstrate), so by the time he was a grown-up twelve-year-old he had experienced all the sort of human things that we experience.

Use the larger tunic with the word 'Humanity' written on it to clothe a twelve(ish)-year-old. All twelve-year-olds start asking questions about God and themselves, and so did Jesus. Part of wearing humanity meant that he developed as a human person and now he was grown-up he was fascinated to know who he was and why he was alive, just as we are. Those questions are important, and need to be asked. They are a sign of growing up. The answers for Jesus (and the answers for us) didn't come all at once. But that visit to the temple seems to have been a very important one for him. He began to understand that he was on earth to carry out God's purposes. That was why he was wearing the clothing of humanity. Perhaps for some of us this Christmas is an important one for finding out God's purpose for us in our lives. We need to come into God's presence wearing the clothes of honesty and openness, and ask our questions.

All-age ideas

- The Gospel can be acted out with a narrator leading the miming.

- The tunic with the word 'Humanity' written on it can be laid down near the altar for people to see and remember as they come to receive communion.

Prayer of the Faithful

Celebrant
We have been called
to pray for one another in God's presence.
Let us settle ourselves to do that now.

Reader
We pray for all who are called to lead and teach
so that the truth of God's love
is shared throughout the world.
We ask for wisdom, energy
and sensitivity to God's prompting.

Silence

Incarnate God:
we love you and we need you.

We pray for all with power
and influence in our world.
We ask for a widespread desire
for those qualities of compassion and integrity.

Silence

Incarnate God:
we love you and we need you.

We pray for all parents and their children,
especially where there are conflicts,
anxious moments and gaps in communication.

Silence

Incarnate God:
we love you and we need you.

We pray for all missing persons and their families,
all who are rethinking their direction,
all who find life full of contradictions
at the moment.

Silence

Incarnate God:
we love you and we need you.

We pray for those who have come to the end
of their earthly life,
especially any who are unprepared.

Silence

Incarnate God:
we love you and we need you.

We make our prayer with Mary,
Mother of the Church:
Hail, Mary . . .

As members of Christ's family,
we name those we know
who are in any particular need.

Silence

Celebrant
Father, we ask you to hear our prayers,
through Christ our Lord.
Amen.

TREASURE SEEKERS

Aim: To get to know the story of Jesus being lost and found.

Starter

Play hide and seek in small groups so that everyone gets the chance both to hide and be found.

Teaching

Talk about how it felt to be looking for the hidden children and how it felt to find them. Today's story is about a time when Mary and Joseph went looking for Jesus.

Using the 'carpet tiles and cut-outs' method tell the story of the visit to Jerusalem with all the mums and dads and children and uncles and aunties and grandparents and cousins. Jesus was twelve years old. Give all the children a cut-out donkey or camel to add to the trail of visitors going up to Jerusalem. Pictures to use in the story are given with the worksheet.

When everyone sets off for home all the trail of animals can be turned over to face the other way, and then Mary and Joseph's donkey will turn back again to find Jesus, before finally joining the others.

Praying

When we are sitting still *(sit still)*:
    we know you are with us, Jesus.
When we are walking along *(walk along)*:
    we know you are with us, Jesus.
When we are playing *(play)*:
    we know you are with us, Jesus.
When we are helping *(pretend to help clean or tidy up)*:
    we know you are with us, Jesus. Amen.

Activities

The worksheet has a searching to find activity and consolidates the main points of the story. The children can also talk over what to do if they ever lose their mum or dad when they are out shopping.

PEARL DIVERS

Aim: To understand that Jesus shared a human childhood, and to look at the kind of experiences he would probably have had.

Starter

Sit in a circle and pass round a toy as each person has a turn to speak. Only the one holding the toy can speak. The first round is 'What I liked best about this Christmas was . . .' Anyone not wanting to speak just passes the toy on. The next round is 'The job I hate having to do is . . .'

Teaching

Have a timeline displayed to help the children place Jesus' birth in its historical context. (Copy this from the timeline drawn on the worksheet.) Have available some library books, travel brochures and Bibles with pictures of Palestine under the Romans and some photographs of the country surrounding Bethlehem. Have a large flat stone or board to demonstrate grinding flour and kneading dough, and a display of some of the raisins and dates and nuts that would have been grown and eaten.

Give the children a 'living museum' experience of what life would have been like for Jesus and his friends, bringing in whatever examples and artefacts you can get hold of. You may for instance be able to borrow some fabric or traditional clothing from the area, or traditional lamps or bedrolls, or you could use the pictures. The more involved the children are the better.

They can find out about sitting crosslegged on the floor and chanting from memory in school, and the kind of local jobs that would be the equivalent of a paper round, such as sheep watching, or helping with the harvest.

Praying

Jesus, you know what it's like
to be the same age as me.
Remind me that I can
talk things over with you
whenever I want
and you always
have time to listen. Amen.

Activities

Use the worksheet to consolidate the teaching, looking at the different areas of life for children in Jesus' time and comparing and contrasting with their own lives. There are suggestions for making a display to put up in church.

GOLD PANNERS

Aim: To explore what it meant for God to be taking on the clothing of humanity.

Starter

Have an assortment of dressing-up items and give each small group a character. Using the items avail-able, they have to dress one member of the group appropriately and the other group(s) try to guess who or what the dressed-up person is supposed to be. Possible ideas: Father Christmas, Minnie Mouse, a pop star, a bride, a mountaineer.

Teaching

Read together the Gospel for today, with different people taking the parts. Focus on what was going on in Jesus' mind while he stayed behind in the temple, asking questions and listening to the teachers. What questions might have been coming into his mind about himself?

They can make a note of the suggested questions on their worksheet. (They may well include things like: Who am I really? What am I supposed to be doing in my life? How am I going to explain this to everyone? Can these writings be talking about me? How could these people have written about me when they don't even know me yet?)

Refer to the way in the starter activity we dressed up to become someone else. The word 'Incarnation' (write it down) means being clothed, or embodied in flesh – in other words, God taking on humanity. Round the word, write some of the things that you all think of about what that meant and how it might have felt, bearing in mind Jesus at twelve years old in the temple. The sort of ideas you come up with might include: risky, dangerous, confusing, humbling, scary, exciting, heartbreaking, puzzling, nerve-racking, thrilling.)

Finally read the Philippians passage which is set out on the worksheet. This draws together the areas you have been exploring and sums them up. These are words worth learning by heart, or practising saying together over a background of music in church as people are receiving communion.

Praying

Thank you, Lord God,
for your willingness
to be born as one of us
so that we could be saved.
Amen.

Activities

Practise the passage from Philippians as suggested above. The worksheet picks up on the inside story of Jesus at the temple and links it with their own questions and growing awareness of God's will for them in their lives.

SECOND SUNDAY OF CHRISTMAS

Thought for the day

Christ is the way God tells people about himself.

Reflection on the readings

Sirach 24:1-4, 12-16
Psalm 147
Ephesians 1:3-6, 15-18
John 1:1-18

If we say someone is wise, we often mean that they are clever, or sensible, or mature. The writer of the Book of Sirach thought of wisdom not so much as a description but almost as a thing or even as a person. 'Wisdom,' he writes, 'speaks her own praises.' Wisdom is one of the ways God speaks about himself and is one of the ways God lets us speak (give praise) to him.

In the letter to the Ephesians, Paul speaks of the glory of God and he encourages the community of those who follow Christ to do the same. Through Christ we can have a new and direct relationship with God, and so receive the grace which makes forgiveness and a new start possible.

John's introduction to his Gospel draws all this together, as he speaks of Christ as the Word – the Message – of God, always present and part of him, and proclaiming God clearly, as a living Message, as he walked about on earth. Today we are given total cinema, so to speak. We are looking at the past, present and future all at once so that God's purpose, and its fulfilment, are seen together. That is the extraordinary truth of the Incarnation: God was, God is, and God will be. And we can see it in the person of Jesus.

Discussion starters

1. John talks of Jesus as 'the Word of God'. Does he mean simply that Jesus lived what he believed, or is there more to the title than this?

2. Why do you think people often shy away from the prospect of having a close relationship with the living God, even when they are quite convinced that he exists?

All-stage talk

You will need a hairdrier or a fan, or a lit candle to blow out.

Start with a riddle. You're thinking of something which is all around us, pressing against our faces and bodies at 15 pounds per square inch. It goes in and out of us all the time we're alive, and there's lots of it right in front of our eyes. What is it? (Air.) But we can't see it, so how do we know it's there?

Put on the hairdrier or fan, or ask someone to blow the candle out. When air moves, we can see what it does. When we try to hold our breath we realise how much our bodies need air to live.

God is here as well, and we can't see him. No one has ever seen God while they are alive on earth. So how can God tell us what he is like, when we can't see him?

There are ways we can see what God is like by what he does and by what he creates. If we look at the world we can see that God must be generous, imaginative, careful, clever, organised, hopeful and happy to let us work with him.

But God had an even better idea. If he could walk among humans as a human, then all the humans who lived at the time or at any time afterwards would be able to see exactly how God behaves. We could see it in our own human language. The language of doing, thinking, feeling and speaking.

In the Gospel today Jesus is talked about as being the Word, or the Message of God. When we look at how Jesus lived and died, we are looking straight at God, even though we can't see God with our eyes.

And what do we see? John describes Jesus as being 'full of grace and truth'. Have this written up on a sheet. Around it you can add other people's ideas. Head the page 'Jesus is' and display it for the rest of the service.

All-age ideas

- Have on a banner or poster the words from John 1:18: 'No one has ever seen God . . . But the Son has shown us what God is like.'

- If you have an OHP, try making up some Christmas cards into acetates as a parish resource. These can be placed behind the words of hymns and carols to reflect their meaning.

Prayer of the Faithful

Celebrant
We have met here
in the real presence of our God.
Let us pray to him now.

Reader
We bring to mind the worldwide Christian Church,
both leaders and people,

as we begin another year.
We ask for a deeper awareness
of God's presence among us.

Silence

Though we cannot see you:
your love surrounds us.

We bring to mind the troubled areas of our world
where corruption, injustice and violence
ruin lives and damage self-worth.
We ask for a renewal of heart and a cleansing grace.

Silence

Though we cannot see you:
your love surrounds us.

We call to mind those we have spent time with
over this Christmas season;
we ask for a blessing upon all our families,
friends and neighbours.

Silence

Though we cannot see you:
your love surrounds us.

We bring to mind all who live away from home,
all refugees and all children in care.
We ask for the security that only the Lord can give.

Silence

Though we cannot see you:
your love surrounds us.

We bring to mind those who have died recently
and all who grieve for them.
We ask for comfort to be given to the dying
and the assurance of the Spirit's presence.

Silence

Though we cannot see you:
your love surrounds us.

We pray with Mary,
who so tenderly nurtured her holy Child:
Hail, Mary . . .

Now, in the space of silence,
we bring to God our Father
our private petitions.

Silence

Celebrant
Heavenly Father,
we ask this through Christ our Lord.
Amen.

TREASURE SEEKERS

Aim: To help them understand that God shows us
he loves us by coming to live with us.

Starter

Have some raisins or chocolate buttons which you
hand round to each child in turn, by name. Point
out that you are fond of them, and wanted to show
them by giving them a little something. God loves
each of us by name, and he had a very good idea
for showing us his love.

Teaching

One day God was looking at all the world he had
made. He smelt the roses, laughed at the monkeys
playing in the trees, smiled to himself as a child
helped his baby brother to play football, and enjoyed
the beautiful sunset. It was a very good world.

Then he got sad as he watched an owner hitting a
dog, two children fighting, and a grown-up stealing
some money. God had made people able to choose
right or wrong, and lots of them were choosing
wrong instead of right, even though God knew it
would make them happier to choose right.

The trouble was that although he was there, the
people couldn't see him. No one can see God. And
God longed to help them.

One day he decided to become a human himself
and live among them. 'And then,' thought God,
'they will understand how to live. They will be able
to follow my example, and I will help them.'

Well, of course God couldn't stop being God
and be a human instead – if he did that all the
world would come to a sudden and nasty end.

So this is what God did. He spoke his great love
for the world and his longing for the people, and
the great love he spoke became a human baby, all
ready to grow up in a human family, and show all
the people what God was really like.

And do you know the name of that baby, born
from the word of great love that God spoke? The
baby's name was Jesus, and we have just been celebrating his birthday! Jesus is God saying 'I love you'.

Praying

Jesus, you show us what God is like.
You show us that he loves us.
Thank you, Jesus! Amen.

Activities

On the worksheet there are instructions for making
a frame to put on a mirror. Whoever looks into the
mirror will see someone God loves. There is also a

dot-to-dot which helps us see something we couldn't see before and a picture which reinforces the teaching.

PEARL DIVERS

Aim: To see Jesus as the Word of God.

Starter

Sit in a circle. Name the children in order round the circle: apple, orange, banana. Remove one chair and stand in the middle. Call 'banana!' and all the bananas get up and change places, while the person in the centre is trying to get a vacated seat. Whoever is left in the middle calls the next fruit, and so on. If the person in the middle calls 'fruit salad!' then everyone changes places.

Teaching

Draw attention to the way that in the game the person in the middle made certain things happen by the word they spoke. What other words in our language set things happening? (Words like 'Silence!' and 'Help!' and 'Quick march!') What word was spoken by God to start our world being made? ('Let there be light.' They can look it up in Genesis 1 and on the worksheet.) Read the first three verses of John 1 so that they can see how important God's word, or message, or communication was. If you have these displayed, the older children and better readers will be able to read it together. Or the children can repeat it after you, line by line.

Now read part of today's Gospel, starting at verse 14, asking the children to listen out for the word 'Word', and try and work out who it means. How can God's Word be in the world?

If they have no idea, remind them that the Word spoken by God at creation was God expressing his love. What person can they think of who expresses God's love, or tells us about God's love? If possible, draw the children to see for themselves that Jesus is the Word of God, rather than telling them outright. All words have power, and God's Word of love is not just sounds, but a person. Jesus is God saying 'I love you!'

Praying

Jesus, you are the loving Word of God.
Speak in my life
and help me to listen. Amen.

Activities

The power of words is looked at on the worksheet, and this leads on to reinforce John's teaching of Jesus expressing God's love in human terms we can understand. Instructions are given for creating a banner on this truth which can be carried into church and displayed for the benefit of the rest of the community.

GOLD PANNERS

Aim: To explore the link between Genesis 1 and John 1.

Starter

Give everyone paper and pencil. One person draws a picture, giving instructions as they go. The others draw from the instructions given, and the results are compared and giggled over. Alternatively instructions can be given for getting your body into a complex position and the results compared.

Teaching

Read the first few verses of Genesis 1, and look for what started creation off at each section (And God said/God's word). This was the expression of God's love and also a command with power in it.

Now look at the introduction to John's Gospel. What links are there with the Genesis passage? (The first words are the same: 'God said' and 'All things were made through the word'; in Genesis, life is brought to being through the word of God, and John says that in the Word was life.) Keep track of these on a flipchart sheet in two columns, headed 'Genesis' and 'John'.

Does John see that word, or expression, of God's love as a kind of holy speech bubble, or something more personal? Who was this Word of God, with a capital W? John sees the Christ as being part of God right from the beginning as the expressed Word and the life-bringer, who later on in time completed the expression of God's love by being made human and living out the love in person. In our drawings, the word spoken enabled us to get an idea of what was in the speaker's mind. (Not that we always got it right!) Jesus is the way God tells us about himself – how he thinks, and how he loves. We know from looking at Jesus that God is prepared to go to any lengths to rescue us. He is prepared to take huge risks for us. He doesn't mind suffering for us. He never stops loving us, and is always willing to forgive us and give us a fresh start. Jesus' life and death prove that we can trust God with our whole lives.

Praying

Word of the Father,
now in flesh appearing,
O come, let us adore him,
Christ, the Lord.

Activities

The Genesis and John passages can be compared in pairs first, using the worksheet, before the ideas are pooled in the whole group discussion. Allow time for questions about the nature of God and about Jesus' identity, as these are areas the group may be questioning at the moment, and it is important that they can air their ideas and doubts. They may like to talk over what some of their non-Christian friends believe as well, so as to work out where they stand.

The worksheet also raises the question of what our own words can express.

THE EPIPHANY OF THE LORD

Thought for the day

Jesus, the hope of the nations, is shown to the world.

Reflection on the readings

Isaiah 60:1-6
Psalm 71
Ephesians 3:2-3a, 5-6
Matthew 2:1-12

Beginning with one person (Abraham) and developing to embrace one family and eventually one nation, God has painstakingly planted the seed of salvation and nurtured it until the whole earth is involved. Isaiah had sensed that day in terms of a sunrise dawning with the light of day on a world of darkness, with all the hope and joy and relief that a new day can bring after a long, dark night. Probably this was one of the prophecies these magi had read as they studied the signs of the sky and wondered about life's meaning. And perhaps it was then that they felt stirring in them a profound calling to be, in person, those visitors who could symbolise the light dawning on the wider world. Certainly they must have been inspired by a powerful sense of urgency and necessity to make such a journey. And as they travelled, both physically and spiritually, towards Bethlehem, bearing the gifts laid down in those ancient scriptures, perhaps they were drawn by much more than a star. Jesus later proclaimed that anyone who sets out to search always finds.

Paul also knows himself to be commissioned to explain God's nature to the Gentiles. He is overwhelmed by the extraordinary way that the Christ has enabled us to approach the great and awesome God with freedom and confidence – as one of the family. And for all of us who are Gentiles, the feast of the Epiphany is particularly one to celebrate, since it marks the truth that we too are part of God's salvation and can share the light of dawn.

Discussion starters

1. Why did Herod find the prophesied birth threatening, while the magi were excited enough to travel many miles to see this child?

2. The Celtic Christians were very aware that the journey is, in a way, the destination. How is this true?

All-stage talk

Beforehand arrange for a knitter to bring a completed garment to church, together with a ball of wool and needles. Also prepare a large paper cut-out of a similar garment, which is folded up so that the first bit that would be made is the only piece showing. Alternatively use the actual garment, folded up at that point.

Begin by showing everyone the wonderful garment that the knitter has made and asking how long it took to make and who it is for. What did it look like at first, when they started making it? The knitter can show the ball of wool and needles, and do a couple of stitches. Hold up the needles with these stitches and point out that it doesn't look much like a jumper/scarf yet! But the knitter went on working at it, knowing that one day it would be ready.

God knew that one day everything would be ready for Jesus to come into the world, but he, too, took a long time making things ready. He started by calling one person, Abraham. (Show the folded garment, but don't refer to it – it is there to be visual reinforcement of what you are saying.) Over the years God went on to prepare all Abraham's family. (More of the garment is revealed.) Until over more years that family became one nation. (Reveal some more of the garment.) But God's plan still wasn't finished. He went on to include not one nation but all the nations and everyone in them. (Shake the whole garment out and display it.) Today is called the Epiphany because the word 'epiphany' means 'showing' or 'revealing' or 'manifesting', and when those wise men arrived at Bethlehem with their presents, God was showing or revealing himself not just to Abraham or his family, not just to the whole nation of Israel, but to all the rest of us in the world as well.

Whatever country you come from, whatever

you look like and whatever language you speak, God is saying to us today that he is there for you and no one is left out. You don't have to have the right ancestors to know God. You don't have to pass any exams to know God.

We sometimes get so interested in the presents the wise men were bringing to Jesus that we forget what brought them there in the first place. It was God who called these wise men from other nations to be there when Jesus was still a baby, so he could welcome them as well. They were there representing all the nations, so when God welcomed them he was welcoming each of us.

All-age ideas

- Today's Gospel can be acted out, preferably with costumes, as these may well be available from a nativity play. I am not suggesting a full-blown production with hours of rehearsal. All that is needed is a sensitive narrator, and the characters to mime what the narrator says.

- The wise men can take the collection and offer the gifts today. This emphasises their role as representatives of all the nations coming to be welcomed and offer their gifts. A globe can be offered at the same time.

- Have a bowl of burning incense, gold and myrrh arranged among flowers as a display either as people come in or near where they will come to receive communion.

Prayer of the Faithful

Celebrant
We are all companions on a spiritual journey.
As we travel together, we pray to God our Father.

Reader
We pray that the worldwide Church
may always be ready
to travel in the Lord's way
and in his direction.

Silence

Light of the world:
shine in our darkness.

We pray for the nations
as they live through conflicts
and struggle with identity.
We long for all peoples
to acknowledge the true and living God.

Silence

Light of the world:
shine in our darkness.

We pray for the families and the streets we represent,
asking for a spirit of generous love,
understanding and mutual respect.

Silence

Light of the world:
shine in our darkness.

We pray for all who are finding their way
tedious, lonely or frightening at the moment;
for those who have lost their way
and do not know what to do for the best.

Silence

Light of the world:
shine in our darkness.

We pray for those who have come
to the end of their earthly journey.

Silence

Light of the world:
shine in our darkness.

We join our prayers with those of Mary,
who showed her Son to the Wise Men:
Hail, Mary . . .

We pray to the Lord, in silence,
for our own needs and cares.

Silence

Celebrant
Father, we commend our lives
to your loving care,
through Christ our Lord.
Amen.

TREASURE SEEKERS

Aim: To become familiar with the story of the wise men finding Jesus.

Starter

Play pass the parcel. At the different layers have old bus and train tickets. The prize at the end is a star-shaped biscuit.

Teaching

Tell the children that today we are going to hear about a journey. It isn't a bus journey or a car journey or a train journey. This is a camel journey. (All pack your bags and get on your camels.) We are very wise people, but we don't know where we are going. We are looking for a baby king. And we are packing presents for him. (Pack gold, frankincense and myrrh.) Produce a star on a stick as you explain how a special star has started shining in the sky and we are sure it will lead us to the baby king. Lead off behind the star, riding your camels, and pretending to go over high mountains, through water, stopping for the night, and going to sleep and so on. At last you reach the town of Bethlehem (stick up a sign) where you find the baby king with his mum and dad. (Have a large picture, or one of the cribs made before Christmas.) We all get off our camels and give the baby our presents. The baby's name is Jesus and we have found him at last!

Praying

This is a prayer the wise men might have said. We have all been invited to find Jesus as well, so we can say it with them.

Thank you, Jesus,
for inviting me
to come and look for you.
I am glad I have found you! Amen.

Activities

To emphasise that the journey of the wise men was probably a hard one, there is a maze to help the wise men find their way to Bethlehem. The star-making activity will need star templates, and ready-cut card for the younger children.

PEARL DIVERS

Aim: To explore why the wise men made their journey and what they found out.

Starter

Who am I? Fix a picture of an animal or food item on everyone's back. They have to find out who they are by going round asking questions about themselves. The others can only answer yes or no.

Teaching

Point out how in the game they had to search for the right answer, and it was like a journey to find the truth. Sometimes people were helpful in that and sometimes they weren't. Today we are looking at some wise men who set out on a quest.

Have two or three adults meeting up as if they are resting on the journey and chatting together about what the day has been like, what they miss, and what they are hoping to find. It is best to try out the conversation beforehand but without any set words as it will then sound natural.

When the wise men have settled down for the night (or gone to feed the camels), show the children a sheet of paper with these headings on it: Who? What? Why? In the different sections brainstorm ideas about who they were (wise men from the East), what they were doing (following a star to find a baby king of great importance) and why they bothered (they had worked out from the signs that this birth was really important for the human race, and they felt a strong urge to be there and pay their respects). Use the children's words, of course.

Now have the wise men on their way back, talking about how they felt about King Herod, what it was like to see Jesus, and why they are going home by a different route.

Praying

Have some incense, gold and myrrh on display during the teaching. As each is brought to the front pray together:

Gold
The wise men brought gold to Jesus.
Jesus, we bring you the gold of our obedience.
Help us to live as you want us to. Amen.

Frankincense
The wise men brought frankincense to Jesus.
Jesus, we bring you the incense of our worship.
You are God and we worship you. Amen.

Myrrh
The wise men brought myrrh to Jesus.
Jesus, we bring you the myrrh of the world's sadness.
Help us to look after one another better. Amen.

Activities

You will need lots of lining paper or rolls of wallpaper. The best present we can give to Jesus is ourselves. Working in twos, the children draw round each other on the paper, cut themselves out and colour them. On the front write:

Jesus,
the best present
I can give you
is myself!

The cut-outs can be offered with the gifts in church and given back at the end of the service for the children to remember at home.

The worksheet has a sequencing activity to consolidate the teaching, and a look at our own journey to Jesus.

GOLD PANNERS

Aim: To understand how the wise men's visit symbolises all the nations coming to worship God.

Starter

A quest for the truth. As with the younger group, this involves having an identity fixed on your back. You can ask everyone else questions to discover your identity but they can only answer yes or no. Instead of pictures have names of famous people for this group.

Teaching

Read the Matthew passage for today, with different people taking the parts. Point out that the wise men were also involved with a quest for the truth. Use the worksheet to jot down all the things that helped them in their quest and all the things which threatened to make it fail. Also think about what made them set off on such a journey in the first place.

Now look at part of the Isaiah prophecy (Isaiah 60:1-4). How do the wise men fit in with this? Help them to see how they are in a way representing all the nations: God's salvation is not only for the nations of Israel but for the whole world.

Praying

Have a world map spread out on the floor. As you play some quiet music or sing a worship song or a Taizé chant, one by one the members of the group light candles in holders and place them on various parts of the world.

Activities

Make a collage for prayer which can be displayed in church or in the hall. Have a selection of newspaper pictures and stories showing some of the areas of need and evil in our world. Arrange them around a central picture (perhaps from a Christmas card) showing the wise men offering their gifts. Have the words from Isaiah 60:1-4 written on the collage.

THE BAPTISM OF THE LORD

Thought for the day

Jesus is baptised, and God confirms his identity and his calling.

Reflection on the readings

Isaiah 42:1-4, 6-7
Psalm 28
Acts 10:34-38
Luke 3:15-16, 21-22

Choosing names for our children is an important job, and one which most family members are more than happy to help with! Using one another's names in conversation is an important way of emphasising our concern for one another as precious and unique. To lovers the name of the beloved is deeply emotive. To be known by name indicates a closeness of relationship which as humans we value. It was hearing her name spoken that made Mary Magdalene realise she was in the presence of the risen Jesus.

As the Isaiah passage reminds us, God has called each of us by name; he knows and loves us as individuals, with our own particular mix of gifts and problems. The redemption he brings is personal and answers our particular deepest needs. It is good to celebrate this on the day we remember the Baptism of Christ, since each person's Baptism is not only their decision to commit themselves to Christ, but also God's calling to each by name.

We are told that at Jesus' Baptism the Holy Spirit descended on him in bodily form like a dove, as he stood praying. God was confirming Jesus' identity as his Son, with whom he was well pleased, and affirming his calling as Saviour of the world.

Discussion starters

1. Obviously Jesus was not being baptised because he needed to repent of his sins and turn his life round. So why did he do it?

2. What is the significance of water in Baptism?

All-stage talk

Using a flipchart, OHP or large sheet of paper and thick pens, collect everyone's suggestions about what water can do. Some of the suggestions can be drawn rather than written, so that the non-readers can also join in.

Read through all the suggestions to celebrate them, and talk about how Baptism picks up on these qualities of water and uses them to teach us spiritual things. When we are baptised we are 'drowned' to the old ways, given new life, washed clean, and refreshed. If it is practical, have water in the font and pour it as you explain each quality and its spiritual meaning.

Remind everyone that today we have heard about Jesus being baptised, and as he was praying the Holy Spirit came upon him, looking rather like a dove flying down to rest on him. And God told Jesus that he was God's Son, and God was well pleased with him.

Point out any dove symbols there are in the church – in carvings, pictures or windows – and have a cut-out dove shape (you can use the picture below) to show everyone. The dove has become a sign or symbol for the Holy Spirit because of what happened at the Baptism of Jesus.

When we are baptised God calls us actually by name to follow him, and sets us apart to love and serve him through the whole of our life. We can only do that with the gift of the Holy Spirit, so that is what we are given. The more we use it, the more it will grow. The sign of the dove will remind us. Whenever we see a dove or a pigeon, or a wild goose, it will remind us that we belong to God, and have chosen to follow him.

All-age ideas

- Give everyone a simple cut-out paper dove as they come in. Ask people to hold their doves in the palm of their hands during the intercessions.

- Decorate the font with flowers to give the sense of a cascade of water.

- Use the Renewal of Baptismal Vows in place of the Creed.

Prayer of the Faithful

Celebrant
Let us pray to the God
who calls us each by name.

Reader
We pray for all baptised Christians
to live out their calling in loving and holy lives.
We pray for those preparing
for Baptism and Confirmation;
for parents and godparents
to be given the grace and perseverance
to keep faithfully the promises made.

Silence

Come, Holy Spirit:
fill our lives.

We pray for peace and integrity
in all our dealings as individuals,
and in local, national and international conflicts;
for openness to hear God's wisdom
and courage to follow his lead.

Silence

Come, Holy Spirit:
fill our lives.

We pray for harmony and understanding
in our relationships with family and neighbours;
for the willingness both to give and to receive,
for the generosity of forgiving love.

Silence

Come, Holy Spirit:
fill our lives.

We pray for those whose weariness or pain
makes it difficult for them to pray;
may they sense the support and love
of the Church of God.

Silence

Come, Holy Spirit:
fill our lives.

We pray for those whose souls
have left behind their frail and broken bodies
and can now fly freely to live in God's company
for the whole of eternity.
May their loved ones be blessed and comforted,
and may we all be brought
to share the joy of heaven.

Silence

Come, Holy Spirit:
fill our lives.

Now we join our prayers with those of Mary,
the Mother of Jesus:
Hail, Mary . . .

In the silence of God's attentive love,
we name those we know
who are in any particular need.

Silence

Celebrant
Father, confident in your love,
we ask these things
through Christ our Lord.
Amen.

TREASURE SEEKERS

Aim: To know that God knows them by name.

Starter

Have a number of pictures or objects set out in the middle of the circle. The children guess the name you are thinking of by the way you describe the object or picture. Start with more general statements and get more specific, like this: 'I'm thinking of something which is round . . . and white . . . and you might put cornflakes in it.' They have to say the name, rather than pointing, unless they are very young.

Teaching

Have the children's names written out carefully on cards with a string attached so they can be worn. Hold up each one in turn and describe the person the name belongs to, by nature as well as looks, and with lots of positives. The children can join in by adding things they like about each one. When all the children are wearing their names, tell them how God knows each of us by name. He already knows all the things about us that we have talked about, and lots more as well.

Show a picture of a baby, a child, and an adult being baptised, and talk about God calling us by name to follow him. They may remember a Baptism in the family, or one of the recent ones in church, and can tell the others what happened. Have a jug and a bowl of water so they can focus on that as they hear about Baptism.

Praying

Dear God,
you know my name
and you know me
and you love me.
I know you by name.
I know you and I love you!

Activities

The name cards can be decorated with coloured sticky paper, finger-painting or with pens. On the sheet there are objects and people to name, and thank God for, and space to draw themselves doing something they like doing.

PEARL DIVERS

Aim: To get to know the story of Jesus' Baptism according to Luke.

Starter

Show pictures of famous people and characters in books, and see how many everyone can identify. Or you could match names with pictures.

Teaching

Bring along some Baptism certificates (a mixture of old and recent ones) and any other signs of Baptism that your church or the children's families have, such as robes, special candles, cards and presents to mark the occasion. It is a very special and important day for us because when we are baptised with water in the name of God the Father, Son and Holy Spirit, we are called by name to follow Jesus, and we decide to follow the Christian way of life.

Today we are going to look at what happened when Jesus was baptised in the River Jordan. Spread out the carpet tiles, or ground- and sky-coloured sheets or towels, with a blue river of paper or fabric running through the landscape. Base your pictures on the ones on the sheet. Put John the Baptist standing in the water, calling the people to make their lives clean, ready for the coming of the Messiah or Christ. Put in the crowds of people listening to him and deciding to put their lives right. Put in some people in the water and move John the Baptist around baptising them.

There was someone there that day who didn't need to clean up his life at all. It was Jesus. (Put him in.) He came with all the other people because he loved them and wanted to show that he was with them. We don't know what Jesus was praying as he went into the water and was baptised, but we do know that when he had been baptised he was filled with the Holy Spirit. It seemed like a pure white dove flying out of heaven to rest gently on him. (Place the dove just above Jesus.) God's voice was heard from heaven, saying to him, 'You are my Son and I love you; I am very pleased with you.'

In a way, Jesus was being told his name. He was being told who he was, and what he was called to be during his time on earth.

Praying

Dear Jesus,
you know me even better
than I know myself.
Help me to grow in your Spirit
day by day, all my life through,
rich with the gift of your love. Amen.

Activities

There are instructions on the sheet for making a model of the Baptism of Jesus. Each child will need a shoe box, cotton, card, colouring pens and glue.

GOLD PANNERS

Aim: To look at what Baptism means to us and what it meant to Jesus.

Starter

Give each small group a sheet of paper with the word 'Water' in the middle. Everyone writes or draws all the things that water does. Then the different sheets can be shared with the other groups.

Teaching

Begin by reading the passage from Isaiah 42, noticing that God chooses and delights in his special servant. Psalm 28 also has a wonderful description of God's great power and majesty expressed in terms of our natural world, his creation.

As you read Luke's account of Jesus' Baptism together, ask them to highlight with different coloured pens what the people were expecting of the Christ or Messiah, and what sign was given from heaven when Jesus was baptised. Do the two match up, or is there a contrast in the pictures used? Draw out the positive, and the gentle nature of the dove and the voice, compared with the thorough and quite aggressive 'cleansing' picture of the harvester sorting the wheat and burning the chaff. Also notice that the dove is a symbol of purity, and both pictures therefore describe a cleansing and saving.

Look at the sheets of paper with the 'Water' words on, and see how the idea of being dipped under the water in Baptism links up with these ideas of washing, drowning and sustaining new life.

Finally read the passage from Acts, and notice how the apostles were concerned that the new Samaritan Christians should have full Baptism, including the outpouring of God's Holy Spirit. How does this pattern link up with the practice in your own church? Discuss any questions they have, and have available some suitable literature for them to take and read if they wish.

Praying

Breathe on me, Breath of God,
fill me with life anew,
that I may love what thou dost love
and do what thou wouldst do.
Breathe on me, Breath of God,
until my heart is pure,
until with thee I have one will
to do and to endure.

(From the hymn by Edwin Hatch)

Activities

Look at a selection of pictures (from the library or local resource centre) showing different ways of being baptised, and talk about the differences and what they all have in common. The sheet has space to record thoughts about the meaning of Baptism for each of us, and also for Jesus.

LENT

FIRST SUNDAY OF LENT

Thought for the day

Following his baptism, Jesus is severely tempted out in the desert, and shows us how to overcome temptation.

Reflection on the readings

Deuteronomy 26:4-10
Psalm 90
Romans 10:8b-13
Luke 4:1-13

We often use temptation as an excuse for sin. It is Satan's whispered lie that when temptation gets too strong we have no hope of resisting and can somehow plead diminished responsibility. So it is quite an eye-opener to watch Jesus in action. After all, the temptations are exceedingly powerful, and the stakes are so high. If the powers of darkness can sabotage God's plan of salvation almost before it has started, then humankind will be gloriously and utterly lost and God will have failed. Arrogance, as well as deceit, is a hallmark of Satan.

So how does Jesus deal with these temptations, and what can we learn from him to help us when we too are severely tempted?

One thing Jesus doesn't do is enter into an argument with Satan. He would lose, because temptations are always cleverly constructed and entirely logical, with enough truth in them to make them appear plausible. What Jesus does is to recognise the motive under the scheming and address this instead, reaching into the secure promises of God and holding firmly on to these.

Using the vulnerability of Jesus' hunger, Satan subtly grafts this on to a challenge to his role and authority so that we can barely see the join. Jesus refuses to get drawn into this, and recognises that the fast is making him vulnerable, so he encourages himself with God's words which affirm what he is doing and its value. In the next temptation Satan attempts to take Jesus' pondering over his mission and his urgent longing for the coming of the kingdom, and to distort this into the need for a quick and immediate answer, which Satan offers to provide. Jesus recognises Satan's apparent generosity for what it is, and reaches into the firm law of God to deliver another simple one-liner: We are to worship only God. End of story, end of negotiation.

In the final temptation, where Satan again homes in on Jesus' longing to draw people to recognise God at work among them, the longing is manipulated into the possibility of bypassing the expensive and time-consuming method of salvation by love. Discerning that Satan's 'helpful' suggestions are really about denying God's sovereignty and total righteousness, Jesus reminds himself as well as Satan of the command not to put God to the test.

All too often we let ourselves get drawn into Satan's arguments. Think of those times your conscience will whisper that you shouldn't be doing what you are, and all the justifications pour into your mind. If we take Jesus' example, we will refuse to listen to these plausible arguments, and reach instead for the deep truths we know of God, recognising that Satan will use our vulnerable areas, and try to distort our noble ones. If we stick firmly with the truths of God, they will reassure and affirm us enough to resist temptation. Contrary to what Satan tells us, temptation can be resisted and overcome.

Discussion starters

1. Jesus must have wanted his disciples to know what had gone on in the desert or he wouldn't have told them about it. Why do you think he thought it was important for them to know?

2. Share any tips you have found helpful in overcoming temptation.

All-stage talk

On matching sets of three graded sizes of card, from A5 to huge, write these two messages, with the print and thickness increasing with the card size.

I want it and I want it now.
Love God and love one another.

Begin by explaining that Jesus went into the desert after he had been baptised, and had a very hard time out there being tempted. We all know what it feels like to be tempted. It's when we want something or want to do something which we know is wrong. (Show the middle-sized 'I want it and I want it now' card.) Ask someone to hold this card, but don't make them stand with their arms in the air for ages.

Jesus was being tempted to turn the stones into bread so he could eat them, but he knew that this would be using his power in a selfish way. He remembered that he loved God and he loved other people (display the largest 'Love God and love one another' sign). Ask someone else to hold this up.

As you can see, the love for God and other people stayed bigger than the temptation, and so Jesus was able to stand firm and not let the temptation get the better of him.

Whenever Jesus was tempted he always remembered that his love for God and other people was much stronger than the 'I want'. Put these signs down.

Now let's see what happens with us. First we get a little temptation inside us. (Give one helper the smallest 'I want' sign.) It isn't very big and we remember the right way to live (give the other helper the middle-sized 'Love God' sign) so we don't give way to the temptation.

But as we think about it more, this happens. (Exchange the small 'I want' for the middle-sized one.) And now there's a battle going on inside us, because the 'I want' is the same size as the 'Love God'. If we're not careful the 'I want' will get even bigger! (Swap it for the largest 'I want' sign.) And when we let the 'I want' get bigger than the 'Love God', even for a minute, we're in danger of falling into temptation, and doing or saying what we really know is wrong.

Jesus shows us how not to do this. As soon as you feel a little 'I want' coming on (show it), remember that you love God and you love other people more than you want what is wrong. (Display the middle-sized 'Love God' sign.) And if the 'I want' gets bigger in you (show the middle-sized 'I want') think hard about how you and God love each other (show the largest 'Love God' sign) so that the 'I want' is less strong and you can fight it; and instead of giving in and doing or saying what you know is wrong, God will be helping you to stand up to temptation and win.

All-age ideas

- On the walls have poster-sized versions of the advertisements below so that people can see how temptations use truth but distort it.

With the posters have a heading: 'Always read the small print!'

- During the first reading have a family bringing baskets of fruit and vegetables to lay in front of the altar.

Prayer of the Faithful

Celebrant
As children of our heavenly Father,
who knows us so well and loves us completely,
let us pray.

Reader
We pray for the Church
as it struggles to steer a straight course
true to the Lord's calling.
We pray for wisdom and courage,
honesty and the willingness to be vulnerable.

Silence

Father, lead us not into temptation:
but deliver us from evil.

Knowing our weakness in the face of temptation,
we ask for strength and protection
so that, though we stumble,
we shall not fall headlong.

Silence
Father, lead us not into temptation:
but deliver us from evil.

We pray for all those
who are fighting temptation
and finding it difficult to resist.
We ask that they may be helped to see clearly,
and be equipped with all they need
to choose what is right.

Silence

Father, lead us not into temptation:
but deliver us from evil.

We pray for those we love,
whose company we enjoy.
We pray too for those who irritate us
and those whom we annoy.

Silence

Father, lead us not into temptation:
but deliver us from evil.

We stand alongside all those who suffer,
all whose lives are in chaos or despair,
and all who live in the dark prison of guilt.
We pray for reassurance and peace,
understanding and compassion.

Silence

Father, lead us not into temptation:
but deliver us from evil.

We pray for the dying,
especially the unnoticed and despised.
We pray for those who have gone through death
and now see the Lord face to face,
that they may receive his merciful forgiveness
and know the joy of living with him for ever.

Silence

Father, lead us not into temptation:
but deliver us from evil.

Now we join our prayers with those of Mary,
the Mother of Jesus:
Hail, Mary . . .

Together in silence,
we name any known to us
with particular needs or burdens.

Silence

Celebrant
Father, we offer you our prayers
in trust and love.
Through Jesus Christ our Lord.
Amen.

TREASURE SEEKERS

Aim: To look at good ways of living.

Starter

Have a selection of balancing activities for the children to try. These could include walking between two chalk-drawn lines, climbing up to stand on a chair without using your hands, walking along a bench, standing on one leg, and walking along a piece of string laid along the floor.

Teaching

Talk about the balancing acts and how we had to try hard to stop ourselves falling and to keep our balance. In the way we live we have to try hard to do what is kind and loving and good. (Walk along the string line as you say this.) Sometimes we fall down on that (wobble off the string here), and end up being unkind and selfish. When that happens we have to put things right and get back to being kind and loving again. (Go back to walking along the string again.)

Have some pictures of people behaving well and badly. Show the pictures one by one, and decide together whether the people are walking God's way or not. If they are, put the picture on the string; if not, place it away from the string. Copy the pictures below or use your own ideas. They need to be pictures your particular group can relate to.

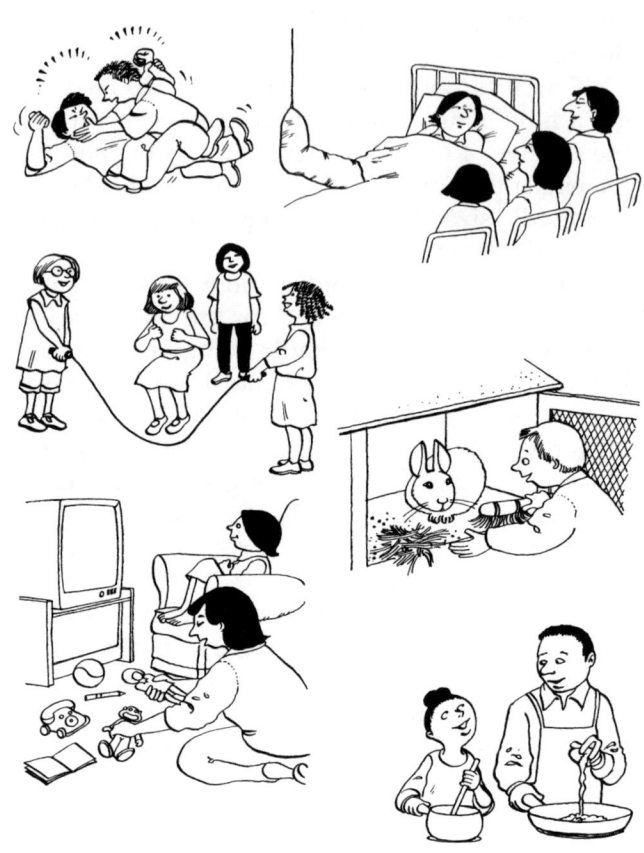

Praying

To the tune of *Here we go round the mulberry bush*. Act out the verses and add or alter them as appropriate for the group. The children's ideas can be incorporated too.

Help us, God, to share our toys,
share our toys, share our toys,
help us, God, to share our toys,
and live as Jesus told us.

Other verse ideas: to help our mums/help our dads; to look after our pets; to tell the truth.

Activities

On the worksheet there is a chart to be filled in through the week to draw attention to their good, brave and honest behaviour, and a 'spot the loving living' activity. They can also be taught Jesus' summary of the law using their fingers. They simply touch each finger of one hand (as if counting) as they say the words 'Love God, love each other'.

PEARL DIVERS

Aim: To know the story of Jesus being tempted and overcoming the temptations.

Starter

Come and sit on my chair. Everyone stands behind a chair except one person who goes out of the room while everyone decides whose chair will be the 'correct' one. When the 'outsider' comes in, everyone tries to make her sit on their chair, and she chooses a seat. If it is the agreed one, the owner of that chair goes outside next. If the wrong chair is chosen she is (very gently) tipped off and can try again. If she gets it wrong three times, someone else goes out and another chair is agreed on.

Teaching

Talk about how we were all tempting our friends to sit on the wrong seat in the game. In real life we are often tempted to do what is wrong, and we sometimes tempt, or encourage, our friends and brothers and sisters to do what is wrong, or avoid doing what is right.

Straight after he was baptised, Jesus was badly tempted too, even before his work had properly begun. If he had given in to those temptations, we would not be here today.

First put a large stone down in the centre.

Jesus was very hungry. He was fasting, going without food, for forty days, as he talked over with God what his work was, and how it could be done. He knew that he could use God's power. Now he was tempted to use it, not to save people but to change the stones around him into bread so he could eat something.

He knew that would be a wrong way of using God's power. So he said to Satan, 'People don't just need real bread to live on – they need my Father's words to live on as well.' Jesus stuck with what was right, so he could go on to feed us with his Father's words of hope and truth.

Now put down a globe.

Satan showed Jesus all the countries of the world, and pretended that he could give them all to him straight away, if Jesus would just worship him. Jesus knew that would be completely wrong, and was a lie, so he told Satan that God is the one you worship, and no one else, no matter what they offer you.

Now put down a first aid box.

Satan suggested that he could win people to him by being a superman, jumping off the top of the temple without being hurt. Satan even quoted from the Bible where it says God's angels will protect you and keep you safe. Jesus said, 'Yes, it does say that,

and it also says, "Don't you dare tempt the Lord your God".' Jesus knew that this wasn't the way to get people to follow God. He had to do it by loving them, even if that took longer and meant he would get hurt.

Praying

Jesus, you know what it is like
to be tempted.
And you never gave in.
Please give me the strength
to stand up for what is right. Amen.

Activities

The worksheet has puzzle activities to reinforce the teaching, and instructions for planting seeds to grow during Lent.

GOLD PANNERS

Aim: To explore the way Jesus stood up to the temptations and overcame them.

Starter

No 'yes and no'. One person is asked all sorts of questions by the group and must reply to them without saying 'yes' or 'no'. If they do, someone else has a go.

Teaching

In the game we were all trying to make the volunteer do the wrong thing. It is very hard to resist temptation, especially in areas where we naturally find ourselves wanting to do the wrong thing. Today we are going to look at how Jesus managed to resist temptations that were very strong.

Read the Gospel for today and then, using three sheets of paper, look at each temptation in turn, under these headings:

1. What did Satan say?
2. What was wrong about his suggestion?
3. How did Jesus reply?
4. Where did his quotation come from?

When you have looked at all three temptations, show a fourth sheet with the heading 'What about us?' Work out together a few hints picked up from Jesus to put into action whenever we are tempted. Some of these may involve getting prepared in advance (such as knowing the Bible well enough to use it). Discuss resources and possible training courses.

Praying

Lead us not into temptation
but deliver us from evil.
Amen.

Activities

The worksheet encourages them to look at tackling temptation in their own lives, and there is a magazine-style questionnaire to see how good they are at standing up for what they believe is right.

SECOND SUNDAY OF LENT

Thought for the day

God's glory transfigures Jesus as he prays on the mountain. Our lives, too, can become increasingly radiant as the Spirit transforms us.

Reflection on the readings

Genesis 15:5-12, 17-18
Psalm 26
Philippians 3:17-4:1
Luke 9:28-36

Those who are not committed Christians will often express disappointment at the selfish or immoral behaviour of churchgoing Christians. They obviously expect that our faith should make a big difference to the way we look, think and behave. I find this quite encouraging. Obviously it needs to be recognised that the Church is a 'school for sinners' and for those who know their need of God, rather than for the perfect. But it also suggests that those who make such remarks hang on to a belief in God's transforming power. And they are right to, because God can and does transform his close followers.

Moses, who communed as a friend with God, came away from the meetings with his face radiant and wears a veil to cover it. The veil prevented the people from seeing the glory of God which terrified them. When we recognise Jesus it is as if the veil is finally lifted, and as we draw closer to God in this new relationship, the Spirit can begin to transform us until our lives begin to shine.

So why don't they? Sometimes they do and we don't notice. It is quite likely that if you told someone you had seen God's love in the way they behaved they would be surprised. It may be that people have seen his radiance in you on occasions. You cannot spend your time regularly in God's company and work at living his way without it changing you and making you beautiful. But we also have to recognise that half measures are not good enough; Jesus always presents us with this challenge: 'Who do you say that I am?' What we reply has a lot to do with recognising the glory shown in the Transfiguration, and that will affect how we decide to spend our time and money and choices.

Discussion starters

1. What do you think the disciples were shown by this mountain experience with Jesus?

2. Why do you think the disciples kept quiet and didn't tell anyone what they had seen?

All-stage talk

You will need a hand mirror.

Begin by asking everyone if they have noticed how people often look like their pets, particularly dogs! Perhaps they choose a pet which reflects their own character. Today we are looking at how spending our lives with God makes us more and more like him.

Use the mirror to catch the light and throw it on to people's faces. Mirrors are excellent at spreading light around, because they are able to reflect light. In the Gospel today we hear of Moses, who was a close friend of God. He was the person who led the people of Israel out of Egypt, where they had been slaves, and through the desert to the promised land. When Moses had been on a mountain in God's company and was given the Ten Commandments, he came down from the mountain with his face glowing and radiant. Like a mirror, he was reflecting some of the glory of God. Sometimes if people are really happy – a bride and bridegroom getting married to the one they love, students hearing they have passed all their exams really well, or children on their birthday – we talk about them looking radiant, or glowing with happiness. How we are feeling and thinking inside changes the way we look.

When Jesus was on earth, three of his close friends were on a mountain with him when he was praying, and they saw him not just with a radiant face, but completely shining, or transfigured. What they were seeing was the glory of God in Jesus, who was and is completely at one with God, his Father. They heard God's voice explaining who Jesus was and telling them to listen to him. Not like listening to music in the background, but really attentive listening, like you would listen to instructions for flying an aeroplane if you were the only person on board able to bring it safely to land.

When we live our lives close to Jesus like this, listening to his quiet voice guiding us, talking over our problems and happiness with him, and working at living a good life, then gradually our faces will start to show some of God's glory, and our lives will start to shine, reflecting God's loving nature like mirrors (flash the light again) reflecting the light.

All-age ideas

- Have a mirror on the floor with a flower arrangement and lots of small candles on it, so that the picture of reflecting light and beauty is expressed.

- During the reading of the Gospel, have music playing, starting at verse 29. This can be provided by the organ or music group, or you could use taped music.

- For the penitential rite, give out small pieces of shiny paper (cut from wrapping paper). Explain that the cleaner, smoother and shinier the mirror, the better it works. Ask people to bring to mind anything in their life which needs cleaning, smoothing down or polishing. Give them time to tell God about it, and receive his forgiveness, so that they are all able to reflect God's love better.

Prayer of the Faithful

Celebrant
As God's people,
let us pray to him now.

Reader
We long to shine with the Lord's light.
May our hearts be set on fire with love for him
and for one another.

Silence

May our lives proclaim:
that the Lord our God is holy.

We pray for lives of light among the darkness
of injustice, corruption and despair;
may those who are already shining
in dark places all over the world
be strengthened.

Silence

May our lives proclaim:
that the Lord our God is holy.

May the Lord come into our homes
and make them places of welcome
where his love is woven
into all our relationships.

Silence

May our lives proclaim:
that the Lord our God is holy.

May those who have to suffer physical pain
or mental and emotional anguish
be given courage
and enabled to draw on the resources of the Spirit
that can transform all our pain and sorrow.

Silence

May our lives proclaim:
that the Lord our God is holy.

May all who have come to the point of death
be welcomed into the kingdom
of everlasting light.
May those who miss their physical presence
be comforted,
and may we all be brought to spend eternity
in the radiance of the presence of God.

Silence

May our lives proclaim:
that the Lord our God is holy.

We make our prayer with Mary,
faithful Mother of Jesus:
Hail, Mary . . .

Knowing that God our Father
hears the prayers of his children,
we pray in silence
our own individual petitions.

Silence

Celebrant
Father, we ask all this
through Christ our Lord.
Amen.

TREASURE SEEKERS

Aim: To look at how lives can shine with God's love.

Starter

Patches of sunshine. Have some cut-out circles of yellow paper scattered on the floor and explain that these are patches of sunshine in a dark wood. The children move and dance around to some music, and when the music stops they go and stand on a sunshine patch. Take away a patch each time so that in the end there is only one patch of sunshine left. Children not finding a patch to stand on are out.

Teaching

Talk about how much we need the sunshine. We need God's love to shine in the world too. God can help us to make our lives shine like patches of sunshine in the dark forest. Put out the sunshine patches again, and this time tell the children to stand in the darkness when you say something which is bad or sad, and go to a sunshine patch when you say something good and loving.

Bad and Sad
People hitting and hurting each other
Being grumpy and sulky
Being a pain
People not having anywhere to live
People telling lies
People not having enough to eat

Good and Loving
People saying sorry
Being friendly
Helping someone
People sharing their things with others
People telling the truth
Giving money to buy food for those who are starving

By physically moving into the sunshine when the 'shining lives' qualities are mentioned, the children will begin to understand the symbolism of radiant light in a spiritual sense. Jesus' life shone because of what he said and what he did. Our lives can shine with his love like patches of sunshine.

Praying

You will need the children to have made their sunshine mats for this. They start by standing on the mat and singing to the tune of *Twinkle, twinkle, little star*. At the darkness section the children move off the mat and walk around it, first one way and then the other, before moving back on to the mat for the last line.

We are sunshine in the darkness,
we are shining with your love.
Help us when we live in darkness,
help us when we live in darkness,
help all those who live in darkness
to shine like sunshine with your love!

Activities

Have some sheets of yellow paper with a wavy outline drawn on. Children old enough to use scissors can cut these out. Others will need help here. Or use white paper and let the children colour them with yellow crayons. The prayer from the sheet can be cut out and stuck on to the mat so that parents can sing the prayer with their children at home. The sheet also includes a drawing activity and a puzzle to see which behaviours belong to the 'light'.

PEARL DIVERS

Aim: To get to know the events of the Transfiguration.

Starter

Pass the smile; pass the frown. Sit in a circle. Someone starts by smiling at their neighbour who then passes the smile on around the group. When it gets back where it started, try passing the frown around the circle. For a real challenge, start a smile going in one direction and a frown in the other.

Teaching

Point out how the way we behave can get passed on to others. People who are happy often spread that around, and people who are gloomy and bad-tempered spread their gloom. The people who spent time with Jesus on earth were changed by being with him. Today we are going to hear two of those friends talking about a rather strange experience they had with Jesus, something they remembered for the rest of their lives.

Have two of the leaders (or two other volunteers imported for the occasion) being Peter and either James or John. You can have three people if resources run to this. They have just met up and are talking about what happened when they went up the mountain with Jesus and saw him shining as he prayed to his Father. Those who are chatting the story need to know the passage very well and talk it through together a couple of times beforehand. Think yourselves into character and talk about it as the real event it was, reminding one another of who you saw there, and what was said, thinking aloud your thoughts about what it meant, and why you were allowed to see it. The children will gain a great sense of immediacy if the conversation is informal but 'real'.

Have a mirror on the floor with several candles standing on it, and as the disciples get to the point when Jesus is deep in prayer have someone quietly lighting the candles. Nothing needs to be said about this, but the visual alongside the story will help touch their senses with understanding of the wonder of what was being seen.

Praying

Lord Jesus,
in your life we see the glory of God.
In our lives

we want to reflect God's glory
by the way we live.
May our lives
shine with love. Amen.

Activities

On the worksheet there are instructions for candle decorating. Great care must be taken to ensure everyone's safety. There is also a Bible study activity to reinforce the teaching and a picture to complete of the Transfiguration.

GOLD PANNERS

Aim: To explore the meaning of the Transfiguration.

Starter

Stand in a circle with everyone holding an unlit candle. One person lights their candle and uses that light to light the candle of the next person, and so on until the light has been passed all around the circle. Then all the candles are blown out. If you come into contact with a flame you get lit up yourself.

Teaching

Recap on Moses being the leader God used to bring his people out of slavery in Egypt and through whom he gave his people the ten commandments. Read Exodus 34:29-30 and talk about the way Moses' closeness to God made his face shine with God's glory.

Now look at the Gospel reading, using different voices for the different parts. On a sheet of paper or flip chart fill in the answers to these questions:

Where?
Who?
When?
Why Moses?
What was Jesus doing?
Who was God speaking to?
What were Jesus, Moses and Elijah talking about?
Why Elijah?
Why Peter, James and John?

This can be done first in twos and then in the full group if some would benefit from the extra confidence this gives. Most of the sections can be filled in by looking at the text, and others are to stimulate discussion. Moses and Elijah represent the Law and the Prophets. Jesus was about to reveal his glory through the cross. How might it help the disciples to see him radiant with God's glory before all this?

Praying

Lord Jesus,
as we gaze on your kingly brightness
so our faces display your likeness
ever changing from glory to glory.
Mirrored here may our lives tell the story,
shine on me, shine on me!

(From *Lord, the light of your love* by Graham Kendrick
© 1987 Make Way Music Ltd)

Activities

The worksheet enables the group to keep track of the discussion, and to think about areas of life which need shining lives to bring God's light into the darkness.

THIRD SUNDAY OF LENT

Thought for the day

The great 'I AM' calls people in every generation to repent so that God's kingdom can be established and grow.

Reflection on the readings

Exodus 3:1-8, 13-15
Psalm 102
1 Corinthians 10:1-6, 10-12
Luke 13:1-9

When God calls Moses from the experience of the burning bush, he refers to himself both as the utterly present – 'I AM' – and also the God of history – 'the God of Abraham, Isaac and Jacob'. God's record of total faithfulness throughout the generations enables us to see that we can trust him completely in every situation of the present. No wonder the psalmists often refer to God as our strong rock, on whose love and compassion, justice and forgiveness we can always depend. Our God will never betray us, let us down or ask of us what we are unable to give.

Moses' daunting vocation and commission eventually resulted in the people of Israel walking out of Egypt to freedom; God's promises are always accomplished. The reading from Paul's letter to the Corinthians reminds his readers of the careful protection and guidance provided for God's people in the desert. But it is a partnership, demanding commitment on both sides. Rather than creating us programmed to work with him in loving obedience automatically, God has graciously given us the power to choose for ourselves between good and evil, life and death. That gives the whole concept of partnership dynamic meaning.

We may know from our own experience the energising peace we discover whenever we are committed to working in partnership with God, and the draining heaviness that weighs us down whenever we have chosen to commit ourselves elsewhere. In today's Gospel we hear Jesus addressing the need we all have to repent; to turn right round whenever we are facing away from God's love and goodness. He firmly rejects the commonly held belief that suffering or violent physical death is punishment for an individual's sin, but teaches that we are all to recognise our need for repentance if we are to choose eternal life with God rather than eternal death.

The teaching is immediately followed by the parable of the hopeful gardener. We are given a wonderful image of God trying everything to prevent us being eternally lost. Like a hopeful and committed gardener, he wants to give us every chance to thrive. God lavishes his compassionate love on us, in the constant hope that we will turn to him and live.

Discussion starters

1. What does Jesus' parable of the hopeful gardener teach us about the way we are to treat others?

2. What is special about Jesus' view of death?

All-stage talk

Bring along a pot plant which is drooping and unhealthy, some plant food and water, a larger pot, trowel and some potting compost. Also a label – 'A Christian' – on a string, and some fruit shapes on strings.

Show everyone the plant and point out how pathetic it looks. Arrange for someone practical and organised to come and pick up the plant, assuring you they'll just get rid of it for you as it's messing up the nice clean church. Protest and stop them taking the plant away, explaining that you still have great hopes for this plant, and you intend doing all you can to help it thrive.

Invite a keen gardener and helper to come and sort the plant out, pruning it, watering and feeding it, and giving its roots more space in a bigger pot. As they do so (protecting the floor as they work), explain how Jesus told a story about a hopeful gardener who did this rather than throw a fig tree out. Jesus wasn't really talking about unproductive fig trees – he was talking about people.

Invite someone to help explain Jesus' story. Stand

them in a pot or bowl and hang a label round their neck which says 'A Christian'. If we were plants, producing fruit, our fruit as Christians would be things like loving kindness, truth, patience, joy, hope, self-control and so on. (Drape labelled cut-out fruits on the person's arms as you speak.) We can all see that this Christian is thriving and producing lots of spiritual fruit. But suppose they never produced any good fruit at all? (Take away the 'fruits'.) Does God just give up on them and have them thrown into hell for ever? What does Jesus' story tell us about this?

Gather ideas, and draw everyone to see that in the story we are shown a picture of what God is like – longing and longing for us to flourish and live, and willing to do everything he possibly can to help us start fruiting.

All-age ideas

- For the Penitential Rite:
  Persistently you call us, and we shut our ears to your voice.
  Lord, have mercy.
  Lord, have mercy.

  Always you are with us, yet we fail to recognise your presence.
  Christ, have mercy.
  Christ, have mercy.

  Patiently you coax us on, as we hold back and make our excuses.
  Lord, have mercy.
  Lord, have mercy.

- Have the words 'I AM WHO I AM' written large on the walls and pillars.

- At the offering of the gifts, invite everyone to offer who they are at the moment, so that the whole church makes an act of commitment to being *available* to God in a new way. As music plays or a hymn or chorus is sung, everyone who wants to writes their signature on a piece of paper and brings it to a basket placed near the altar. Everyone can then join in the prayer of offering – 'Blessed are you, Lord God of all creation, of your goodness we have ourselves to offer . . .'

Prayer of the Faithful

Celebrant
Remembering the faithfulness of God our Father, let us pray to him now.

Reader
God our Father is the God of Abraham, God of Isaac, God of Jacob; we thank him for his love and faithfulness in every generation.

We pray for the Church – the community of faith – for its leaders and teachers, for all the baptised; may we hear God's word and will for us, and have the grace to act on it.

Silence

Lead us:
Heavenly Father, lead us.

God our Father is God of the present, the past and the future; we pray that his kingdom of love may come in every place and every heart, to bring the healing and hope which he alone can give.

Silence

Lead us:
Heavenly Father, lead us.

May God our Father teach us to be family; may he be present in our homes, not reserved for some special place but in every room and relationship.

Silence

Lead us:
Heavenly Father, lead us.

We pray that the Lord of peace may anoint the crushed and oppressed with the balm of his presence, to uphold and encourage, to redeem and transform.

Silence

Lead us:
Heavenly Father, lead us.

We commend to the Lord of life our own loved ones who have died, in the sure knowledge that death to this life is not the final end many fear but the gateway to eternal life.

Silence

Lead us:
Heavenly Father, lead us.

We pray with Mary, who heard and believed God's promises:
Hail, Mary . . .

In the stillness of our hearts let us pour out to our listening God whatever hangs heavily on our hearts or uplifts us in thankfulness.

Silence

Merciful Father, we ask you to hear our prayers, which we make through Christ our Lord. **Amen.**

TREASURE SEEKERS

Aim: To understand that God wants to help us grow in love and goodness.

Starter

Have a selection of balls and bean bags, enough for each child to have one. Encourage them to practise their throwing and catching, so that they get better and better at it.

Teaching

Gather everyone in a circle and share with each other what you were all practising, and how you got on. Be encouraging and make certain that you are praising the way they have all been working hard at difficult things, rather than praising one 'expert'.

Following Jesus is something we can get better and better at as we practise, and we can all help one another along, encouraging each other in being loving and thoughtful, and trusting God.

Now tell them this story, which they listen to with their eyes closed. During the story quietly place a small vase of fresh flowers down in the middle of the circle.

This is a story about you. You are opening a big gate that leads into a secret garden. You walk through the gate and feel the soft grass under your feet. Colourful butterflies are flitting about, and the sun feels warm on your back. You can see your shadow on the grass, and a tiny ladybird climbing up a stalk. All around you are flowers – daisies and buttercups in the grass, red and yellow roses and blue forget-me-nots in the flower beds. There are apple trees and weeping willow trees. You can hear the bees buzzing and you feel happy in the garden.

You sit down on the grass and watch the gardener watering the flowers, snipping off dead bits of the plants and clearing the ground around them all in order to help them grow well. You see the gardener stop and look carefully at one plant which is looking rather a mess. You think to yourself that he might as well throw this plant away, as it hasn't grown any flowers or fruit for ages.

But the gardener is carefully looking after the plant. He's digging in some plant food around the roots, clearing away some strong weeds, and cutting the plant back a bit. Now he's giving it a good long drink, to make sure it has everything it needs to grow well. You think to yourself that the gardener must be very fond of all his plants to spend all that time on one which hasn't even been flowering. No wonder the garden feels a happy place to be. All the plants must know that the gardener loves and cares for them and will do everything he can to help them grow well.

You pick a few flowers and take them with you through the big gate and out of the garden. You take the flowers home and give them to someone you love. Then you suddenly find yourself back in the Treasure Seekers group at church, with the leaders and the other children, and there, in the middle of the circle, is a little bunch of flowers from that secret garden!

Praying

Dear Father God,
you are like a good gardener,
the way you look after us all
and love us
and help us to grow well.
Thank you! Amen.

Activities

On the sheet there is an outline of the garden, and the children can draw in the flowers and trees which the gardener loves and looks after, or they can stick on ready-cut shapes of coloured paper for flowers, with green wool stalks.

PEARL DIVERS

Aim: To look at the parable of the hopeful gardener and explore its meaning.

Starter

If the location and weather are suitable, take the group out to look at the way some plants are beginning to push shoots up from the earth, and others look like dead twigs but will soon be in bud. Look, too, at which plants seem to be strong and healthy, and which are not thriving at all. If you can't go outside, use house plants and walk around the room as if it's a garden.

Teaching

Back inside, share ideas about the state of all the plants. If they were the gardener, what would they do with the plants which seemed to have given up flowering or fruiting? (No right or wrong answers here.)

Explain that Jesus told a story with a secret meaning (a parable) about a gardener. You will tell them the story Jesus told, and then they can all be

detectives and work out what the secret meaning of the story is.

If you can, use a short sound-effects tape of bird song in the country to introduce the reading, and read the passage so it sounds like you talking it, rather than reading it. Then ask everyone these questions:

- Why did the gardener not want to cut the fig tree down straightaway?
- When are we like the fig tree in this story?
- If it was a thinking and feeling fig tree, what might it think and feel about the gardener?
- What do we learn from this story about the way God feels about us?

Praying

The Lord is compassion and love,
slow to anger and rich in mercy.
For as the heavens are high above the earth
so strong is his love for those who fear him.

(From Psalm 102)

Activities

On the sheet they are encouraged to see how God provides us with everything we need to become fruiting trees. They can then check how much they are making use of God's help. They will all need some tracing paper to make the window picture, celebrating God's love and care.

GOLD PANNERS

Aim: To explore the different perspectives of earthly and eternal death.

Starter

Sit them all around an object and have a go at sketching it from the different perspectives. Then share the varied responses.

Teaching

Point out that our view of the object depended on where we were viewing it from, and today Jesus is helping us to view death from a rather different perspective. Normally we are tied into viewing bodily death as the end of life, and very final. Keeping fit and alive at all costs is all part of this viewpoint. Jesus revels in full life and health, but today we hear him challenging the way we view death.

Read today's Gospel together. Today we have little problem with recognising that those who die tragically are in no way being punished for sin they have committed. But we're still hung into bodily death as being the BIG FINAL END, and find that pretty scary. Jesus is saying it's more like the curtains closing at the end of a play, which you then realise is only part of a much bigger play where the curtains are still well and truly open; it's the eternal life or death we need to be looking at very seriously, rather than putting all our energies into avoiding the bodily death section.

So how do we get fit and stay healthy in terms of eternal life and death? Jesus says it's all a question of repentance – turning our lives around constantly to be facing in the direction of the life that lasts for ever, or can be cut off for ever. If we are to survive (in the real sense of everlasting life), that turning Godwards of our lives is an absolute must. And the hopeful gardener story shows how keen God is to help us do it.

Praying

My soul, give thanks to the Lord,
all my being, bless his holy name.
My soul, give thanks to the Lord,
and never forget all his blessings.
It is he who forgives all your guilt,
who heals every one of your ills,
who redeems your life from the grave,
who crowns you with love and compassion.

(From Psalm 102)

Activities

On the sheet they will be looking further at Jesus' perspective on death. They are also encouraged to think through the process of repentance.

FOURTH SUNDAY OF LENT

Thought for the day

Be reconciled with God. He is waiting to welcome us.

Reflection on the readings

Joshua 5:9-12
Psalm 33
2 Corinthians 5:17-21
Luke 15:1-3, 11-32

The readings from the book of Joshua and the letter to the Corinthians both reflect on the way God lovingly provides for us and actually transforms us in the process, and this is dramatically floodlit with the familiar and well-loved story of reconciliation from Luke.

When the young man in today's Gospel has recklessly spent all his father's money and is sitting in rags, minding the pigs, he has sunk to about the lowest status in his society. Coming to his senses, driven there by hunger and despair, is like a sudden faint memory lighting up who he really is, who he was born to be, and where he came from. It is this memory of his true identity which enables him to rationalise his position. He plans to go back to his father directly, not creeping in disguise to be hired on the farm but as the son he has remembered himself to be. As a wayward son, he plans to live out his rightful punishment.

But, of course, this second part of his plan gets swallowed up in the father's reaction to his son's homecoming. Joy in their reconciled relationship cancels out the expected ongoing punishment. The important thing, as far as the loving father is concerned, is that his son is at last alive to him again.

What an amazingly powerful story this is for all of us who have wandered off squandering the riches of our God's creation, thinking ourselves totally independent of our creator, and forgetting entirely who we really are. The moment we come to our senses, and that faint memory of our true heritage and destiny as children of a loving God lights up inside us, we are started on the road back to our Father. It is the road of honest, candid dialogue with God, recognising the true state of ourselves, and our unworthiness to be treated as the heirs we have remembered ourselves to be.

Jesus' parable shows us the reaction we can expect from getting real with the living God; the extraordinary force of welcoming, forgiving and accepting love nearly bowls us over.

Discussion starters

1. Why does it seem to be more important to God than anything else that we are real with him?

2. What makes people 'come to their senses'?

All-stage talk

Bring along some balloons and party streamers, hiding them out of sight until the right moment!

Talk about how we all have times when we fall out with someone in our family, or with one of our friends, or with someone we work with. It feels rather as if a big crack has opened up between us and this other person. Sometimes it just lasts a few minutes, and sometimes, sadly, there can be unhealed rifts between people for years. Invite everyone to think of times we've fallen out with someone, and remember how we get to make up again, or seal up the gap that has opened up between us.

Collect suggestions of things we've found help heal those gaps. (These might include such things as saying sorry, or the other person apologising, making a joke of it, some kind of gift or kind letter, playing a different game, talking it through.) As humans we can get quite good at ways of making up because we get lots of practice! We often think it's worth the hard work of making up with people because we don't actually like the feeling of living with a great chasm between us and someone else.

In our Gospel today we heard Jesus' story about the young man who decided to come back to his father, even though he knew he'd really made a mess of things in his life. As that young man set off to walk back to his father's house, he wasn't pretending he hadn't done anything wrong. He hadn't come to ask for a loan or a new set of clothes so he could go back and carry on spending again. What actually happened was that the young man had suddenly realised what a mess he was in, and who he really was – the son of a wealthy and generous farmer. So then it made sense to go back home and ask to be treated not like a son, but like one of his father's servants.

And what happened? Bring out all the balloons and streamers as you remind everyone of the way the Father welcomed his son back home again, because he loved him so much and was so very happy the gap between them could be healed. God our Father is waiting to welcome every person who has got to the point of realising there's a gap between them and God, and who badly wants things to be put right.

All-age ideas

• An alternative Penitential Rite:

Let us go to our Father and say, 'Father, we have sinned against heaven and against you'.

Lord, have mercy.
Lord, have mercy.

Let us go to the One who welcomes sinners and eats with them.

Christ, have mercy.
Christ, have mercy.

Let us come, trusting in our Father's mercy and forgiveness.

Lord, have mercy.
Lord, have mercy.

• Have the Gospel acted out as it is read.

Prayer of the Faithful

Celebrant
Gathered together as children in God's family, let us pray.

Reader
We pray for the insight and discernment we need in our church community.
May we learn to have a greater love for the Lord as we learn to live and work in harmony, focused on him and not on our divisions.

Silence

God our Father:
supply our needs.

Into the unease and weariness of our world may the Lord pour the reality and wholesome truth we need, that we may learn mutual trust and support one another in love.

Silence

God our Father:
supply our needs.

Into the laughter and tears of family life may the Lord pour the freshness of his living presence, as we work at our relationships and deepen our love for one another.

Silence

God our Father:
supply our needs.

Into the loneliness and pain of those who feel rejected and unvalued may the Lord pour his compassion and reassurance, that each person may know the full extent of his love for them.

Silence

God our Father:
supply our needs.

May the dying know, and find comfort and hope in the Lord, and may those who have died in faith live for ever in the beauty of his holiness.

Silence

God our Father:
supply our needs.

Mary opened her life to the loving power of God; we make our prayer with her:
Hail, Mary . . .

We know that our merciful Father hears us;
let us pray in silence now
for our individual needs.

Silence

Celebrant
Father, hear our prayers,
through Christ our Lord.
Amen.

TREASURE SEEKERS

Aim: To know that God our Father is welcoming and forgiving.

Starter

Play a welcoming circle game. Everyone sits in a circle and the leader starts describing someone in the group. Everyone says together, 'I'd like to meet that person – who can it be?' The person concerned stands up and says, 'It's ME!' Everyone shakes hands with them or claps, before the leader describes someone else.

Teaching

Tell the children this story.

Yow Bear lived with a boy called David, who loved him very much. When David pedalled his car, Yow was always there sitting beside him, hanging out over the side and watching the pavement racing past underneath them. When David went to bed at night, Yow Bear snuggled in beside him. Sometimes he went exploring once David was asleep, but when that happened he couldn't quite manage to jump up on the bed again, so David would wake up to find Yow Bear lying on the floor.

If David was ever very cross or very sad, Yow Bear would either get stamped on a lot or cried on a lot, so he was quite a floppy bear and had been mended many times.

Yow Bear was a well-travelled Bear as David tucked him under his arm and took him with him everywhere he went. So Yow had been on a ferry (and hoped he wouldn't be dropped in the water), he'd been to school to see David's sister in a play, he'd been in buses and trains and cars.

One day there was jam tart and custard for pudding and David suddenly said, 'Can Yow Bear have . . . Where *is* Yow Bear?' And Yow Bear was lost. He wasn't under the bed or in the bath. He wasn't in any of the places he sometimes hid in. Everyone searched the whole flat, and nobody found him. Everyone was so sad that they didn't feel like eating the hot jam tart and custard.

Then Mum remembered where they had all walked that morning, watching a tractor at work, so she went outside to search for him there. David cried into Dad's sweater and hated the world.

After a while everyone heard the door open, and Mum's feet climbing the stairs to the flat. 'Growl, growl!' said Mum in Yow Bear's growly voice. David shot off Dad's lap and grabbed Yow very tight, hugging him and beaming away through his tears. Everyone was smiling and laughing and so happy that Yow Bear was home again. And everyone decided they'd like some jam tart and custard after all!

Praying

God our Father,
we belong to you and love you
and know that you love us.
Being with you makes us happy.
Amen.

Activities

The worksheet can be made into a 'welcome home' poster which they decorate with scrunched-up tissue paper, or an assortment of shiny and colourful scraps of paper, foil, and wool. The poster can then be hung up at home to welcome anyone who has been away.

PEARL DIVERS

Aim: To get to know the parable of the lost son.

Starter

Dear Mr Crocodile. Mr Crocodile stands at one end of the room and everyone else at the other end. They all say, 'Dear Mr Crocodile, may we cross your shining river?' Mr Crocodile then replies, 'Only if you're wearing blue/green/yellow/brushed your teeth this morning/write with your left hand . . .' All those in his particular category can take a step forward, and so on. When some of the children reach the other side of the room, they can welcome the next arrivals.

Teaching

Today we are going to hear one of Jesus' stories which is all about a journey home. Choose someone to be the father in the story, and others to be his two grown-up sons. Tell the story from the Bible passage, but using your own words, rather than reading it, so that the children can act it out. The rest of the group join in with all the partying, and they can also be pigs and servants.

After the story, thank all the actors, and ask the

children what they think Jesus might want to tell us through this story. Explain that Jesus would often tell stories and then leave everyone to think about them, rather than 'decoding' it all for them, because he wanted to get them thinking. Collect their ideas and talk together about them.

Praying

Father God, when we wander away from you
give us the grace to come to our senses
and start our journey home to your side,
knowing that your arms are open in welcome
because you love us so much.

Activities

Using the sheet they can make a model of the son returning to his father. For extra strength, the sheet can be mounted on thin card.

GOLD PANNERS

Aim: To explore what it means to be reconciled to God.

Starter

Mark out a crevasse on the floor with chalk, two or three metres wide. Either as a whole group or in pairs they are going to work out a way of bridging the gap. (It's an exceedingly deep crevasse.) Provide them with string. They can use the chairs in the room if they wish.

Teaching

Write the word 'Reconciled' on a card and talk about what it means to be reconciled to someone. Have some ideas ready to throw in, such as being at one again, being friends again, a rift between people being healed, the gap between them being bridged, a sense of new-found harmony and peace.

Read 2 Corinthians 5:17-21, preferably from *The Message* which makes the meaning very clear. Highlight for them the main ideas that God put the world right with him through Jesus, giving us a completely fresh start; that we're given the task of telling others what God's doing; and that we're called to persuade people to drop their differences and make things right between them. That's God's work, and we do it as friends of God.

Then read today's Gospel, seeing reconciliation in practice.

Praying

God our Father,
Jesus spoke your peace to a sinful world,
giving us the grace to be at one with you.
Teach us, as his followers,
to do the same,
turning hatred to love, conflict to peace
and death to eternal life. Amen.

(Adapted from today's Collect)

Activities

On the sheet are various situations where reconciliation is badly needed, and they can think over some ways to bring God's peace. They are also encouraged to look at areas in their own lives where there needs to be reconciliation with another person, or with God.

FIFTH SUNDAY OF LENT

Thought for the day

It is not God's wish to condemn anyone, but he longs for us to turn to him and live.

Reflection on the readings

Isaiah 43:16-21
Psalm 125
Philippians 3:8-14
John 8:1-11

Today's passage from Isaiah, written during the time of exile, speaks hope to a broken people. Through his prophet, God reminds his children of how in the past he led them out of a terrible situation into freedom. With that memory in their minds to help them trust, he draws them out of their present misery to hear about a future which is full of images of new life, growth and beauty. If God can make all things new, then there is hope for us in even the most appalling darkness and suffering. God's nature is to redeem; to compost our experiences, both sweet and bitter, and turn them into rich and fertile soil.

This means that we need not spend our time dwelling, full of guilt and shame, on past sins; we can instead bring them all to God and he will forgive us, effectively lifting from us the weights that bow us down and hold us back. It is freedom which

God offers us, the freedom of travelling light so that we can run more easily and lightly through life, with our hearts happy and at peace.

We see such freedom being offered in today's Gospel. We are not told anything about the woman in question, or indeed the man involved! It is possible, since this was a test situation, that the woman was well known to Jesus, and those offended at him keeping such company wanted to confront him with proof of her sinfulness so as to see how he could possibly retain any kosher 'cred' now that one of his friends had been caught in the act.

Certainly Jesus refuses immediately to be drawn into any debate; he gives everyone, including himself, a bit of time to calm down. His eventual reply forces everyone present to look at things differently. Mercy triumphs over judgement, and Jesus succeeds in persuading the entire angry crowd to act with mercy, born of their own recognition of need for God's mercy.

When he finally turns to the woman it is to offer her the freedom of walking into the future unimpeded by her past or the burden of sin. And that is what God offers to each of us.

Discussion starters

1. Why do you think Jesus answered the crowd the way he did, even though the people were right in saying that the lawful punishment would be stoning to death?

2. Are there some occasions when we doubt that God can really 'do a new thing' in our lives or habits? And in the church? And in our world?

All-stage talk

You will need some lengths of rope, chain or thick string, a blindfold and a bicycle security chain with padlock.

Talk about how we often tie our lives up in knots. We may remember having done something wrong and then having told a few lies to cover up. Or there may be someone we've once had a row with and now we dread bumping into that person ever again. Those kinds of experiences are rather like pieces of rope tying us up and preventing us from moving freely. (Ask a volunteer to help explain this by allowing you to tie them up here and there.)

There are other things which chain us as well. Pick out a really strong rope or chain and explain how selfishness ties us up and restricts our movement dreadfully – we're so busy thinking about ourselves, our own needs and wants, our own rights and so on, that we can't reach out to other people at all. (Tie up the arms firmly.)

Arrogance and vanity make us think we're so wonderful that they stop us seeing the truth about ourselves (put on blindfold), and fear and guilt can make us too terrified to move forward (tie up the legs). So we end up spiritually trussed up, living a compromise and never living life as fully as we could.

God loves us and hates seeing us like this; he yearns to set us free. We heard that message loud and clear in all our readings today – God is not out to condemn us, but to set us free to live. As soon as we hesitantly let him into our lives he will start untying our ropes of selfishness, taking off our blindfolds of arrogance and vanity and prejudice, unchaining our fear and guilt (do this as you talk), until he has set us free to live happily and love others. (The volunteer can leap and run around a bit to demonstrate.)

All-age ideas

• Write out the following message with the words on separate pieces of card: LET IN JESUS AND HIS LOVE WILL SET YOU FREE. Mix the words up, lay down the first word in place, and then, during one of the hymns, invite some of the children to put the words in order to make an important message. If they arrange this on the floor near the altar, everyone will see it as they come to receive Communion.

• Cradle one hand in the other. Love that hand and its owner as Jesus does, with understanding and affection. Then use those same hands to reach out to others in the sharing of the Peace.

Prayer of the Faithful

Celebrant
God is present with us now.
Let us bring him our prayers and concerns
for the Church and for the world.

Reader
We pray that the loving Lord
may continue to breathe his life into the Church,
so that we may speak his love to the world
and be willing to suffer and prepared for sacrifice.

Silence

Lord, through your love:
transform our lives.

We pray that the loving Lord
may breathe his peace into the world,
so that we may work together co-operatively,
sensitive to one another's needs and differences.

Silence

Lord, through your love:
transform our lives.

We pray that the loving Lord
may breathe his patience and forgiveness
into our homes and all our relationships,
so that we may learn
to cherish and respect one another,
and act with generosity.

Silence

Lord, through your love:
transform our lives.

We pray that the loving Lord
may breathe his encouragement
into every suffering and every sadness,
so that the dark and painful times
become places of strong spiritual growth.

Silence

Lord, through your love:
transform our lives.

We pray that the loving Lord
may breathe his welcome
deep into the souls of the dying,
so that death is only the door
leading to the joy of eternal life.

Silence

Lord, through your love:
transform our lives.

We make our prayer with Mary,
who knew the fullness of God's merciful love:
Hail, Mary . . .

Confident in God's forgiving love,
we pray our personal petitions
to him in silence now.

Silence

Celebrant
Father, accept these prayers,
helping us to follow
your example of forgiveness,
and to love others as you love us.
Through Christ our Lord.
Amen.

TREASURE SEEKERS

Aim: To see that God is in the sad and hard times as
well as the happy ones.

Starter

Have an assortment of junk, crayons, paint, wool
and glue. Tell the children that all this is stuff that
no one wants. It's stuff that people have thrown out
as rubbish. But we can use it to make things. Set the
children free to transform the junk, and then share
and admire what we all managed to make.

Teaching

Talk about the fun we've had with some old boxes
and thrown-out rubbish. God never thinks of anything or anybody as rubbish. He can make beautiful
things out of everything. Show some seed. What does
God make out of this dried up, dusty stuff? Flowers!
(Show some pictures from a seed catalogue.) Show
some vegetable peelings and old tea bags. What can
God do with this smelly old stuff? Compost to help
the tomatoes grow! (Show some ripe compost.)

It's the same with people. God doesn't think,
'Oh, they're too small for me. I can't work with
them.' He thinks, 'Ah, good! Some small people to
cheer someone up, or give their mum a hug, or
teach the grown-ups. Just what I needed!' And he
doesn't think, 'Oh, they're no good to me now
they're old and can't get out much.' He thinks, 'Ah,
good! Some old people who can't get out much, so
they've lots of time to think and pray for the holiday club. Just what I needed!' For God nothing is
rubbish and nobody is rubbish.

God can even use the times we are sad. He can
even use the bad things like accidents and wars, and
make something good come from them. Nothing
and nobody is too bad for God to use, because he
loves us all.

Praying

Loving God,
I am glad you love us so much.
I am glad I can help you now
as well as when I am grown-up.
You can use my sadness as well as my happy times
whenever you like. Amen.

Activities

If the children need more time to finish their junk
models they can do that now. The worksheet helps
them think about the good that God can bring out
of such things as moving house, a rainy holiday,
and a time in hospital. Make sure they understand
that God never makes bad things happen to us, but
when they do happen he always works to use them
for some good.

PEARL DIVERS

Aim: To understand that God does not condemn, but forgives, setting us free.

Starter

Have some wild creatures in a suitable container to look at together. (Snails, worms and beetles, for example.) After talking about them and enjoying them, explain that the creatures aren't able to live freely if we keep them caged up like this, so we need to set them free to enjoy living their lives outside again. Then go out and set the creatures free.

Teaching

Have one of those magic slates and draw someone with a really grumpy expression on it. If we decide that we don't want to have anything to do with such a grumpy picture, we can just slide the slate out and in to clear the screen completely. Now the grumpy picture is wiped away for ever. It's the same with computer screens – we can delete all our mistakes so no one would ever know we'd made them.

Today our readings from the Bible show us that God can do the same kind of thing with us. God doesn't want us to be walking through life weighed down with all our sins so that we can hardly move. God is full of love and mercy, and that means he has the power and authority to forgive us and set us free. Forgiving us is like wiping all our past mistakes and deliberate sins, so that they aren't there any more. There's an example of Jesus doing this in the Gospel today.

(Have a shallow tray of dry earth on the ground in front of you, and a number of rectangular building bricks, or chess pawns which you can place and move around as people.)

To set the event in context, ask everyone what kind of friends Jesus had – were they all good people? No, Jesus was well known for spending his time with people who behaved quite badly, and some of the religious leaders didn't think he should. They thought a good teacher should set a good example by mixing with good, well-behaved people.

One day Jesus was teaching in the temple and a crowd of people were listening to him. (Arrange a crowd of 'people'.) Suddenly there were shouts and screams, and some other people came in dragging with them a woman who had been caught committing a crime. (Arrange more 'people', together with one 'person' on their own.) The teachers shouted at Jesus, 'Our law says this woman should be stoned to death for committing such a crime – what have you got to say about that?'

Everyone waited to see what Jesus would do. Would he go along with the law and join in the stoning of this criminal? Would he say the sacred law was wrong?

In fact, Jesus didn't say anything. He just bent down and started writing on the dusty ground with his finger. Perhaps he kept rubbing his writing out, as God rubs out our sin. He knew everyone was really steamed-up, and it gave them all some space to cool off and calm down. But they insisted that he should answer them, and eventually Jesus looked up at them (you look up at the faces around you), and said, 'Let the person here who has never done anything wrong be the person to throw the first stone.'

First of all no one moved. Then the oldest person realised that they had done things that were wrong, and walked quietly away. (Remove one of the 'people'.) One by one, other people remembered that they weren't perfect either, and moved away (move all the others away), until in the end the woman was left standing there all on her own.

Jesus said to her, 'Where are they all – didn't any of them condemn you to death?'

'No one, sir,' replied the woman.

Then Jesus looked at her and said, 'I don't condemn you either. You're free to go . . . and don't sin any more.'

So the woman was set free to live. Her crime had been wiped out, and now she was given a completely fresh start.

Praying

Lord God, I know that I am not always loving.
Sometimes I am unkind and want my own way.
But I am sorry about this.
Please forgive me and make me more loving.
Amen.

Activities

On the sheet there is a picture to colour and make into a jigsaw puzzle, so that they can experience the way God mends broken lives and puts people together again when we get messed-up. Mount the picture on thin card before cutting it into pieces, and provide an envelope for each child so they can take their puzzle home with them.

GOLD PANNERS

Aim: To know that God is not in the business of condemnation but forgiveness.

Starter

Bring along a jigsaw puzzle for everyone to work on. God is in the rebuilding business.

Teaching

Read the passage from Isaiah, first placing it in the context of the people's disappointment and grief; Jerusalem, their holy city, has been destroyed, and they are forced to live in exile. How would this passage have filled them with hope in their suffering? Point out the way God is promising to bring about something new, which will change the whole world.

As you read from Philippians 3, show a picture from a newspaper sports page of athletes racing. What is the race we are running in? What is the prize we're aiming for?

Now read today's Gospel, trying to help them see both why the law demanded death and why Jesus is more concerned with a sinner's future. What does all this tell us about the nature of God?

Praying

Lord God, give us clear sight to see
when we are in the wrong,
courage to come to you in penitence,
and trust to receive your total forgiveness. Amen.

Activities

On the sheet are examples of punishments for the same crime in different countries, and there are questions for them to try answering about trusting God's forgiveness but not presuming upon it.

HOLY WEEK

PALM (PASSION) SUNDAY

Thought for the day

As Jesus rides into Jerusalem on a donkey, and the crowds welcome him, we sense both the joy at the Messiah being acclaimed, and the heaviness of his suffering which follows. Jesus' mission is drawing to its fulfilment.

Reflection on the readings

Liturgy of the Palms:
Luke 19:28-40

Liturgy of the Passion:
Isaiah 50:4-7
Psalm 21
Philippians 2:6-11
Luke 22:14-23:56 or Luke 23:1-49

It is no accident that the Isaiah reading, the Psalm and the passage from Philippians prepare us to hear the Gospel narrative of the Passion with our hearts as well as our ears. They have been chosen to work on our understanding and bring us to the point where we sense deep truths and echoes of hope, right in the centre of the gruelling and disturbing events of the Crucifixion. And even before these readings we will have joined with the crowds of Jerusalem in waving our palm branches and celebrating Jesus' entry into the city. It is a day of mood changes and can feel quite emotionally draining.

The Isaiah passage introduces us to the concept of the Saviour being a vulnerable, suffering servant, obedient to God's will, and utterly faithful to his calling, in spite of the rejection he receives and the way his mission is misinterpreted. Then the Psalm expresses firm trust in God's loving goodness which continues for ever. This is not a shallow feel-good factor, but a steady pulse of assurance which works in the bewildering and distressing times, as well as the times of relief and lighthearted happiness.

The letter to the Philippians focuses our attention on the amazingly generous nature of Christ's humility. With the Isaiah passage fresh in our minds, we realise that Jesus is taking on that suffering obedience of the loyal servant which is bound to bring with it rejection and worldly failure and misunderstanding.

So when we come to the story of the Passion in today's Gospel, all the echoes from Isaiah, the Psalm and Philippians are there, enabling us to grasp something of the cosmic proportions of what we are witnessing; something of the extraordinary love and provision, gracious humility and total faithfulness of our God.

Discussion starters

1. Was there any way the suffering and death of Jesus could have been avoided?

2. Reading the account of the Passion, what do we learn about the nature of God?

All-stage talk

Ask about football matches people have watched which have been really memorable and exciting. If you happen to have any players in the congregation, ask them to talk about a particularly memorable moment of triumph, and how it felt to have the spectators sharing the exhilaration.

When Jesus rode into Jerusalem all the crowds were on his side, cheering, waving and singing, pushing for the best view, and excited not just with Jesus as a hero but at what was a turning point for their side – their country. There would have been some there on that first Palm Sunday who saw it as a political statement, others as religious revival, others as a festive carnival of some kind.

So why did Jesus ride into Jerusalem on a donkey?

He was doing something the scriptures had said would happen to the promised Messiah. This meant he was giving a very strong hint to the people about who he was. He was saying that the Messiah had now come and was entering the holy city of Jerusalem as a king. But instead of all the rich clothes and grandeur of an earthly king, Jesus was riding on a very humble animal that was often piled high with people's luggage and shopping. It was a bit like using a shopper bike rather than a Rolls Royce, stretched limo or BMW.

All the crowds that day cheered Jesus, but a few days later, once he didn't look like a winner any more, many of the same people had turned against him and were yelling for his blood.

What kind of supporters are we? Do we support our team only when it's doing really well, or do we hang in there even after a run of lost games? Do we stick with our friends even when they go through a bad patch? Do we keep trying even when a marriage gets shaky? And, perhaps most important of all, are we happy to sing God's praise in church on Sunday but ignore him or deny him by our behaviour and language and choices during the week?

These are Palm Sunday questions which we need to ask ourselves today.

All-age ideas

- Give the children coloured crêpe-paper streamers to wave in the procession, and choose songs which are joyful and don't need books for at least part of the route. Encourage the children to shout and dance and sing – children were very noticeable on the first Palm Sunday.

- Look at some imaginative ways of presenting the Gospel using different voices, singing it, using slides as a visual focus, changing the lighting during the narrative, or using expressive mime during the narration.

Prayer of the Faithful

Celebrant
As we recall Jesus entering Jerusalem,
let us gather our thoughts to pray.

Reader
As the crowds welcomed Jesus,
we pray that many more will welcome him
into their hearts and lives over the coming year.
We pray for opportunities to spread the good news
and courage to take them.

Silence

Lord, you are our God:
we welcome you!

We recall the donkey Jesus rode on,
and we pray for that real humility in our hearts
which treats status and image casually,
and truth and loving service seriously.

Silence

Lord, you are our God:
we welcome you!

The children sang and shouted in praise;
we pray for the children in our homes,
our city and our land.
May we not fail them
in the support and teaching they need.

Silence

Lord, you are our God:
we welcome you!

The crowds were responding
to the healing love
they had seen in action in Jesus.
In our love and prayer
we now bring all those
we would have brought to Jesus for healing and help.
May they be given comfort and reassurance,
wholeness and hope.

Silence

Lord, you are our God:
we welcome you!

Jesus knew he was riding to his death.
We pray for all on that last journey,
especially those burdened with fear and guilt.
We commend to God's eternal love all who have died.

Silence

Lord, you are our God:
we welcome you!

We make our prayer with Mary,
who shared her Son's sorrows:
Hail, Mary . . .

Together in silence,
we name those known to us
who need our prayers.

Silence

Celebrant
Father, hear our prayer;
may we praise you not only with our voices
but in the lives we lead.
We ask this through Christ our Lord.
Amen.

TREASURE SEEKERS

Aim: To introduce them to the story of the entry into Jerusalem.

Starter

Stop, wave, shout hooray! When different signs are displayed the children 'Stop!' (a red circle), 'Wave!' (a cut-out or real palm branch), and 'Shout hooray!' (a crown). You can also sing a praise song, such as *Sing Hosanna*.

Teaching

Using upturned bowls and pots and a green cloth or large towel, let the children help make a model landscape. Boxes covered in white paper make the Jerusalem buildings, and the path down into the Kidron valley is a length of brown crêpe paper or material. Cut out coat shapes of fabric which the children can lay down on the road in front of Jesus, and have a card cut-out of Jesus riding on the donkey which you can move along as you tell the story. Let the children all wave their paper palm branches, standing around the model. They will feel as if they are all part of the story.

Praying

Hooray for Jesus,
riding on a donkey!
Hooray for Jesus,
he is our King!
Hooray for Jesus,
coming to Jerusalem!
Hooray for Jesus,
he is our King!

Activities

Today the children may be joining in the parish procession, with streamer-waving, singing and dancing. They will also be preparing the model. Have large palm leaves drawn on green sugar paper. Older children can cut these out themselves, and those just mastering the scissors technique can make random cuts along the sides of the basic shape. Pictures to help with this and the houses are given on the worksheet. There is also a picture of the event which the children can complete by drawing in the people cheering Jesus on his way.

PEARL DIVERS

Aim: To get to know the events of Palm Sunday and think about its significance.

Starter

Stop, go, cheer! Make a red 'Stop' and a green 'Go' sign, and a crown. Have the words for shouting written up large and with a festive feel. When the red sign is shown they have to freeze; when the green sign is shown they can move around the room; and when the crown is shown they shout 'Blessed is he who comes in the name of the Lord! Hosanna in the highest!' Sometimes the green sign and the crown can be shown together.

Teaching

The children's classic book *Donkey's glory* (Nan Goodall) includes the story from the donkey's point of view, and the Palm Tree series includes *Jesus on a donkey* which tells the story from the point of view of one of the children. Pictures to accompany the telling can be copied on to acetates and shown on an OHP, or simply held up and shared.

Praying

Holy, holy, holy, Lord,
God of power and might!
Heaven and earth are full of your glory;

Hosanna in the highest!
Blessed is he who comes in the name of the Lord.
Hosanna in the highest!

Activities

On the worksheet there are instructions for making a picture in relief using aluminium foil and the template provided. The children may also be joining in with the parish procession, waving streamers, singing and dancing. Another activity on the sheet involves decoding a message which can be checked by reading Luke's account of the entry into Jerusalem.

GOLD PANNERS

Aim: To look at the statement Jesus made by his entry into Jerusalem and the mixed reactions to it.

Starter

Tales of the unexpected. Sit in a circle. Each person in turn adds one word to make a group story. Draw attention to the way the story ends up quite different from what you expect from the word you added, because different people have different ideas and plans.

Teaching

Have a large sheet of paper with a picture of the entry into Jerusalem in the middle. Round the out-side of the picture work together on comments and questions which different people might have made at the time. What might the children have thought and wondered? What about Peter, Judas, Mary, Lazarus, the Pharisees, and the Romans? Put their suggestions in speech bubbles, identifying the speakers.

Now read the Luke version of Jesus' entry into Jerusalem with different people reading the parts, and everyone being the crowd. Then read Philippians 2:6-11 noticing how that Palm Sunday procession acted out Christ's character.

Praying

Thank the Lord because he is good.
His love continues for ever.
I was in trouble. So I called to the Lord.
The Lord answered me and set me free.
I will not be afraid because the Lord is with me.
People can't do anything to me.
The Lord is with me to help me.

(From Psalm 117)

Activities

Make a short radio documentary with an interviewer asking various representatives what they think against the crowd background and a commentator describing what is happening. The worksheet provides a short script to use and adapt.

GOOD FRIDAY

CHILDREN ON GOOD FRIDAY

Many churches organise separate worship and teaching for children on Good Friday. It is important that they are enabled to be part of this time, and Easter cannot really be celebrated with meaning unless we have also stood at the foot of the cross.

Whether you are planning to create a children's 'way of the cross', in and around the church, a prayer trail, craft activity, or dramatic presentation of the events, bear in mind that young children need to have the whole story, including the Resurrection, rather than being sent home with the pain and suffering of Jesus and no mention of Easter. We also need to be sensitive about dwelling on the horror of the Crucifixion, and it may be necessary to split the children into age groups for part of the time, even if you have very small numbers in each group. Hot cross buns with a drink can be part of the event, and they need to come away with some sense of the amazing love of God.

EASTER

EASTER DAY

Thought for the day

It is true. Jesus is alive for all time. The Lord of life cannot be held by death. God's victory over sin and death means that new life for us is a reality.

Reflection on the readings

Acts 10:34, 37-43
Psalm 117
Colossians 3:1-4
John 20:1-9

Throughout the whole world today Christians are celebrating the most extraordinary event. Death, the most final thing we know as humans, has been the setting for the greatest regeneration story of all time. Jesus of Nazareth, handed over to the Roman authorities for execution and a cursed death, has been raised to a kind of life never before experienced. He has a body, the scars are still visible, he talks, listens and eats. Yet he is no longer bound by space or time.

In Christ's risen nature we sense the stirring of a new life, freed from all the tragedy and pain of mortal life, and full of hope, joy and overwhelming fulfilment. But the Resurrection stories are about people who are emotionally confused and drained. The exhausting events of the past week have them seeing but not recognising, wondering and agonising but not immediately able to make sense of anything. And that is so human and reassuring for us to read.

So often it takes us years of living before we eventually grasp something of God's involvement in our journey or our pain. So often the evidence of his real, loving presence is staring us in the face, and yet we assume any number of other factors are responsible. Peter was wallowing so deeply in his own misery and pessimism that he probably wouldn't have noticed Jesus if he had been standing there next to him. It may well have been that Jesus was!

With great gentleness and courtesy Jesus holds back on revealing the full power and vibrancy of his new life, so as to lead people at their own pace to recognise the astounding truth. He lets them see only what they are capable of assimilating, for he loves them, and has no desire to scare or overwhelm. That is just as true for us today. The more we seek this risen Lord, the more of him we will notice, recognise and delight in.

Discussion starters

1. What difference does it make to you that Jesus is alive for all time since that first Easter Day?

2. How can we help others to recognise the living Jesus in this generation and in this location?

All-stage talk

Take along a few Easter cards you have received, and show them around, describing the pictures on them. There are probably some fluffy new chicks, young lambs skipping about in the spring fields, lots of flowers, and some decorated eggs. And we probably all gave and received a chocolate Easter egg today. So all this says that Easter is a happy, festive occasion, in tune with the new life of spring-time, with all the new birds, animals and flowers.

What else? Some cards have a garden with an empty tomb, and three crosses on a hill in the distance. Others have made all the flowers into the shape of a cross. So what do these cards tell us about Easter? They tell us about another kind of new life, which doesn't happen naturally every time winter is over, but only ever happened once. It wasn't an ordinary thing at all. It was so completely amazing and impossible that people are still talking about it two thousand years after it happened! Do you know what it was? (Let them tell you.)

Well, that's impossible, surely. People can't come back to life again. It just doesn't happen. The fact that it actually did happen – that Jesus really did die on the Friday, and he really was alive again on the Sunday – shows us that Jesus must be more than a human being. He must be God as well as human. And he must be still just as much alive now as he was then. No wonder we want to celebrate and give one another flowers and cards and Easter eggs! Spring is nice to celebrate, but this is the most wonderful event ever. It means that nothing, not even death itself, is out of God's reach for saving and transforming.

When you eat your chocolate eggs, and open your Easter cards, remember what we're really celebrating today: Jesus is risen. Alleluia! (Everyone can shout back: 'He is risen indeed. Alleluia!')

All-age ideas

• Have one flower arrangement consisting of three levels. The lowest arrangement has rich dark purples with only a few hints of gold. Gradually the colours blend into the gold, yellow and white of Easter at the top arrangement. This will be a visual reminder of the journey to Easter through the suffering of Good Friday.

• Part of the children's day during Holy Week

could be given over to creating a banner proclaiming the message of Easter. This can be made of fabric, with the design stuck (with double-sided sticky tape) or appliquéd on to the background, or of heavyweight wallpaper using either paint or collage work.

- The Easter garden presents a wonderful opportunity for different age groups to work together. Consider having a garden outside the church as well as inside.

- Encourage everyone to bring bells to ring in a burst of praise with the organ or music group just before singing the Gloria.

Prayer of the Faithful

Celebrant
With joy in our hearts,
come, let us pray together.

Reader
We remember with gratitude
the presence of the Church
in remote and highly populated areas
all over the world.
We pray for all other Christians rejoicing today
in the wonder of the Resurrection.

Silence

Life-giving God:
give us new life in you.

We pray that we may recognise the risen Lord
as we walk through our days,
and we ask that he may remove anything
which blurs our spiritual vision.

Silence

Life-giving God:
give us new life in you.

We pray for the courage to speak out
against injustice and oppression;
we pray that our leaders may establish and uphold
right values and sensitive legislation.

Silence

Life-giving God:
give us new life in you.

We pray that those of our families and friends
who have not yet met the risen Lord
may be drawn into his company and introduced,
so that they can enjoy his faithfulness and love.

Silence

Life-giving God:
give us new life in you.

We remember those whose lives
are filled with pain, anxiety or sorrow,
and ask that the risen Lord may come alongside them
and speak their name.

Silence

Life-giving God:
give us new life in you.

With the words of Resurrection fresh in our minds,
we commend to the Father's eternal love
those who have died,
that they may live with him for ever.

Silence

Life-giving God:
give us new life in you.

We join our prayers with those of Mary,
in her Easter joy:
Hail, Mary . . .

In and through the power of the risen Lord,
we make our private petitions and thanksgivings.

Silence

Celebrant
Father, in grateful thanks,
we pray we may be worthy
of all your gifts and blessings.
Hear our prayer through Christ, our risen Lord.
Amen.

TREASURE SEEKERS, PEARL DIVERS AND GOLD PANNERS

If possible, it is recommended that the children and young people are in church with the other age groups today. Use and adapt some of the all-age ideas, and involve the young people in some of the music and in the decorating of the church.

TREASURE SEEKERS

Aim: To enjoy celebrating that Jesus is alive.

Starter

Have an Easter egg hunt, preferably outside if this is safe and practical.

Teaching

Palm Tree publish a version of the Resurrection story called *Jesus is risen*; or you could tell the story gathered around an Easter garden that the children have helped to make.

Praying

Jesus died for us
  (arms out, head down)
Now he's alive for us
  (jump up and clap hands over head)
Hip, hip, HOORAY!
Jesus is alive today!
  (raise arms)

Activities

Use plasticine or playdough for the children to make their own models of the garden, and the women coming to the empty tomb. On the worksheet there is a picture of the women visiting the tomb early on the first Easter morning.

PEARL DIVERS

Aim: To teach them about the first Easter.

Starter

Have an Easter egg hunt, preferably outside if this is safe and practical.

Teaching

Have two leaders as the women, talking over what happened that morning. It needs to be in a chatty, informal style, rather as two friends might talk over their experience of bumping into someone really famous who helped them pick up the shopping they had dropped. Only this experience of meeting the risen Jesus is so extraordinary that both of them are still fairly dazed by it.

Praying

Christ has died.
Christ has risen.
Christ will come again.
Alleluia!

Activities

On the worksheet there are instructions for making a cross of flowers. Each child will need a piece of oasis and access to either a garden or a selection of small flowers. There is also a picture of the first Easter morning to complete and colour.

GOLD PANNERS

Aim: To celebrate the good news of Easter.

Starter

A time of praise, with everyone playing instruments and/or singing music suitable for this age group.

Teaching

Read Acts 10:34, 37-43, and then the John account of the empty tomb. Talk together about how each of those involved might have felt, and compare the way Peter talks in Acts with what we hear of him in today's Gospel. What had made the difference?

Praying

Lord, it's gradually dawning on me
that you were completely dead on that Friday,
and now you are completely alive.
Total victory over sin and death!
I want to share your risen life
for the rest of my life. Amen.

Activities

The worksheet helps to keep track of the discussion and gives instructions for making flags which can be used when they go into church.

SECOND SUNDAY OF EASTER

Thought for the day

Having seen Jesus in person, the disciples are convinced of the Resurrection. We too can meet him personally.

Reflection on the readings

Acts 2:42-47
Psalm 117
1 Peter 1:3-9
John 20:19-31

People will often say, 'If I hadn't seen it with my own eyes I'd never have believed it!' Sight is the sense we trust most for evidence and proof. There are many who assume God does not exist because they cannot see him with their eyes, and it is interesting that God has chosen to withhold from us that very proof of existence that we prize most highly. It's almost as if he is challenging us to be less dependent on this sense because our very mastery in sight can blind us to other kinds of perception.

The disciples had the women's eye-witness account to trust, but they didn't trust it. They were only convinced of the Resurrection when Jesus suddenly appeared right there in the room with them, talking with them and fully alive. We may think we are convinced of the Resurrection, but supposing the risen Christ suddenly appeared visually in the middle of our worship, and spoke to you, and looked you straight in the eye. I suspect our conviction would suddenly rocket, and we would be bursting to tell everyone about it.

The really exciting thing is that we can also meet the living Jesus personally. We may not be able to see him visually, but there is no doubt that he is with us in person whenever we gather to pray, whenever we share the Eucharist, and whenever we 'wash one another's feet' in loving service. Sometimes his presence is full of peace, sometimes reassuring, challenging or affirming, and as we become more attuned to his company, we come to realise that sight isn't the most important proof after all.

Discussion starters

1. How do you think the apostles felt when they found Jesus there among them for the first time since the last supper?

2. What would you say to someone who felt they could only believe in God if they could see him?

All-stage talk

Beforehand place a tape or CD in your pocket. Begin by telling everyone that you have got an orchestra in your pocket and asking them if they believe you. Then show them the tape or CD. Now they have seen with their eyes they know exactly what was in your pocket. And now that they understand what it is, they can see that you were right – you did have an orchestra in your pocket, but not in the way they expected!

Jesus had told his friends that he would have to suffer and die before rising to new life, and they hadn't understood what he meant. Even when Jesus was dying, nailed to the cross, they didn't realise that this had to happen if we were to be saved from sin and death. Instead they felt miserable and let down and lost and confused. They didn't believe because they hadn't seen for themselves. (Put the tape back in your pocket.)

Then, on the first Easter evening, Jesus was suddenly there with them. He was alive, talking with

them and they were so excited and overjoyed to have him there again. Now that they had seen him they knew it was true that he was alive. (As you say this bring out the tape from your pocket again, but don't refer to it. It will simply help them make connections.)

But it was also different from what they might have thought. Jesus wasn't exactly the same as before. With this new life he was able to be there without having unlocked the doors. He could appear and disappear. But he was a real person, not a ghost. He didn't make the disciples feel scared; he filled them with peace and happiness.

At last they began to understand what he had meant when he had talked to them about dying and rising again. They began to understand that God's love had to go right through death, loving and forgiving the whole way, so as to win the battle against evil. When Jesus came through death and out into the light of new life, he was like a butterfly coming out of its chrysalis – the same but completely different, free and beautiful.

Thomas and the others needed to see Jesus with their eyes for quite a few times after the Resurrection. They now had to learn that he was always there with them, even if they couldn't see him.

All-age ideas

• While singing the *Caterpillar* song, have a few children with painted net butterfly wings and wrapped in green towels to look like caterpillars. They are squirming around, pretending to eat plants and then curling up during the chrysalis part. Then they throw off their towels and fly about all over the church, ending with arms raised in front of the altar.

• Today's reading works well with different voices and a narrator.

Prayer of the Faithful

Celebrant
In the knowledge that God is here present with us, let us pray.

Reader
We pray for our bishops, priests and deacons, in their demanding ministry of love, that they may be given all the support, grace and anointing they need.

Silence

Open our eyes, Lord:
to see things your way.

We pray for the gifts of discernment and integrity
among all those who govern, advise and lead.
May all self-centred ambition be cleared away
so that our leaders are free to serve.

Silence

Open our eyes, Lord:
to see things your way.

Whenever we have eye contact with family, friends,
neighbours or colleagues,
we pray that the Lord may be there
in that communication,
and remind us of our calling to love one another.

Silence

Open our eyes, Lord:
to see things your way.

We call to mind those whose eyes are wet with tears
or tense with pain.
May they sense the Lord's reassuring love
which can bring us through the darkest of valleys.

Silence

Open our eyes, Lord:
to see things your way.

Jesus is the firstfruit of the new and eternal life.
In gratitude for the privilege
of knowing them here on earth,
we pray for those
who have recently walked through death
into that promise.

Silence

Open our eyes, Lord:
to see things your way.

Together with Mary,
the Mother of our Redeemer,
we make our prayer:
Hail, Mary . . .

In the name of the risen Lord,
we name our own particular cares
and concerns.

Silence

Celebrant
Father, we know that you are here present;
hear the prayers we make,
confident of your love.
Through Christ our Lord.
Amen.

TREASURE SEEKERS

Aim: To experience that something can still be there
even if we can't see it.

Starter

Play a peep-bo game with the younger children
and a hunt-the-slipper game with the older ones.
Point out that the slipper was there all the time,
even before we found it.

Teaching

Spread out a towel, sheet or carpet tiles on the floor
and copy the pictures below on to thin card. Gather
the children around and tell the story of today's
Gospel, using the pictures.

Praying

Dear Jesus,
I can't see you
but I know you are here.
I know you can hear me,
and I know you love me.
Thank you, Jesus! Amen.

Activities

On the worksheet there is a dot-to-dot picture of Jesus
to complete, and a picture to colour. Also there is
an activity which helps the children appreciate
their senses, and realise that sight is not the only
way of knowing something is true. Possibilities for
the seeing but not touching category would be the
sun, moon and stars; hearing but not seeing might

be someone's heartbeat, the wind, or thunder; touching but not hearing might be a table or a sandwich; and all three might be a person.

PEARL DIVERS

Aim: To help them see the reality of Jesus being alive again.

Starter

Play detectives. Everyone stands in a circle with one person in the middle. A ball or balloon is passed around the backs of everyone and the detective in the middle has to discover where the ball has got to. When they think they know, they point to the person they suspect. If they are right, this person swaps as the next detective. It was when the detective picked up the clues and actually saw the ball that they knew for certain where it was.

Teaching

Beforehand a leader and a child prepare a short informal conversation in stage whispers, talking together about Peter and the other friends of Jesus, about all the healing that's going on, and the way they are sure that Jesus is very much alive. They are whispering because it's dangerous to be heard talking about Jesus as if he's still alive.

Now Peter (another leader or invited helper) comes in, singing to himself, and the others rush up to him and ask him how he can be so sure that Jesus – who was so completely dead – is completely alive.

Peter explains to them and the children how they know because they've met with Jesus in person. He explains in his own words, and from his own point of view, the events on that first Sunday when Jesus was suddenly there with them, and how he came again the following week, when Thomas was there as well.

Praying

Jesus,
I have heard the witness
of those who saw you alive
after the Resurrection,
and I believe they told the truth.
You are alive,
and I can live my life
in your company!
Thank you, Jesus.

Activities

On the sheet there are pictures in speech bubbles so they can pretend they are Peter and Thomas, and some of the healed people, explaining why they know Jesus is really alive. There is also a blank speech bubble for the children to draw in a situation where they know Jesus is really alive (such as receiving Communion at Mass; helping them be loving when they want to be nasty; calming their fears).

GOLD PANNERS

Aim: To look at the importance we place on seeing in order to believe, and how Jesus honoured this for Thomas and the other apostles.

Starter

Use the 'Convince them' exercise on the sheet, where they have to try and persuade their partner that a tall story is true.

Teaching

Look at the account in John's Gospel. As in our starter activity, the disciples were trying to convince Thomas of something he wasn't sure was true. The apostles were actually eye-witnesses of the risen Jesus, and so they knew they were speaking about something that had really happened.

Use the sheet to guide you in the discussion about it, so that they are able to draw out some of the factors involved in being convinced, and in recognising and perceiving things with or without the aid of visual evidence.

Praying

Lord Jesus,
Thank you for helping Thomas believe.
Please help my friends,
especially . . .
to know you are real
and always here with us. Amen.

Activities

Talk over particular situations in their lives and friendships where there is scepticism, doubt and disbelief. Pray for one another and for the people mentioned.

THIRD SUNDAY OF EASTER

Thought for the day

Those who know Jesus and recognise that he is the anointed Saviour are commissioned to go out as his witnesses to proclaim the good news.

Reflection on the readings

Acts 5:27-32, 40-41
Psalm 29
Apocalypse 5:11-14
John 21:1-19

This week the readings invite us to see the consequences of the Resurrection both from a heavenly and an earthly point of view at once, which is a very three-dimensional experience! In the passage from Apocalypse we see through the eyes of the visionary the ecstatic and eternal welcome given by the inhabitants of heaven to the triumphant Lamb of God, who has proved worthy of all honour, glory and praise through his total sacrifice, self-expending and loving obedience.

From the earthly point of view we have the disciples, so wonderfully human and well-meaning and bumbling, going back to the safe place they came from as a natural reaction to the trauma and turmoil of the present. We recognise the symptoms, as we remember our own tendency to settle into old established behaviour patterns if God's new direction for us is proving too challenging or too open-ended.

So, typically, our God makes his appearance in a place we will be bound to meet him: the place we are fishing in. And as Jesus sets up his camp breakfast on the beach, he gives those friends he loves so fondly the opportunity to discover him, recognise him, and recommit themselves to his way of living. Gently and deliberately Jesus leads Peter to undo those denials and face the dangerous consequences of commitment realistically. There is a maturity about Peter's commitment now which is quite different from his previous enthusiastic claim that he would never forsake his Master. This commitment is quieter, and made with more self-knowledge. Peter is growing up.

Whenever Jesus meets us and challenges us, we become his witnesses and are drawn into a commission which carries great responsibility. Those who have not met Jesus will judge him by the way we behave and speak.

Discussion starters

1. What do you think was going through Peter's mind at each stage of his conversation with Jesus on the beach?

2. What does Jesus' approach to Peter teach us about our way of evangelising others?

All-stage talk

Beforehand prepare some masks from thin card, and mount them on sticks so that they can be held up in front of people's faces. Here is the pattern.

Begin by asking for two volunteers (of different age groups) and giving them a brief interview: What is your name? What is your favourite colour? What do you enjoy doing? How did you get to church today?

Explain that it's nice for us all to know who these people are, and suggest that we all get to know the name of someone in church today. We may see them there regularly but have never actually discovered their name!

Notice how Jesus made a point of calling Simon Peter by his name in today's Gospel. 'Simon, son of John, do you love me?' And on the first Easter Day when Jesus met Mary in the garden he called her by her name, and that's when she recognised him as Jesus.

Produce the 'happy' mask and ask for a volunteer to 'wear' it. Talk about the way we sometimes pretend we're different from the person we really are, because we think God and other people will like us better. This person is pretending to be happy. But if we are pretending, and God knows that inside we are really feeling very grumpy or sad, then the mask we are wearing makes him sad. This person is pretending to be very holy and good. But if we are pretending, and God knows that inside we are feeling angry and resentful, then the mask we are wearing makes him sad.

Jesus wants us to trust him with our real selves, even the bits where we make mistakes and get our lives in a mess. He speaks to us by our real name and will spend our lifetime teaching us who we really are. (Take the mask away.)

All-age ideas

- Have this written on the handout, or displayed

on the OHP so that each person is able to join in with the responses.

Leader	My child, where are you?
All	Here I am, Lord, right beside you.
Leader	That is not the person I know and love. Where is the real you, my child?
All	Here I am, Lord. Surely you recognise me now?
Leader	I recognise the face you wear, but where is the real you that I love?
All	Suppose I showed you and it was unacceptable?
Leader	It is the real you that I love.
All	Then just as I am, O Lamb of God, I come!

- Alternatively, this can be done by a hidden voice and someone wearing a mask, which is put aside at the end.

- The Gospel can be mimed as it is narrated.

Prayer of the Faithful

Celebrant
Let us gather with our prayers
before the God who knows each of us by name.

Reader
We pray for the newly baptised
and those who have recently returned to the Lord.
As the Church, may we support them well
and delight in them as members together
of the Body of Christ.

Silence

Here I am, Lord:
send me!

We pray for strength and protection
against all hypocrisy and double standards
in our society.
We pray for a spirit of genuine service
among all who lead and in all areas
where we have authority.

Silence

Here I am, Lord:
send me!

We pray that our homes and our relationships
may be places where people know,
by the way we look at them and treat them,
that they are valued, cherished
and respected for who they are.

Silence

Here I am, Lord:
send me!

As we call to mind all who have learned
to regard themselves with contempt,
we pray that the Lord may draw near to them
and whisper their true name,
so that they discern the truth
of his love and respect for them.

Silence

Here I am, Lord:
send me!

We pray for the dying
and those who have recently died,
commending them to the joy
and safe-keeping of God's love.

Silence

Here I am, Lord:
send me!

We share Mary's Easter joy
as we join our prayers with hers:
Hail, Mary . . .

In silence filled with love,
we name our particular prayer burdens.

Silence

Celebrant
Father, may we, who confess Christ as Lord,
live in his strength.
Through the same Christ our Lord.
Amen.

TREASURE SEEKERS

Aim: To get to know the story of today's Gospel.

Starter

Going fishing. Borrow or make the kind of magnet rod and lines which can catch paper fish with paperclips on their mouths. Have the paper fish cut ready so the children can decorate them and add the paperclips. Put the fish in a carton pond, and let fishing commence!

Teaching

Tell the story with the children all acting. They push the boat into the water, throw the net out into the water, wait, inspect the net, wait some more, and get fed up. Then catch sight of a man on the beach, cup your hand to your ear to hear what he says, pull in the net, throw it in the other side and haul in the massive catch. Realise that the man on the beach is Jesus, give a great shout, wade to shore and enjoy breakfast together.

Praying

Dear Jesus,
thank you for coming with us
to the shops / on the bus / to the dentist.
Wherever we go
you are always there for us. Amen.

Activities

If you get enough small cartons, each child can colour one to make a complete fishing set to take home. The worksheet has the outline for a collage picture which can be completed by sticking on cotton wool clouds, shiny paper fish and a red shiny paper fire on the beach. There is also a fish jigsaw with the words 'It's Jesus!' on it.

PEARL DIVERS

Aim: For them to connect Peter's previous denial with today's commitment and commissioning.

Starter

Sit in a circle and go on a campfire-style 'lion hunt'. The journey to the cave – through short grass, long grass, sticky mud, water and so on – is repeated at speed in the other direction on the return journey. Today we're going to look at the way we sometimes have to go back the way we came to put things right in our lives.

Teaching

Have a fishing net (such as a net curtain), some shiny paper fish, some driftwood and matches, and a mirror, explaining that all these come into today's story. Read the story from the *International Children's Version* or the *Good News Bible*, asking the children to listen out for when the objects are mentioned. This will help to focus their listening, and they will also notice that the matches are there as a sign of the driftwood being a fire, and there is no mention of a mirror. Explain that the mirror is, like the matches, a sign for something that is going on in the story.

Show people their faces in the mirror and point out that by doing this you are helping them to see for themselves what they look like. In our story Jesus is helping Peter to see what he is really like, and in our lives Jesus helps each of us to see what we are like as people. Some things we know already. You probably know if you are a kind person, or if you worry a lot, or if you get easily upset, or if everything makes you laugh. You might already know whether you are good or bad at telling the truth, making up quickly after an argument, or cheering up your friends. That's good. Jesus wants us to get to know ourselves.

Sometimes people get frightened by what they find out about themselves. Perhaps they would like to think they were kind, but they find out that really they are quite unkind. Peter wanted to be the kind of person who would stick up for Jesus however dangerous it became, but he found out on Good Friday that he was actually a bit of a coward. Three times he had denied he even knew Jesus.

Jesus wanted to show him that he still loved him, and it was OK to be like he really was, so long as he didn't pretend he was different. That way Jesus could help him learn to be the brave person he wanted to be. Three times Jesus gave Peter the chance to say he loved him, so that the past was put right.

And Jesus says to us, 'It's OK to be the person you are. You don't need to pretend you're different. Together we can work on the things you find hard.'

Praying

Jesus, you're right.
There isn't any point in pretending with you,
because you know me as I really am.
I'm glad I'm me, if you're glad I'm me!
Let's work together
on those things I find hard. Amen.

Activities

The separate figures on the sheet can be coloured and cut out and stuck on to a background of blue and yellow sugar paper. Other things can be added, such as pieces of net and shiny fish, to create a collage picture. There is also an activity on the sheet to link Peter's denial with this fresh chance to put things right.

GOLD PANNERS

Aim: To look at the way the risen Jesus meets, calls by name and commissions, and how we should be prepared for this in our own lives.

Starter

Using the worksheet, each person writes their Christian name. The pages are swapped around and each one writes a positive and realistic adjective beside the letters, like this: Dave becomes Daring, Adventurous, Vocal, Enthusiastic.

The sheets are then swapped back for people to read their personalised name. Or people can write their own, or work in pairs.

Teaching

Begin by reading the passage from Apocalypse, working out who the Lamb is, and why he is being given such a welcome into heaven.

Having established that we are talking about Jesus, look together at the fish for breakfast story, to see how the humans on earth are coping with the Resurrection. Help them to see the importance of the way Jesus calls Simon by name each time, as he gives him the opportunity to heal the hurts and have a fresh start.

Our name stands for who we are, without any masks.

Praying

Lord,
give me the courage
to come to you just as I really am,
recognising my need of you
and willing for you to work
in me for good. Amen.

Activities

Use the masks on the sheet to think about the kind of cover-ups we put in place as humans to try to kid ourselves, or those we want to impress, or God. And those individualised names can be written out and decorated appropriately and given to the person they celebrate. All of these can be worked on as a group activity, so that each person is affirmed by the whole group.

FOURTH SUNDAY OF EASTER

Thought for the day

Jesus, the Good Shepherd, leads his flock into eternal life.

Reflection on the readings

Acts 13:14, 43-52
Psalm 99
Apocalypse 7:9, 14-17
John 10:27-30

As we continue to celebrate Easter, today's readings help us to view the whole of life through eyes of eternity. The Resurrection showed Jesus to be the Good Shepherd he had claimed to be, leading his people through death into the meadows of life in all its fullness with no end, no suffering and no evil at all.

In the Gospel we hear Jesus expressing his faithful care of his sheep, and the love bond which binds them to him and keeps them eternally safe. It is such a liberating truth to know that, whatever happens to hurt the body, Jesus the Good Shepherd will always protect his sheep from ultimate hurt.

The reading from Acts shows some of that temporary and temporal hurt happening to Paul and Barnabas in the form of persecution for proclaiming the Gospel. Just as it starts to look hopeful that God's good news is being heard and understood by large numbers of people, the opposition sets in, disrupting, confusing and undermining, so that Paul and Barnabas end up being aggressively expelled from the city. But evidence of the Good Shepherd's ultimate guiding and care shines out in the way that they are filled with joy and the Holy Spirit, even as they meet complete 'failure', insult and rejection.

Such a reaction is extraordinary, and was in itself an amazing witness to life which is altogether larger and more full of meaning than anything imprisoned in the limits of time and space. The Good Shepherd has already led them into eternity, and they live the eternal life even while they continue to live in time as well.

In the passage from Apocalypse we are seeing all this eternal living from the other side of the grave. Those known to the Good Shepherd – those who follow him and listen to his voice – emerge into the realm of life beyond physical death, suffering and evil, to live for ever in the presence of God.

Discussion starters

1. If someone asked you why you were convinced Jesus was alive today, what would you offer as evidence?

2. What do you think Jesus meant when he said, 'I and the Father are one'?

All-stage talk

First ask for an intrepid explorer and blindfold the valiant person who volunteers. Now set out an obstacle course which ends with building a tower of three cartons at the far end, which are to be brought through the obstacles one by one.

Ask for three other volunteers and explain to the explorer that s/he can choose any one of these guides to help them build the tower by going through the obstacle course. The first guide is blindfolded and has his legs tied together. The second guide can see but can only see the place where the tower will be built. The third guide can see and is able to move around wherever s/he likes. The big question is . . . which guide will the explorer choose? Before the explorer chooses, invite everyone to tell someone near them which guide they would choose and why. Then ask the explorer to decide and set them off, timing their task to create urgency.

Afterwards explain how Jesus the Good Shepherd is like the guide who can see and move anywhere he likes. He is both in time and eternity, and this makes him by far the wisest choice in our lives, because he can see the whole situation. He knows where we are and what our limitations and weaknesses are. He can come alongside us and help us through even the most frightening or difficult times in our lives, and, at the time of our death, he can lead us safely into heaven. To be part of his flock we have only to listen to his voice and to follow him wherever he leads us.

All-age ideas

- Have two or three 'stations' of prayer focus on situations where Christians are being harassed or persecuted for living and preaching the Gospel. While music is playing, invite people to walk round and look at the displays, adding their names to encouraging letters provided, or writing letters or cards to those in authority.

- Include a sheep and/or a shepherd's crook in one of the flower arrangements today, and have some wheat and spring meadow flowers, with a written heading: 'Jesus the Good Shepherd leads his sheep through life into eternity.'

Prayer of the Faithful

Celebrant
As members together of the Body of Christ,
let us pray to the true and living God.

Reader
We pray for the nurture
of each member of the Church;
for the newly baptised and for all
in ordained and lay ministry,
that our love for one another may show
as we work for the coming of the kingdom.

Silence

Direct our hearts, O Lord:
to love you more and more.

We pray for the gift of discernment,
so that we recognise God's presence,
and reverence his face
in the faces of those we meet.

Silence

Direct our hearts, O Lord:
to love you more and more.

We pray for our civil rulers
and all those who govern our country
and make its laws,
that we may act responsibly and with compassion,
attentive to real needs and good values.

Silence

Direct our hearts, O Lord:
to love you more and more.

We pray particularly for homes
filled with suspicion and envy,
and ask for the healing of old hurts,
together with hope and perseverance
as people set out on paths of reconciliation.

Silence

Direct our hearts, O Lord:
to love you more and more.

We pray for those whose capacity for trust and love
has been damaged by other people's sin.
We long for the healing and forgiving power of the
    Spirit,
so that all who are imprisoned by their past
may walk freely with the Lord.

Silence

Direct our hearts, O Lord:
to love you more and more.

We pray for those who have recently passed
through death,
that they may be judged with mercy,
so that, made whole in God's love,
they may know the joy of eternal life.

Silence

Direct our hearts, O Lord:
to love you more and more.

We pray with Mary,
Mother of the Good Shepherd:
Hail, Mary . . .

In a time of silence,
we share with God our Father
our personal burdens, joys and sorrows.

Silence

Celebrant
Father, hear our prayer;
in joy may we follow the way of Christ,
who alone has the words of eternal life.
Through the same Christ our Lord.
Amen.

TREASURE SEEKERS

Aim: To know that Jesus is like a shepherd to us and we are like his sheep and lambs.

Starter

Lay on the floor a blue sheet to be water and some green paper clumps of grass. The children crawl around being sheep and lambs, and one child is dressed up (in nativity play costume or dressing-gown and tea-towel) as a shepherd who leads them around the room, taking them to the water for a drink, and the grass to graze.

Teaching

Show the children some pictures (from books or calendars) of shepherds with their sheep, and talk about the way the shepherd is there to look after the sheep and lambs, and take them safely to green pastures and fresh streams of water.

Now show them a picture (from a children's Bible) of Jesus with some children. Jesus is like a shepherd to us and we are like his sheep and lambs. All through every day of our whole life, Jesus leads us safely, and one day, when we die, he will lead us safely into heaven.

Praying

Loving Shepherd, lead me
through each day of my life.
Lead me safely to heaven.
Amen.

Activities

The sheet can be made into a mobile of sheep with their shepherd. Each child will also need cotton wool or chopped white knitting wool to stick on the sheep, wool or string to hang the sheep and shepherd and prayer, and a metal coat hanger.

PEARL DIVERS

Aim: To know that Jesus is the Good Shepherd whom they can trust to lead them.

Starter

Play 'follow my leader', with the leader pretending to be different animals in turn. Everyone else copies the leader. Swap leaders a few times and accompany the game with a praise tape.

Teaching

Beforehand record a few voices which are well known to the children. Some are famous people, and others are local, familiar voices, such as the priest, a teacher at school, or a parent. Play the voice recordings, one at a time, and see if the children recognise them. Explain that today we are going to look at something Jesus said about recognising voices.

How did they recognise the voices on tape? Because they were used to hearing those people – they knew what their voices sounded like, even if they hadn't heard them saying those words before.

Ask them to listen out for the answer to this question: 'Who recognises the Good Shepherd's voice?' as you read them today's Gospel. Read it slowly and clearly, with short pauses between the phrases to help them take in the meaning. (The answer to the question is the sheep that belong to the Good Shepherd.) Who is the Good Shepherd? Jesus. And who are the sheep who belong to him and recognise his voice? Those who follow Jesus – people like us! Just as a good shepherd leads and guides all his sheep and lambs and keeps them safe, Jesus, our Good Shepherd, leads and guides us safely through all the dangers and evils all the days of our life and, when we eventually die, he goes on leading us safely to heaven.

Praying

Jesus, our Good Shepherd,
when you call us, we will follow,
where you lead us, we will go,
because we know your voice of love
will lead us safely
all the way to heaven. Amen.

Activities

On the sheet there is a game to make and play, where they only obey the instructions given by the shepherd. For counters the children make a small model sheep from playdough, or they can cut out the sheep pictured.

GOLD PANNERS

Aim: To know that even though our Christian witness may cause us trouble, the Good Shepherd will keep us eternally safe.

Starter

Play any ball game which involves one team trying to get goals while the other team is doing their best to stop them.

Teaching

How much easier it would be to get goals if we didn't have the opposing side always trying to stop us scoring! In our spiritual journey as Christians, we will sometimes find ourselves in situations where we seem to be battling against injustice, prejudice, teasing or even persecution, all because of our faith. Read the passage from Acts to see an example of this happening in the Early Church, and talk over any times when they feel that good starts have been thwarted by people being persuaded not to support but instead disrupt progress.

How could Paul and Barnabas be filled with joy after being treated so badly? Discuss their ideas and then read together the passage from Apocalypse, where we are standing at the other side of the door of death, seeing those who have stayed faithful coming into the joy of heaven. Notice the encouragement and comfort which is offered here to Christians presently going through persecution.

Finally look at the Gospel for today, with Jesus' promise to lead the sheep who belong to him, so that they will be eternally safe, whatever happens to them. How does this passage encourage us in our own life journey? Might it make us braver about living the Christian life, even when the going gets tough?

Praying

God and Father of our Lord Jesus Christ,
though your people walk in the valley of darkness,
no evil should they fear;
for they follow in faith the call of the shepherd
whom you have sent for their hope and strength.
Attune our minds to the sound of his voice,
lead our steps in the path he has shown,
that we may know the strength of his outstretched
   arm
and enjoy the light of your presence for ever. Amen.

Activities

On the sheet there are examples from Acts and from present-day Christians who are prepared to face opposition and rejection in order to live as followers of Christ. They are encouraged to pray for those in such situations at the moment, and recognise in their own lives when following Christ is right even if it is dangerous or uncomfortable.

FIFTH SUNDAY OF EASTER

Thought for the day

Christ, breaking through the barrier of sin and death, allows us to break into an entirely new way of living which continues into eternity.

Reflection on the readings

Acts 14:21-27
Psalm 144
Apocalypse 21:1-5
John 13:31-35

Today's readings continue to help us see events from several viewpoints at once. Rather like those remarkable holograms which burst into three dimensions from a flat surface, we are seeing the Crucifixion and Resurrection of Christ from beforehand, afterwards and in eternity, and these viewpoints, clustered together like this, throw into relief for us the powerful and cosmic significance of those events.

In the Gospel reading, just after Judas has gone out into the night, Jesus looks ahead to the imminent suffering, degradation and failure, and paradoxically claims that the Son of Man is about to be glorified. This is followed by the command given to his disciples to love one another. It is in their self-giving love that people will recognise their allegiance to the God who is glorified by this total expending of self about to be displayed on the cross. God will be glorified by the living-out of forgiving love without limit.

The reading from Apocalypse enables us to see from heaven's point of view, standing aside from the confines of time, and looking with the eyes of the visionary. There are images of accomplishment and victory over all evil for all time. There is the beginning of what is new, as if we are watching with the shepherds the self-emptying of God in the baby on manger straw, and the sense of that full completion at the end of time when all tears will be wiped away for ever. And stretched across time and space is the God of life, focused in the stretching-out of Jesus' arms for us on the cross.

Barriers crumble in the face of such love, and we see an example of this ongoing process in the reading from Acts, as Paul and Barnabas continue to spread and reinforce the Good News. God's saving love is not confined to the Jewish people but is freely available to us all, however distant in years or miles we may be. As Christ breaks through the barrier of death, all new things become possible. If we are resurrection people, our lives will act this out and gather others into the kingdom through the way we refuse to live by the old order of sin, the old prejudices, the old values. Love, though expensive, is the new way to live, and we are to spread it liberally and lavishly without boundaries or exceptions.

Discussion starters

1. How many examples of barriers being broken down can you find in today's readings?

2. How will people know that we are Christ's disciples?

All-stage talk

Beforehand ask a family to help you by providing a couple of clothing items which are now too small for their child to wear. Or you could borrow a cub/brownie sweater which once you would have been able to get into. Also find a sprouting acorn, or a similar example of life bursting out of confines.

Begin by talking about the way we grow out of our clothes. Sometimes we like a sweater or jacket so much that we want to go on wearing it even when it's a bit short or tight, but eventually we realise that we just can't get into it any more, and we'll have to hand it down to someone younger or smaller. As you talk about this, use the children and their skimpy clothes to illustrate how silly it looks and how uncomfortable it feels to wear something which is much too small for us, and then try the same garment on someone it fits to see the difference.

Remind everyone that we are spiritual as well as physical, and we can grow out of things spiritually as well. Some of the early Christians thought that it wasn't right for non-Jewish people to be allowed to join the Church. Today we heard how Paul and Barnabas set off to continue preaching the Gospel to the Gentiles, those who weren't Jews. God wanted everyone to be part of his love, with no one left out. So the early church very sensibly took off that out-grown idea.

When we are very young, we are taught to pray prayers we can understand. That's wonderful. But if we are still praying like a three-year-old when we are thirteen or twenty-three, or fifty-three, we are wearing skimpy spiritual clothes that we have really outgrown. Unless we realise that, and take them off, and find ways of praying that fit, we won't be able to move forward where God wants us to go.

Take a look at the acorn. Acorns are lovely to hold and play with, just as they are. But the oak tree can't become its huge, leafy self unless it breaks out of the acorn, and leaves that behind.

Jesus gives us all a rule, or command. We are to love one another. As soon as we start this kind of responsible, caring love for one another, we are bound to start growing. Sometimes the growing hurts. Sometimes the growing feels exciting. Sometimes the growing is hard work. And always the growing will be breaking out of where we were before. This means that, like children growing taller year by year, we will not be able to keep wearing the same old spiritual clothes. God won't let us get set in our ways because he goes on having exciting plans for us right through our lives, no matter how old we get.

All-age ideas

• Have a display of Paul's missionary journeys.

• Have everyone holding hands, either as they sing *A new commandment* or during the Lord's Prayer.

Prayer of the Faithful

Celebrant
It is God's love that has drawn us here together.
Let us pray to him now.

Reader
Wherever Christians are fussing and arguing,
living outside the Father's will,
we pray for a deep cleansing, healing and renewing,
so that we may truly be the Body of Christ in our
     world.

Silence

Lord, you show us:
what loving really means.

Wherever injustice stifles human growth,
and selfish ambition distorts leadership,
we pray for right and good government
throughout the world,
born of wisdom and humility.

Silence

Lord, you show us:
what loving really means.

As we watch our children growing,
may they learn from our example
to grow more loving
in the ways we deal with conflict,
approach difficulties,
and address the needs of those we meet.

Silence

Lord, you show us:
what loving really means.

In the places of long-term pain
and sudden shock,
of weariness, disappointment and fear,
we pray for peace which only God can give
and the comfort which speaks of hope.

Silence

Lord, you show us:
what loving really means.

May the physical death of those we now recall
be nothing less than the gateway
to a new and lasting life in God's love and protection.

Silence

Lord, you show us:
what loving really means.

We join our prayers with those of Mary,
whose life was guided by love:
Hail, Mary . . .

In silence,
we make our private petitions to God,
who knows all our needs.

Silence

Celebrant
Father, confident in your boundless love,
we place these prayers before you.
Through Christ our Lord.
Amen.

TREASURE SEEKERS

Aim: To know that Jesus' friends love one another.

Starter

Sit in a circle and give everyone a chance to talk about their friends – what their names are and what they like playing together. Then play a circle game as friends together, such as 'The princess slept for 100 years', or 'In and out of the dusky bluebells'.

Teaching

Explain that today we are thinking about friends, and we're going to find out about Jesus and some of *his* friends. The children can do all the actions as you talk about the way Jesus and his friends went for walks together, listened to each other (cup hand to ear), talked together (open and close hands to make them 'chat'), laughed together and cried together. They sometimes went to parties and ate nice food together and drank refreshing drinks together. At the end of the day they got tired together (yawn).

Jesus loved his friends and he said to them, 'I want you to love one another like this. Even when you don't feel like it, I want you to be kind to one another and look after one another.' And that's what all Jesus' friends try and do.

Jesus has lots of friends. There are the friends who lived with him in Galilee, and there's all of us who follow Jesus today. We can be his friends as well – when we walk together, listen to each other, talk together, laugh together and cry together. And when we eat and drink, and when we get tired at the end of the day, Jesus is still with us, loving us.

Praying

I have a friend who is deeper than the ocean,
I have a friend who is wider than the sky,
I have a friend who always understands me,
whether I'm happy or ready to cry.
Jesus is my friend who is deeper than the ocean,
Jesus is my friend who is wider than the sky,
Jesus is my friend who always understands me,
whether I'm happy or ready to cry.

Activities

The worksheet has pictures to encourage the children to explore what it means to live in the loving way which marks us out as Jesus' friends, and they can fold, cut out and colour a string of Jesus' friends who are holding hands.

PEARL DIVERS

Aim: To explore the nature of friendship and what it means to be God's friend.

Starter

If you can borrow a parachute, some parachute games would be excellent, as they help develop the qualities of sharing and co-operation. Alternatively play some circle games, such as passing the smile or passing the hand squeeze, and place-changing. (In this everyone makes a drum roll with hands on thighs, and chants, 'Is it you, is it me, who will it be? Who will it be?' Then the leader calls out the category, such as those who ate Sugar Puffs for breakfast, those who are wearing stripes, or those who have a sister, and these people get up and change places.

Teaching

Explain that Jesus told his disciples they were to love one another. The way other people will recognise that we are Jesus' friends is by the way we love one another. If we don't live like that, it really means we are not his friends. Who do you think can be one of Jesus' friends? Is it only those brought up to go to church? Or only the ones who don't have bad tempers? Or only the ones who can read the Bible? (They can think about this; we'll talk about it after the story.)

Tell the story from the Early Church of how Paul and Barnabas had to make new friends in new places, and how people had to recognise that they were Jesus' friends.

After the story, go back to the question you left the children to think about, and in a circle, so that all have a chance to speak, share their ideas.

Praying

Jesus, you are my friend
as well as my Lord and Saviour.
Please teach me to be a good friend
to others
all my life. Amen.

Activities

On the worksheet the children are encouraged to look at the qualities of a good friend, and I have included several things which may or may not be considered necessary, as well as some obvious choices. It is valuable for children of this age to start looking at the values they are living by, so that they learn to make thoughtful choices in the way they live.

GOLD PANNERS

Aim: To explore the nature of God's loving friendship with us and its implications for us in our relationships.

Starter

Bring along a selection of newspapers and cut out any stories and headlines which they feel are about a breakdown of love between individuals, groups and countries. Share the findings with one another.

Teaching

Draw attention to the fact that they have collected plenty of evidence to suggest that people find loving quite difficult. Look at John 13 to see if Jesus can throw any light on this for us. Presumably, if Jesus' followers are going to be noticeable by their loving, it's likely that most people will not be behaving in this way, and that ties in with what we have seen in the newspaper. The fact that the unloving behaviour is news, however, suggests that there are still lots of people who are living lovingly; they don't make the news because this is still considered normal

behaviour, and that has a lot to do with our Christian heritage, and the spark of God's love in our human nature.

Have a brainstorm of the kind of behaviour Jesus might have had in mind when he talked about us loving one another, and collect the ideas on paper. The worksheet will help to see how these ideas slot in with the different popular meaning of the word 'love'. Look at how godly loving breaks down barriers between people and is never destructive or possessive, and then look at how this links with the words of Jesus that God would be glorified through the Crucifixion. Help them to see that Jesus' total love was shown on the cross in the way he was prepared to go on loving unselfishly whatever the cost.

Read the story from Acts which gives a practical example of the way God's loving leads us on into new places all the time, as God helps us understand him better through our own particular situations and problem-solving.

Praying

Help me, Lord,
to understand what real loving means
in my own situation.
And, when you have shown me,
give me the grace to try it out. Amen.

Activities

The worksheet enables them to explore the question of what real Christian loving is, and there is space to record their ideas. Using the stories picked out from the newspapers, make a display of these and accompanying prayers which can help people visiting the church to pray.

SIXTH SUNDAY OF EASTER

Thought for the day

The continuing presence of God, as Holy Spirit, leads us, as Jesus promised, into a personally guided outreach to all nations.

Reflection on the readings

Acts 15:1-2, 22-29
Psalm 66
Apocalypse 21:10-14, 22-23
John 14:23-29

During this time between the Resurrection and the Ascension Jesus continues to prepare his friends for something which is completely beyond their experience. In today's Gospel we hear how he introduces them to the idea of God's personal involvement through the power of the Holy Spirit. The prospect of having to carry on without Jesus in person among them must have been bleak and daunting to the disciples. Jesus speaks into those fears and assures them of this faithful presence once he has gone from their physical sight.

There is a section of the Bayeux tapestry which is called 'William comforts his soldiers'. This strikes me as a somewhat wry comment, as the picture shows William comforting them by jabbing at their backsides with a sharp weapon! Forceful comfort, indeed. But there is in this image an acknowledgement that fear can prevent us from doing what we know is right, and at such times a prod or two sharpens our determination to get the better of our fear.

When Jesus has given us full assurance of God's presence, we are told not to let our hearts be troubled. I suspect this has a sharper edge which is often missed, and we are actually being told not to allow ourselves to be perturbed or shaken by circumstances. Satan can so easily sidle in through our fear, self-doubt and trepidation, and start whispering the lie that whatever we are facing is far too difficult and we are bound to fail. We can prevent that, in God's strength, by refusing to allow such undermining fears access.

In the Acts reading we can see the promised guiding power of the Holy Spirit in action. God's close involvement with his people means that, whenever Christians are attuned to him and make themselves available, they will be led at the right time into the right circumstances where they can be best used for the work of God.

There is an urgency about outreach. We have before us that great vision of all peoples gathering to acknowledge their Creator, and worship the one true God, and whenever we pray the kingdom in, in the Lord's prayer, we voice our longing for the vision to be accomplished. Yet there is still so much to do, so many lives to touch, and each of us has only a lifetime.

Dare we waste any more of it with our own priorities?

Discussion starters

1. How do we allow the Holy Spirit a voice in settling disputes in the Church, at work or at home?

2. Do we pray for the kingdom out of habit, or are we aware of the responsibility it lays on each of us?

All-stage talk

First fill the space of the centre aisle with chairs and obstacles. If yours is a fixed pews building, have people to sit down as obstacles in the aisle. Remind everyone of how, in today's Gospel, Jesus was talking to his friends at the last supper they had together before he was crucified. Jesus knew his friends were dreading the future without him being there with them. Perhaps they thought it would be a bit like this.

Ask for a volunteer and blindfold them, twizzle them round and send them off down the aisle. As they walk hesitantly, bumping into the obstacles, you talk about Jesus' friends thinking that living without Jesus around would be like trying to get round the difficulties of life blindfolded, and with no one to help or guide them.

Rescue the volunteer and remove their blindfold. As this person knows, you don't feel very safe all on your own and unable to see where the obstacles are. It is frightening and could be dangerous. Sometimes our life can feel like that, and it isn't a comfortable place to be.

What Jesus wants his friends to know is that God doesn't have that in mind for them at all. Although Jesus knew he wouldn't be there physically with his friends for ever, he promised them that they (and we) would have a personal guide right there with us. Let's see how that changes things for us.

Blindfold the volunteer again, but this time appoint a sensible, caring guide who steers them round the obstacles, talking to them and helping them along. (You may want to have primed this person beforehand.)

Watch them together, and then talk alongside the rest of their journey about God's Holy Spirit being with us to teach and explain things to us, to guide us and help us through the dangerous parts of life, so that we are not left alone, but working in partnership with our loving God.

All-age ideas

- Have labelled paper flags from many different nations displayed around the church. Or focus on a few countries and have displays of the needs and problems facing the people there, examples of their bread, and pictures of their people, together with the national flag. During the intercessions people can be encouraged to walk around the church, praying for the needs as music from the countries is played or sung.

- The meaning of the reading from Apocalypse is brought out well if it is read chorally by a group of people who have prepared it prayerfully, splitting the phrases among different voice tones – high, medium and low. If you have an OHP consider making some acetates from coloured pictures of light and water to show during the reading.

Prayer of the Faithful

Celebrant
Drawn by the Holy Spirit,
we have arrived at this moment,
when we can pray together for the Church
and for the world.

Reader
As members of the Church in this generation,
we ask for guidance and blessing
for all our deacons, priests and bishops,
and all in training for lay and ordained ministry.
As the people of God, we ask for the gifts we need
for the work we are called to do.

Silence

Lord, you are with us:
every step of the way.

This fragile, vulnerable planet is so beautiful,
and in such need of guidance;
we pray for a deeper valuing
of our universe and of one another;
for the kingdom to come on earth as in heaven.

Silence

Lord, you are with us:
every step of the way.

May our homes be centres of love,
acceptance and welcome;
we pray that the Spirit will make his home among us
in each room and each relationship.

Silence

Lord, you are with us:
every step of the way.

We pray for all who are weighed down
with doubts, fears and misgivings;
all who are haunted by the past
or scared by the future.
We ask for them awareness of the Spirit's constant
    presence
and the courage he brings.

Silence

Lord, you are with us:
every step of the way.

As we remember those
whose earthly life has come to an end,
we pray that they, and we in our turn,
may be received into heaven
and live for ever in divine light.

Silence

Lord, you are with us:
every step of the way.

We make our prayer with Mary,
tranquil Mother of Jesus:
Hail, Mary . . .

Upheld by God's peace,
we pray now in silence
for any needs known to us personally.

Silence

Celebrant
Heavenly Father, accept our prayers
through Christ our Lord.
Amen.

TREASURE SEEKERS

Aim: To introduce them to the idea of going where God the Holy Spirit leads us.

Starter

Follow my leader. Choose several children to take turns at leading everyone around to music, walking, hopping or dancing in the way they choose.

Teaching

Talk together about when we say goodbye, and practise waving to one another and blowing kisses. Talk about feeling sad when the time comes for saying goodbye to friends or grandparents and we don't want them to go.

Explain how Jesus' friends didn't want him to go, and when the time came to say goodbye they were sad. They didn't look forward to being without him. Jesus wanted them to know that he would not be leaving them on their own. The Holy Spirit of God would be coming to be with them and lead them in the right direction.

Praying

As you lead the children through a drawn or marked pathway, lead them also line by line in this prayer:

Spirit of God,
lead me along the paths
of kindness
and love. Amen.

Activities

The idea of leading is continued in the worksheet where they can take their finger for a walk through the country. There is also a matching activity to start you talking about keeping in touch with God so that we know where we are being led. Give the children the opportunity to ask for God's help and guidance in any areas of their life which they are a bit scared about, or which make them sad. Their recording of these places visually will be part of the prayer, and you can talk later about how God answered them. Children need to know right from the start that God can work with them and through them.

PEARL DIVERS

Aim: To look at God's provision for us in the leading and guidance of the Holy Spirit.

Starter

Pair the children up and blindfold one of the pair. They take it in turns to lead the blindfolded one around the grounds, taking great care to protect each other from danger.

Teaching

Talk over how it felt to be unable to see, and how it helped to have a friend to help us travel safely. When Jesus was with his friends at the last supper he talked to them about having to leave them. They were very sad and rather anxious at the thought of living without their good and wise friend there in person. Jesus had always been able to sort out their fears, cheer them up, get them to make up after arguments, and point out the right things to do. How on earth would they be able to cope without him? And how would they be brave enough to tell other people about him when they knew that would put them in danger?

Read the Gospel for today, asking them to listen out for a promise Jesus gave. They can put their hands up when they hear it, and John 14:23 can be displayed for everyone to read together. So the disciples (and that includes us) were not going to be left like orphans to manage on their own. Somehow God would be with them, in a real and personal way, even though it wouldn't be a person they could see physically.

To get just one idea of how this worked out, tell the children about a time after the Resurrection, when Paul and his friends were travelling round telling people about the God of love. Tell them how the Spirit stopped them going to some places they planned, and led them straight to another place, where some people were ready to hear the good news and become Christians. All over the world, and in each century, God the Holy Spirit is there, guiding people to understand God's will and open doors and nudge in the right direction.

Praying

You could sing *Waiting for your Spirit* by Mick Gisbey (see page 213 for the words and music), and have this prayer during the music interlude between verses:

Lord, I want to go wherever you need me.
Train me to notice
your quiet voice
showing me
the right way to live. Amen.

Activities

There is a short quiz and drawing activity on the worksheet to get the children thinking about the way loving involves taking thought and care for people. This may be an opportunity to recognise that rules their parents make may sometimes seem a pain but really they show that our parents care about us. There is also an opening to learn the need to listen to God's Spirit, and to practise this during the week. If there is time the children can colour some flags of different countries with the words 'God loves you' written in the appropriate language. These can be laid on the floor around the altar for people to see as they gather for communion.

Here are some languages to start you off:

French:	Dieu vous aime
German:	Gott liebt dich
Italian:	Dio ti ama
Spanish:	Dios te ama
Swahili:	Mungu anakupenda

GOLD PANNERS

Aim: To explore the nature of the guiding of the Holy Spirit.

Starter

Borrow a game of Mastermind, or play a simple searching type of game, where you are gradually guided to the correct solution by the feedback given.

Teaching

Point out that in the game you worked in partnership with the feedback to reach the solution, though all the time you were free to take the advice or ignore it. Today we are looking at the help Jesus promised would be available to all his friends, including us, when he was no longer walking physically around the planet. Read today's Gospel to see what Jesus said about this help.

Now look at an example of it working out in practice. I suggest you read Acts 15, showing how a problem had arisen and how they planned to deal with it.

Then read the 'letter' and show how the decision, a solution to the problem, involved the Holy Spirit.

Praying

Holy Spirit of God
come and lead our Church.
Put your good ideas
into our minds
and train us to hear your guidance
so that God is glorified
in all we do. Amen.

Activities

The worksheet helps them learn from Acts the way the Holy Spirit can sometimes guide us in our own lives, and there is space to record any thoughts that come up about God's leading. Picking up on the spreading of the good news to all the peoples of the earth, make a display from pictures and products of a few countries which focuses on their character and their needs. This display can be used in church during the week as a prayer focus.

THE ASCENSION OF THE LORD

Thought for the day

Having bought back our freedom with the giving of his life, Jesus enters into the full glory to which he is entitled.

Reflection on the readings

Acts 1:1-11
Psalm 46
Ephesians 1:17-23
Luke 24:46-53

The Ascension marks the end of Jesus' appearances on earth and his physical, historical ministry. It is also a beginning, because this moving away from the confining qualities of time and place means

that Jesus will be present always and everywhere. It also means that the humanity of Jesus is now within the nature of the wholeness of God. Our God has scarred hands and feet, and knows what it is like to be severely tempted, acclaimed and despised.

In a way, it is at the Ascension that the value of all the risk and suffering involved in the Incarnation becomes apparent. The saving victim takes his rightful place in the glory of heaven, and only that can enable God's Holy Spirit to be poured out in wave upon wave of loving power that stretches to all peoples in all generations.

Amazingly our own parish, our own congregation, is part of this glorious celebration with its far-reaching effects. Each of us, living squashed into a particular time frame lasting merely a lifetime, can be drenched in the power of that Spirit, and caught up in the energising nature of it.

As we celebrate the Ascension we, like the disciples, are expectant with joy at the prospect of the gifts God has in store, and yet still mulling over the breathtaking events of Easter. It is like being in the still centre, in the eye of the storm.

Discussion starters

1. Why were the disciples returning with great joy, even though Jesus had left them?

2. Why do you think Jesus made sure that his final leave-taking was definite, and actually witnessed by the disciples?

All-stage talk

Begin by staging a Mexican wave, which runs through the whole church or assembly. Point out how it only worked so well because all of us as individuals were working together as a unit of energy.

Remind everyone of the events leading up to today, giving them a whistle-stop tour of Jesus' life, death, Resurrection and post-Resurrection appearances. Explain how the disciples needed that time to get used to Jesus being alive and around, though not always visible or physically present.

Now they were ready for the next stage in the plan. Jesus leads them out of the city and he gives them his blessing, telling them to hang around Jerusalem without rushing off to do their own bit of mission work. (Enthusiasm is wonderful but it can sometimes make us race off to start before we've got everything we need.) The disciples have got to wait because God is going to send the Holy Spirit to empower them and equip them for the work they will be doing. It will make it possible for the news of God's love to spread out through the world like our Mexican wave.

When Jesus had finished giving the disciples their instructions and his encouragement, we are told that the disciples watched him being taken into heaven, until a cloud hid him from their sight. Those are the only practical details we have, so we don't know exactly how it happened. But we do know that the disciples were in no doubt about where Jesus had gone, and they were full of joy and excitement as they made their way back to the city to wait for the Holy Spirit, as Jesus had told them to.

A lot of years have gone by since Jesus ascended into heaven – about two thousand years. But that isn't much if you aren't stuck in time as we are, and God isn't stuck in time. He's prepared to wait to give us humans the chance to turn to him in our lives, and we don't know the date when Jesus will return. We do know that in God's good time he will come back, and everyone will see his glory together, both the living and those who have finished the earthly part of their life.

In the meantime, we have been given the Holy Spirit, so that God can be with us in person every moment of our life, helping us and guiding our choices, steering us safely through temptations, and teaching us more and more about our amazing God. All he waits for is to be invited.

All-age ideas

- Any artwork or writing that the children have done on what the Ascension is about can be displayed around the building.

- Have a beautiful helium balloon at the ready. Write on it an Ascension message that the children would like to send. After the service two representative children can let the balloon float away.

- Children can wave white and yellow streamers during some of the hymns.

Prayer of the Faithful

Celebrant
As we celebrate together, let us pray together.

Reader
As we celebrate this festival
of Jesus' entry into heaven as Saviour and Lord,
we pray for unity in the Church
and reconciliation and renewed vision.

Silence

God of love, both heaven and earth:
are full of your glory.

We pray that the God of our making
may draw us deeper
into the meaning of life.

Silence

God of love, both heaven and earth:
are full of your glory.

We pray for all farewells and homecomings
among our families and in our community,
and for all who have lost touch with loved ones
and long for reunion.

Silence

God of love, both heaven and earth:
are full of your glory.

We pray for those who are full of tears,
and cannot imagine being happy again;
we pray for the hardened and callous,
whose inner hurts have never yet been healed.
We pray for wholeness and comfort and new life.

Silence

God of love, both heaven and earth:
are full of your glory.

We commend to God's eternal love
those we remember who have died,
and we pray too for those
who miss their physical presence.

Silence

God of love, both heaven and earth:
are full of your glory.

We make our prayer with Mary,
sharing her joy at her Son's Ascension:
Hail, Mary . . .

We pray in silence, now,
for our own particular needs and concerns.

Silence

Celebrant
Father, accept our prayers;
fit us for heaven,
to live with you for ever.
Through Christ our Lord.
Amen.

TREASURE SEEKERS, PEARL DIVERS AND GOLD PANNERS

It is likely that Ascension Day services for schools will not need a separate programme for children and young people. However, in the books for TREASURE SEEKERS and PEARL DIVERS I have included a drawing and colouring activity for today.

SEVENTH SUNDAY OF EASTER

Thought for the day

Jesus lives for all time in glory; we can live the fullness of Resurrection life straightaway.

Reflection on the readings

Acts 7:55-60
Psalm 96
Apocalypse 22:12-14, 16-17, 20
John 17:20-26

As we reach the final part of Jesus' great prayer before his arrest, recorded with perception and empathy by John, we cannot fail to be moved by the heartfelt yearning shown there. Jesus truly loves this untidy band of companions, and longs passionately for them to become bound to their God and to one another as they have already begun to in his company. And then we suddenly find that we, too, are being prayed for by our Saviour on the night before he dies. We are the ones who have come to believe through the witness of the apostles, and the years between melt away as we become aware of the personal handing-on in succession, one to another down through the generations from these friends to whoever it was who introduced us to Jesus.

There is a great air of excitement in the readings today, because we don't have to wait to start living this new Resurrection life Jesus promised. Pentecost is only a week away, the Lord reigns, Jesus in glory is also close with us, and the joy of living the risen life is infectious.

In these days before celebrating Pentecost we see the effects of Pentecost, graphically described by Luke. Stephen faced danger, rejection and death but he was so filled with the Holy Spirit that he had the strength to face this ordeal with the eyes of his faith fixed firmly on the glory of God. The Holy Spirit would come to work wonders with the complicit witness, here named Saul. Later, as Paul, he would go on to live out the 'new life' with extraordinary results.

Discussion starters

1. Can you think of Christians whose reactions to suffering and disaster have allowed you to catch sight of where their treasure lies?

2. Are we living this new life yet? (If not, think about preparing for this year's Pentecost with real longing to receive the Spirit of God afresh.)

All-stage talk

Beforehand ask a few people to bring awards they have been given. These should include things that probably lots of others have as well, such as a five-metre swimming badge and a driving licence. There may also be a darts cup or a music certificate.

Begin by showing the awards and talking briefly to the award-holders about how these have been well earned, and give us an idea of the standard that has been achieved, so they are something to celebrate. Probably lots of us have similar awards that we have been honoured with, which is well worth celebrating. (A round of applause may be in order.)

When Jesus entered heaven, about forty days after he had come back to life on the first Easter Day, the whole of heaven gave him a hero's welcome. They said he was worthy to receive power and wealth and wisdom and strength, honour and glory and praise – everything good they could think of.

They wanted to honour him like this because Jesus had managed to do such an incredible thing. He had lived a human life and gone on loving all the way through it without once giving in to temptation, turning against God's will or putting his own wants first. Through loving people enough to die for them, he had been able to break the hold death has over all of us, so we can live freely and happily in God's company. (Another huge round of applause for Jesus.)

Now go back to the swimming badge. This badge proves that Susie is able to swim. What God is saying to us today is that Jesus has won the victory for us, so we are all able to live this incredible new, free and happy life in his company.

It is as if there's a wonderful pool just waiting for us to enjoy, but perhaps we're only holding our badges at the edge of the pool, instead of getting into the water and using them. Let's plunge into the life Jesus has won for us and enjoy it to the full!

All-age ideas

• Banners celebrating the fullness of God's glory in heaven and earth can fill the church with colour today, and the flowers, too, can express the colour and variety of full life in Christ.

• If you have some banners in church, don't leave them leaning against walls. Have them carried round the church during the entrance hymn, interspersed with others proclaiming the words: 'The Lord reigns!'

• The Acts reading needs to be really imaginatively read so that everyone is caught up in the excitement and drama of it. Have it acted out, or read with different people taking the parts.

Prayer of the Faithful

Celebrant
Let us pray to the God who gives us so much
and loves us so completely.

Reader
We pray for a fresh outpouring of the Spirit
in all areas of the Church,
till our lives are so changed for good
that people notice and are drawn to the Lord.

Silence

We are your people:
and you are our God.

We pray for godly leaders and advisers
all over the world,
and for the courage to speak out
against injustice and evil.

Silence

We are your people:
and you are our God.

We pray for those affected
by our behaviour and our conversation,
that we may in future
encourage one another by all we say and do.

Silence

We are your people:
and you are our God.

We pray for those as yet unborn,
that the good news will reach them too;
we pray for those who have rejected God
because of the behaviour of his followers;
we pray for all who have lost their way.

Silence

We are your people:
and you are our God.

We pray for the dying,
especially those who are unprepared or frightened.
May all who have died in faith
be welcomed into the kingdom.

Silence

We are your people:
and you are our God.

We join our prayers with those of Mary,
who was filled with the Holy Spirit:
Hail, Mary . . .

In silence, we pray to the Lord
for our own intentions.

Silence

Celebrant
Father, trusting in your love
we lay these prayers before you
through Christ, our Lord.
Amen.

TREASURE SEEKERS

Aim: For them to know that Jesus is in heaven, and explore what heaven is like.

Starter

Sit in a circle and describe different children and objects by giving clues about them. The children have to guess who or what is being described. (I'm thinking of something that is warm . . . and colourful . . . and has a hole to put your head through. What could it be?)

Teaching

Young children may not have been involved in Ascension Day services so tell them today about the friends of Jesus getting used to seeing him alive after Easter. Now the time has come for Jesus to go into heaven, and his friends won't see him any more. Use pictures cut out of card and move them around on carpet tiles or towels on the floor, with the children gathered round the outside of the landscape. Pictures to copy are given below. Cut out a large cloud to hide Jesus from their sight, and then take the friends back to Jerusalem rejoicing, before you add in the angels welcoming Jesus into heaven.

Praying

The angels said,
'Hallo, Jesus. Well done!'
I want to say it too:
'Hallo, Jesus.
Well done!'
Amen.

Activities

On the worksheet is a pattern for making angels. For the very young these will need to have been already copied and cut out. If you want to have lots of angels for each child use the template and cut the angels from that, perhaps using different colours of paper. Cotton or wool can be attached to the heads either by tying, or with sticky tape. Use shoe boxes for the surroundings of heaven, and white paper with cotton wool on it for the cloud.

PEARL DIVERS

Aim: To see the new life in action, through Stephen's story.

Starter

Sitting in a circle, pass round a trophy type of cup. As each person holds it they name something they are able to do. Everyone responds, 'Thank you, God, for making us!' We are all equipped for whatever God wants us to do, and the gifts we are given are there to be used in the very best way.

Teaching

Remind the children that we have just celebrated Ascension Day. Tell them about this last time the disciples met with Jesus, what he said to them, and where he was going. On a calendar they can work out how long Jesus had been around in his risen state since the Resurrection.

Today we are going to see an example of the kind of life Jesus' followers were living after Jesus had returned to heaven, and the Holy Spirit had been sent to equip the disciples for God's work.

Introduce an invited guest (one of the leaders dressed up) to tell everyone his story. He is holding a stone, which he fingers as he talks. He tells them how Stephen was one of those followers of the man Jesus who had been executed by crucifixion, but these followers of his were convinced he had come back to life, and was the promised Messiah. The teller had tried his best to stamp out this group of people – known as 'followers of the Way'. How could this Jesus be the Son of God? How could the Son of God end up dying a cursed death on a Roman cross?

He explains how Stephen had something about him which did seem to point to him speaking the truth, and he had worked hard to prove his claims about Jesus from Scripture, but it just wasn't right for these Jesus-followers to be going about happy as if Jesus really was alive and had power to live in them.

He explains how he had joined the others with stones to throw at Stephen and put him to death, but something had stopped him throwing his stone. It was the way Stephen had stood there, with stones hitting him, and gazed up into heaven as if he really could see into it. And as the stones knocked him to his knees, Stephen was actually praying for God to forgive those of us killing him! He describes how Stephen's example has made him think again about Jesus, and he's decided to find out more about being a follower of the Way. He's going to keep the stone he nearly threw to remind him.

Praying

Thank you, Jesus,
for the new life
you have won for me.
Fill me up
with the Spirit of God
so that I can live life
to the full. Amen.

Activities

The worksheet reinforces the teaching with space for them to draw in what Stephen could see. They will need a Bible for this. There is also a question about the quality and direction of their own lives to think over, either in small groups or on their own during the week.

GOLD PANNERS

Aim: To see the new life being lived out in the followers of Jesus like Stephen.

Starter

Share some 'worst moments ever' with one another.

Teaching

Look first at the Gospel reading, and make a note of what and who Jesus is praying for. Consider why he prayed so much for this, thinking of the Church's history to give you some ideas.

Then recall the events of the Ascension, and the new phase which that entry into glory made possible. Presumably we should be able to look at some records of what happened after the coming of the Holy Spirit to see this new life in action. Read the events in Acts 7, dramatising them with different voices and sound effects. Then, using the worksheet, think about the story from the viewpoints of the different people involved.

Praying

Jesus, Lord and Saviour,
reigning in heaven,
we give you thanks and honour,
praise and worship,
both with our voices
and with our lives. Amen.

Activities

Turn the discussion of different viewpoints into role-play, using the notes they have made to help them. The different speech bubbles can be written out and mounted on coloured paper with the Bible reference as a heading and used to introduce a parish Bible study.

PENTECOST

Thought for the day

As Jesus promised, the Holy Spirit is poured out on the apostles and the Church is born.

Reflection on the readings

Acts 2:1-11
Psalm 103
1 Corinthians 12:3-7, 12-13
John 20:19-23

In the ancient story of Babel a deep human puzzle was explored. Why is it that, whenever we let our skills and gifts divert us into pride and ambition, we end up bickering and losing our capacity for mutual co-operation? It is a story which provides a useful foil to the events of Pentecost.

For here we have God's answer, and in the story from the Acts of the Apostles, where there is no longer division caused by language, the Babel story turned on its head. God's Holy Spirit, residing in our whole being, opens up the possibility of living as God intended – in harmony with our Creator. That new relationship is bound to spill out into our relationships with one another, and work against the destructiveness we know so well and despair of overcoming.

As the force of the Spirit, coming in great power, surges like wind and fire into the place where the apostles are expectantly waiting, they are completely drenched in the waves of God's energising love. 'Drenched' is perhaps an odd word to use in the context of tongues of flame, but in terms of the Holy Spirit it makes sense, because air (breath or wind), water and fire – those raw experiences of natural power – are all linked with the physical expressions of the presence and power of God among his people.

It is God's nature to warn us ahead of time if something is coming up that he wants us seriously to attend to. The disciples have taken Jesus' prophecy to heart, and have been waiting watchfully and prayerfully for the last nine days since the Ascension. So often we miss God's voice because we are not expecting to hear it. We miss the outpouring of his Spirit in our lives because we are not expecting him to act. Yet as soon as we set ourselves faithfully and expectantly to ask for it and wait for it, God honours the honesty of our longing, and makes his presence known.

Discussion starters

1. Do we really want God's Spirit to fill us, or does the thought terrify us so that we are actually asking God to keep a safe distance?

2. Why is Jesus saying, 'Peace be with you', linked to his showing his hands and his side? What does this mean for us as peacemakers?

All-stage talk

Beforehand make five red, yellow and orange flame shapes (about 30 centimetres high) and hide them around the church.

Begin by asking for examples of flames, such as on a gas hob, bonfire, forest fire, log fire, candle, acetylene torch, fire-eater, house on fire, match, oil lamp, steel works, steam engine, lighter, Bunsen burner. Draw people's attention to the tremendous power of some of these and the quiet, gentle nature and soft light of others. Fire is something we all have to respect, as it can burn and destroy as well as giving us light and heat.

Send the children off to search for the five flames that are hidden in the church, and tell the adults about our need to seek out the Spirit expecting to find, just as the children are doing now. They trust that what they have been told to search for will be there, and it will. We need to believe that if we seek God we will find him – and we will.

When the children return with the five flames, you can remind everyone of the way the Holy Spirit is described as being like tongues of fire, with the sound of a rushing wind. (You can get everyone to make this sound as the flame-carriers move round the church.)

Like fire, the Spirit can be strong and powerful in our lives. (The first flame is held up.) Sometimes the Spirit is gentle and quiet, whispering deep into our needs and telling us what is right. (The second flame is held up.) Like fire, the Spirit is warming, spreading love and a real desire to put things right, and stand up for goodness and truth. (The third flame is held up.) Like fire the Spirit is purifying, burning away all that is evil and selfish in us, so that we can become like pure refined gold, glowing with the light of God's love. (The fourth flame is held up.) And, like fire, the Spirit is enlightening, shedding light for us on the Bible, our conversations and relationships and the events of our lives, so that we can see God more clearly through them. (The fifth flame is held up.)

All-age ideas

- Make three flags using yellow, orange and red lining material and bean sticks. During one of the hymns have three people standing in a triangle waving the flags gradually upwards and downwards. Or they can be used individually at different parts of the church to express worship as people sing.

- Have each side of the congregation facing each other and praying for each other to receive the Holy Spirit in their lives afresh. They can pray silently or aloud, or in unison with this prayer, said once loudly and then whispered softly.

  Holy Spirit of God,
  come upon these people
  whom you know and love so well,
  and fill them to overflowing!
  Amen; let it be so.

- Have a time of shared expectant quietness after the prayer, with some quiet music being played and sung by the music group or choir.

- Have the church decorated with flame-coloured flowers, ribbons, streamers and balloons.

Prayer of the Faithful

Celebrant
As the Spirit enables us,
let us gather ourselves to pray.

Reader
May all Church leaders,
ordained ministers and the laity
be filled to overflowing
with love for all God's people,

and kindled with fresh zeal
for spreading the good news of the Gospel.

Silence

Spirit of the living God:
fall afresh on us.

May all those negotiating for peace
in the delicate areas of national conflict,
industrial disputes and entrenched bitterness,
be blessed with the peace of God,
tranquil and patient beneath the pressures.

Silence

Spirit of the living God:
fall afresh on us.

In our homes and places of work,
our schools and hospitals,
may there always be time
for the warmth of loving concern
and the comfort of being valued.

Silence

Spirit of the living God:
fall afresh on us.

May all rescue workers be strengthened and kept safe;
may all who are trapped in damaged bodies or minds,
in poverty or tyranny, in earthquakes, floods or storms,
be brought to freedom and safety
and be aware of God's love for them.

Silence

Spirit of the living God:
fall afresh on us.

We pray for those who have died
and all who mourn their going;
may the fears of the dying be calmed.

Silence

Spirit of the living God:
fall afresh on us.

The Holy Spirit came down on Mary,
and with her we pray:
Hail, Mary . . .

Alive to the Holy Spirit,
we name those we know
who are in any particular need.

Silence

Celebrant
Father, accept these prayers
through Christ our Lord.
Amen.

TREASURE SEEKERS

Aim: To celebrate the birthday of the Church.

Starter

Jack in the box. Have everyone crouching down. The leader says, 'Ready, steady, Jack in the box!', and everyone springs up. Vary the length of time between the 'ready' and the 'steady' so the children are hanging on the leader's words, ready to spring into action, but not sure when to.

Teaching

Explain how Jesus' friends had been told to wait for the coming of the Holy Spirit after Jesus had gone into heaven. They were praying and waiting, and waiting and praying for over a week, and then suddenly the Spirit came to them all.

Bring in a birthday cake with two candles on it. If possible, have the cake in the shape of a church, or have a picture or model of a church on it. Explain to the children that today is like the birthday of the Church, not just of St Andrew's but all the churches everywhere in the world. Light the candles, each of which stands for about a thousand years. It is now about two thousand years since the Holy Spirit of God was poured out on Jesus' friends and the Christian Church was born.

As you talk about the handing-on of the Gospel, use a set of Russian dolls, and keep taking another one out. Those few people told lots of others about Jesus, and those others told lots more, and their children and their grandchildren, and then the grandchildren grew up and they told their friends and their children and their grandchildren. And soon more and more people all over the world knew about Jesus and the love God has for us. And they went on telling other people until eventually someone told us! So now we know about Jesus and God's love for us, and through our lives we'll tell our friends and our children and our grandchildren so they will know as well.

Sing 'Happy Birthday, dear Church', blow out the candles and share the cake.

Praying

Happy birthday, dear Church,
Happy birthday, dear Church.
Jesus' love is for ever,
Happy birthday, dear Church!

Activities

Have some fairy cakes already iced, and let the children decorate them ready to give out to everyone as birthday cake after the service. The worksheet has a picture to colour of the Church being born at Pentecost.

PEARL DIVERS

Aim: To become familiar with the events at Pentecost.

Starter

Play a game where the children are waiting expectantly but can only act when they hear the instruction. Here is one example. Everyone finds a space to stand in and the leader calls 'One . . . two . . . three . . . hop to the window / crawl like snakes / pirouette round the table / score the winning goal.' (Choose a variety of activities to suit your group.)

Teaching

Remind the children of how, at the Ascension, the disciples had been told by Jesus to wait in Jerusalem for the gift of the Holy Spirit to come. They went back and spent time praying together so they would be ready for the Spirit when it came.

Have some of the children to be the apostles, waiting and praying together. As you read or tell them about the way the Spirit came, the other children can make the sound of an orchestrated rushing wind, and some can be given red crêpe-paper streamers to whirl around the place where the apostles are sitting. As the wind dies away and the disciples are left alone, tell the children how the Spirit had made them full of excitement and joy. They were longing to tell everyone about Jesus, and the way God loves us.

The apostles can now come running and dancing out to the crowd in the street, telling them that Jesus of Nazareth, who had been crucified, was the promised Messiah, the Christ, the Son of God. End with the people asking to be baptised and become his followers.

Praying

Fill my life,
Holy Spirit of God,
with joy and love and hope.
Live in me so I can show others
how much you love them. Amen.

Activities

Using the template on the worksheet the children can cut out lots of flames in red, yellow and orange. These can be given out to the rest of the congregation after the service. There is also a Pentecost wordsearch to reinforce the teaching. Finding words from 'Pentecost' will also help to familiarise them with this word.

GOLD PANNERS

Aim: To look at the continuing coming of the Holy Spirit.

Starter

Have two large sheets of paper, one with the word 'Fire' in the centre and the other 'Wind'. In small groups work on drawing and writing all the things they can think of associated with these words. Share the sheets with everyone.

Teaching

Recap on the way the disciples were waiting for the Spirit promised by Jesus, and they were expecting something to happen, though they didn't know what it would be. Then read the passage from Acts together, involving everyone for the crowd, and for the sound effects. Ask them to close their eyes. Take them travelling through time, imagining that they are in the room with the disciples. Draw on the use of senses – what they can hear, smell and see, how their clothes feel and the heat in the room, and how it feels to be among these people who have walked about with Jesus and are all really praying.

Lead them to imagine the sound of that strong wind approaching, and then the experience of being surrounded with this powerful presence of God and the wind and flames of fire. Bring them back into the present and talk about the experience.

Praying

Come, Holy Spirit,
fill the hearts of your people
with the fire of your love!

Activities

On the worksheet there is a quiz based on Acts 2:1-11, for which they will need a Bible. There are also some testimonials of people talking about how it felt when the Holy Spirit came upon them. These can be used as a basis for discussion, and a meeting arranged in the week for those wanting to know more about Confirmation and/or being more open to receive the Spirit in their lives.

FEASTS OF THE LORD

TRINITY SUNDAY

Thought for the day

The unique nature of God is celebrated today, as we reflect on the truth that God is Creator, Redeemer and Life-giver.

Reflection on the readings

Proverbs 8:22-31
Psalm 8
Romans 5:1-5
John 16:12-15

The actual word 'Trinity' does not occur in the Bible, but that is not to say it is not mentioned. As we get to understand the nature of God more and more, it becomes clear that we are wrestling with understanding something quite beyond our human experience. Even though God can make himself and his will known clearly to us along the way of life, there is no way that we will ever be able to grasp exactly who God is and what he is like, at least during our time on earth.

But that's no reason for not trying! Trying to get to grips with the truth about God's nature is all part of our journey into the depth of his being, and as such is immensely valuable. Our readings today are a good starting point.

First we have the poetry of Proverbs, expressing something of the 'community' of God's nature; the way that Wisdom, described as a personality, has been present from the very beginning, and was part of the creative loving process that brought all things into being. There is a sense of harmony and shared delight, along with the everlasting 'now', which we, being time-trapped, find hard to imagine.

Psalm 8 catches the song of Proverbs and dances with it, amazed at the nature of creation and the attitude of God towards it. Humankind is so privileged in having the ability to marvel.

In Romans we sense the orchestration of God; the way that in Jesus it all comes together, and we as humans can be drawn into God's life-giving power which transforms our attitudes to the trials and troubles we are likely to face. God is both transcendent and immanent.

So, when we read in John about Jesus referring to the Friend – the Spirit who will take his followers by the hand and lead them into the truth – in the same breath as he speaks about the Father and himself sharing all things, we can begin to glimpse something of the dynamics of God. Rather as you may look at a speck of microfilm and see it first as a dot which then explodes into a wealth of information when properly viewed, so our initial glimpses of God are going to burst into a dynamic, unimaginable richness which is sensed and worshipped, rather than understood.

Discussion starters

1. What symbols in our churches are used to try to express the three in oneness of God?

2. Is the 'Trinity' nature of God reflected in our own nature as humans?

All-stage talk

Beforehand prepare a cake. Also get together two eggs, a bag of sugar, a bag of flour and some margarine, and a mixing bowl, cake tin and wooden spoon.

Set the cake tin down and tell everyone that today we are going to have a cake again, because it was so nice last week having the children's cakes, and today is another important day, Trinity Sunday. So we are going to have a Trinity cake. Ask various helpers to bring the eggs, sugar and flour and margarine and place them in the cake tin.

Proudly present the cake, inviting everyone to take a slice, and let the children point out to you that you haven't got a cake at all. You've just got the ingredients. But isn't a cake just ingredients, then? Let them help you understand that you'd have to mix them together and cook them before you had a cake.

Now let it suddenly dawn on you that it's a bit like that with the nature of God. God is the Father who created the world, Jesus Christ who saved us, and the Holy Spirit who gives life to the people of God. But they aren't separate from each other, any more than these separate ingredients are a cake. To be a cake all the ingredients need to be co-operating and working together. Then they become something which is not just eggs, flour, sugar and margarine. Produce the real cake and point out that you wouldn't say, 'Have a slice of eggs, flour, margarine and sugar with your cup of tea.' You'd call it by its name: a cake.

In the same kind of way, when we talk about God we are talking about our Maker, and we're talking about the risen Jesus who has rescued us from sin and death, and we're talking about the Holy Spirit who brings us into new life. We know that the word 'God' means all three persons in a wonderful harmony, a community which is still One.

Give the Trinity cake to whoever is in charge of refreshments after the service, so it can be shared out then.

All-age ideas

- Use three different voices for the Proverbs reading. Work through the text prayerfully and listen to the places where single voices or a group of voices seem to be indicated. Split the single voice sections between the three people, according to the sense of the phrases and linking meaning with voice type.

- Put clover and shamrock among the flower arrangements today to express the 'three in one' nature of God.

- Use the baptismal statements of belief for the Creed.

Prayer of the Faithful

Celebrant
Let us pray to the Father,
in the power of the Holy Spirit,
through Jesus, the Son.

Reader
We pray for all theologians
and those who teach the faith
throughout the Church.
We pray for Godly wisdom and human insight.

Silence

Holy God:
help us to know you more.

We pray for peace and co-operation,
harmony and mutual respect
in all our dealings with one another
locally, nationally and internationally.

Silence

Holy God:
help us to know you more.

We pray for those who depend on us,
and those on whom we depend,
for our physical and spiritual needs.
May we be enabled to honour one another
as children of God's making.

Silence

Holy God:
help us to know you more.

We pray for those who feel fragmented;
and for those forced to live apart from loved ones
through war, political unrest,
natural disasters or poverty.
We commend their pain
to the comforting of the Spirit.

Silence

Holy God:
help us to know you more.

We remember those who told us of God
through their words and lives;
we think of those who have died in faith
and ask that we may share with them
the joy of God's presence for ever.

Silence

Holy God:
help us to know you more.

Joining Mary, the Mother of our Lord,
we make our prayer:
Hail, Mary . . .

We pray in silence
to our heavenly Father
for our own personal intentions.

Silence

Celebrant
God our Father, hear our prayer;
may we be led by the Spirit
to a deeper knowledge of you.
Through Christ our Lord.
Amen.

TREASURE SEEKERS

Aim: To help them appreciate the wonder of God.

Starter

Let them make something, such as a picture, from all kinds of bits and pieces, such as wool, bottle tops, toffee wrappers and feathers. Or they can paint or print a picture. This activity needs to be fairly unstructured, so they express themselves in their pictures.

Teaching

Display all the pictures and admire them. Talk about how when we enjoy thinking of things and making them, we are doing what our God loves doing. He loves making things that are beautiful and huge and tiny. He loves making people, and watching over us as we grow and learn to do all sorts of things for ourselves, using the brain he has given us.

Pass round a few things God has made for the children to look at, touch and smell. Talk together about how lovely they are. (You might have a stone, a shell, a feather and a flower.)

Praying

Lord God,
I love the things you have made.
They show me your love. Amen.

Activities

Give the children large letters to colour and stick these with their pictures on to a long roll of wallpaper which can be displayed in church. The finished message reads: 'Our God is wonderful!' The worksheet also has this message, together with a dot-to-dot which again puts them in the role of creator so they can appreciate God as Creator.

PEARL DIVERS

Aim: To understand more about the nature of God.

Starter

Set out different colours of paints and help them to do colour sums, like this:

Red + Yellow =
Yellow + Blue =
Red + Green =

Teaching

Beforehand prepare the word 'Trinity' on two pieces of card, with 'Tri' on one piece and 'Unity' on the other.

First look together at the colour sums, and point out the way that although we put clear yellow and clear blue in, you can't see them any more once they've turned green. They have become something different.

Today is called Trinity Sunday, and we're going to look at what that means. Show the cards as 'Trinity'. Then put the 'Unity' bit down and concentrate on the 'Tri'. Talk about words they know which have this in them, such as tricycle, tripod and triangle. Between you work out from these words what TRI means. What has three got to do with God? Draw three dots on a sheet of paper and name them with their help, God the Father, God the Son and God the Holy Spirit.

Now pick up the 'Unity' section. Block off the 'y' and ask what words they know with 'unit' in them, such as united, unit, and unite. If anyone can count in French you can ask them what 'un' means in French. Work out together the meaning of 'Unity'. What has this got to do with God? Draw lines joining the three dots together to form a triangle and explain that there is only one God. But unlike the colours we made, we can still see the three different 'colours'

of God in his nature. That's why the Church has squashed the two words 'Tri' and 'Unity' together, to make a word that tries to understand God better. Fix the two pieces of card together again, and put the word next to the drawing.

Praying

Glory be to God the Father,
Glory be to God the Son,
Glory be to God the Spirit,
Holy Trinity, three in one!

Activities

There are instructions on the worksheet for making a Trinity bookmark using clover leaves and sticky-backed plastic. An alternative method is to use clover-leaf shapes cut from green paper. There are some other puzzles to solve, and a story of Patrick and the child on the beach.

GOLD PANNERS

Aim: To understand more about the nature of God.

Starter

Give out packs of drinking straws and sticky tape, and give everyone the challenge of making a tower out of straws in a set time. Use an oven timer with a loud ring.

Teaching

Admire the towers and draw attention to the importance of the triangles for strength and stability. Think of how triangles are used in other structures.

Explain that there is also a triangular feel about today, as it is Trinity Sunday, and is the day we celebrate the 'three in one' nature of God. Using the worksheet to jot down notes as they go along, read the passages from John, Romans and Proverbs, picking out the references to the 'three persons' of God and talking over any difficulties or questions they have.

Praying

Give them some examples of Celtic 'Trinity' prayers and then try making one of your own between you.

Activities

Using squares of green lining material and bamboo canes they can stitch or staple flags to be used in worship, or design an altar frontal to express what they understand by the Trinity.

CORPUS CHRISTI

Thought for the day

Jesus is the Living Bread, who brings us eternal life through Communion with him.

Reflection on the readings

Genesis 14:18-20
Psalm 109
1 Corinthians 11:23-26
Luke 9:11-17

Today we celebrate with deep thankfulness the gift given by Jesus of himself. In the Gospel we hear that familiar, extraordinary story of thousands being fed from what was available and offered, so that everyone went away satisfied. In traditional fashion, Jesus the prophet acts out his teaching of God's care and provision, in an amazing blend of compassion and generosity, order and co-operation. The provision is such that there is plenty left over; we are left with the sense that the feeding can go on and on and on, throughout the whole of the twelve tribes of Israel and on out to reach the entire world.

And that is exactly what is happening, because the feeding is still continuing. At every Eucharist in every age and place of worship, whether huge crowds or simply two or three are gathered together, the living bread goes on being blessed and broken, shared and received, so that all are satisfied.

Paul's account of the Last Supper reminds us afresh of the Passover meal Jesus ate with his friends, just before his arrest. The Lamb of God is about to be sacrificed, and Jesus uses the ancient words of the Passover to show his disciples the meaning of what is soon to take place. He offers himself, in the sacramental form of bread and wine, telling them to go on celebrating this gift whenever they eat and drink in God's company, so that they may remember him.

We have become used to the word 'remember', so that its full meaning is no longer obvious; but to 're-member' is actually to reconstruct, or to put the parts together, so that we are able to relive what we re-member. Christ comes to us in the breaking of bread as fully now as at that Last Supper, the Christ who has entered into total death and been raised to unending life. Day by day, through lifetimes and generations, the feeding of the living bread continues, sustaining us through time into eternity.

Discussion starters

1. Why bread and wine? How are these particularly helpful in understanding the significance of the Mass?

2. How is the feeding of the five thousand a parable as well as a miracle?

All-stage talk

Give everyone a stalk of grass or wheat, and ask them to look at the seeds on it. For thousands and thousands of years the earth has been producing this stuff, all over the world. Our great-great-grandparents would have been able to pick stalks like this, and so would their great-great-grandparents. And there will still be plenty there for the great-great-grandchildren of the youngest child here! That's quite a lot of grass, and it's all done by the grass seeds falling into the earth and growing more seeds which fall into the earth and grow more seeds . . . Bread is made out of flour, and flour is squashed posh grass seed. (Produce some bread.) It's good food – very tasty and full of energy to keep you alive. It was bread and fish which Jesus took to feed all those people in the Gospel reading today. First he accepted the bread which was offered (and it wasn't very much at all), then he looked up to heaven and thanked God for what they had, and started to break it up to share it out among everyone. And the love that wanted all those people to be fed was so strong in Jesus that he went on breaking and sharing out, breaking and sharing out, until every person there had eaten as much as they needed – and *still* there was more!

Today we've gathered to meet with Jesus in our particular country, in our particular town, on this particular date, at this particular time of day, just like all those people beside the lake. We've come because we know that God is worth knowing, and we love him.

So, in a very special way, we are all part of that big picnic by the lake. When we bring bread and wine to the altar we will be offering to God what we have – all that we are and all we've done and said, and all the time ahead of us. When the priest takes the bread and thanks God for it, consecrates it, breaks it and shares it with us, we are reliving Jesus doing what he did at the lake, and then in a special way at the last meal he ate before he was crucified. That breaking and sharing of the bread has been going on and on right down through the centuries, and there's still plenty of Jesus' life for every one of us to share it!

All-age ideas

- If you have anyone who bakes their own bread, they could make a loaf to be part of a flower arrangement on the theme of the day, which can be shared afterwards.

- Precede or follow the Mass with a time of shared silent prayer in front of the Blessed Sacrament.

Prayer of the Faithful

Celebrant
Gathered as the Body of Christ,
let us pray together to our heavenly Father.

Reader
As we celebrate Christ's sacramental presence among
    us,
we rejoice that we can feed on him
and be nourished with his life.
We pray that the people of God
in every part of the world
may grow in holiness and love.

Silence

Feed us, Father:
with the Living Bread.

We pray for those who know deep spiritual hunger
and for the spiritually complacent;
for a world where loneliness and fear
distrust Christ's promise of hope;
for the kingdom of God to come.

Silence

Feed us, Father:
with the Living Bread.

We pray that through our feeding
the communities we live and work in
may be blessed and nourished;
that our homes may be places of prayer,
and that we may have the courage to be vulnerable.

Silence

Feed us, Father:
with the Living Bread.

We pray for all who receive Communion
in hospital or in their own homes;
that they may find strength and healing
through encountering Christ's love.

Silence

Feed us, Father:
with the Living Bread.

We pray for those whose earthly lives
have come to an end,
that in God's eternity they may find
lasting peace and joy.

Silence

Feed us, Father:
with the Living Bread.

We make our prayers with Mary,
who brought the Living Bread into the world:
Hail, Mary . . .

Let us be still in the presence of God
and bring to him the needs and concerns
that weigh on our hearts.

Silence

Celebrant
Heavenly Father,
you nourish us by the body and blood of Jesus,
so that we can share the life of heaven,
both now and at the end of time.
Hear our prayers and provide for us all.
Amen.

TREASURE SEEKERS, PEARL DIVERS AND GOLD PANNERS

It is likely that Corpus Christi services for schools will not need a separate programme for children and young people. However, in the books for TREASURE SEEKERS and PEARL DIVERS I have included worksheets for children in church today.

ORDINARY TIME

SECOND SUNDAY OF THE YEAR

Thought for the day

As a marriage celebrates the beginning of a changed, new life for the bride and groom, so our loving, faithful God has chosen us and is ready to transform our lives for the good of the world.

Reflection on the readings

Isaiah 62:1-5
Psalm 95
1 Corinthians 12:4-11
John 2:1-12

Today the nature of our relationship with God is expressed in terms of marriage. Starting with our experience of the best in human love, we can use this to imagine the totally loving, totally faithful nature of our God. Really, of course, it is the other way round: being made in the likeness of God we share, in part, his capacity for faithfulness and loving which is often expressed in the decision to marry the object of our deep love and affection.

At a marriage celebration there is in many cultures a symbolic change of name, to signify that there has been a fundamental life change and that the two are now one. In a similar way God first loves us and chooses us, and then calls us onwards into so changed a life in him that it is often referred to as being born again into a new life.

The passage from 1 Corinthians explores how this new life in the Spirit manifests itself. Paul is anxious to make it clear that there is no rigid format for our new life. It is as varied and diverse as we are, reflecting all the richness of individual gifts. But for all the differences there is a bond of unity, because all these gifts are expressions of the one Spirit. We can get ourselves unnecessarily worked up about the distribution of such gifts. If, instead, we keep our eyes on Jesus, the gifts can be received and valued wherever and however they happen to show up.

The transformation of our lives could not be shown more dramatically than in the Gospel event of the water being transformed into wine at the marriage in Cana. The ordinary is turned into the remarkable through contact with and obedience to the word, or Word, of God.

Discussion starters

1. Why do you think the servants did as Jesus said? How do you think they felt as they poured out the wine?

2. Are we ready to 'do whatever he tells us'? What holds us back?

All-stage talk

Beforehand ask someone in the congregation who still has their wedding dress or bridesmaid's dress to bring it along. Several people could do this – they won't have to wear them unless they want to! Ask a happily married couple to be prepared to talk about their wedding day.

Introduce the people and their wedding dresses, bringing out how special they are because of it being such a special day in their lives. Talk to the married couple so that they show how their love for one another brought them to marriage and how the wedding day emphasised the important step they were taking. If there are couples soon to be married, this would be a good time to pray for them as they start their new life together.

Through the prophet Isaiah, God tells his people that his love and faithfulness is a bit like that of a devoted bride and groom. We have been loved and called, and chosen to live a new life together with our God. He will take us just as we are and gradually change us into being more richly ourselves than we could ever be on our own.

Today's Gospel was all about something changing. Water was changed into wine. That happens naturally every year as the rain falls and gets drawn into the vine to make grape juice, and then the grape juice is fermented carefully to make that new drink – wine. But that wedding day in the town of Cana was different because the change happened straight away. Ask the married couple if they had ordered enough wine for their wedding, and then go over the wedding story and the way Jesus transformed the whole situation. John, who wrote this account, tells us that it showed the disciples they could put their trust in Jesus.

That is true for us as well. Whatever has gone wrong in your life, whatever makes you really sad or angry or disappointed, God will take and change so it can be used for good. Nothing you have to suffer will ever be wasted if you stick with Jesus, and do as he tells you.

All-age ideas

• Have the main flower arrangement with a wedding theme, with ribbon and a framed wedding photograph, a bottle of wine and two glasses among the flowers.

• Have the Isaiah passage read chorally with a group of men, women, boys and girls. Work through the passage together, listening for ways to bring out both the meaning and the poetry through the different combinations of voices. The easiest way to record this is with different coloured highlighter pens on copied sheets. Arrange for one of the group to take the lead and that will keep everyone together.

Prayer of the Faithful

Celebrant
Drawn by God's love and constant faithfulness to us, let us pray.

Reader
We pray for all those who would love to believe but cannot yet trust in the living God.
We pray for those who have rejected God because of the unloving behaviour of his followers.

Silence

Fill us, Lord:
fill us to the brim.

We pray for all who give orders and have influence over other people.
We pray that all peoples may be led justly and with sensitivity.

Silence

Fill us, Lord:
fill us to the brim.

We pray for all our relationships which need God's transforming love;
we pray for those we irritate and upset and those who have hurt and upset us.

Silence

Fill us, Lord:
fill us to the brim.

We pray for those whose lives feel empty and lacking real meaning.
We pray for those whose frailty, pain or illness makes it difficult to pray.

Silence

Fill us, Lord:
fill us to the brim.

We pray for those who are dying and those who have completed their life on earth, that they may be brought to peace and everlasting joy.

Silence

Fill us, Lord:
fill us to the brim.

We join our prayers with those of Mary, chosen Mother of our Lord:
Hail, Mary . . .

In silence,
as God our Father listens with love,
we name our own particular cares and concerns.

Silence

Celebrant
God our Father, hear our prayer;
may the richness of your transforming Spirit refresh and renew our lives.
Through Christ our Lord.
Amen.

TREASURE SEEKERS

Aim: To be introduced to the story of the wedding at Cana.

Starter

Water play. Protect the floor and have a number of washing-up bowls with water, containers and sieves. Let the younger children enjoy filling and emptying. Older children can be encouraged to see how many small containers it takes to fill a larger one.

Teaching

Talk with the children about any weddings they may have been to and taken part in. Show a few wedding photos (preferably amateur ones which show people enjoying themselves rather than in set poses). Now tell them about the time Jesus and his mother were invited to a wedding. When you get to the part about the water jars, fill a large jug with water. Pour some into a wine glass as you tell them about the servants pouring it out. The fact that it is of course still water can lead on to what happened in Cana. I think this is far preferable to the red colouring stunts which only turn it all into a magic trick.

Praying

Thank you for the falling rain.
(wiggle fingers downwards)
Thank you for the rising sap.
(draw fingers upwards over body, as if a tree)
Thank you for the juicy fruit.
(hold arms out with fingers hanging down)
Thank you for my favourite fruity drink! Amen.
(pretend to drink it)

Activities

On the worksheet they will be changing things and making them special, and this forms a basis for thinking about how God works in our lives. Instructions for making a clay or plasticine water pot are given on the sheet.

PEARL DIVERS

Aim: To see the wedding at Cana as a sign of God's glory shown in Jesus.

Starter

A tasting survey. Have a number of different fruit drinks and some drinking cups. Blindfold some volunteers and give them the different drinks to taste, asking them to name them. Record their opinions on a chart and then let them take off the blindfold and reveal the identity of the drinks.

Teaching

Explain how we are going to hear about some people whose drink gave them a rather nice surprise. Have one of the servants telling the story. S/he can be holding a water jar and wearing appropriate clothing or headcovering to add to the effect. Whoever is telling the story needs to know the events well, and see it all from the servant's point of view. You can then slip in bits of hearsay about this man, Jesus, and comment on how you felt as he told you what to say and what it was that made you prepared to go along with what he told you to do. The aim is to help the children see what happened as if they were there as well.

Remind the children of the meaning of the Epiphany, and talk over with them what was being shown about God in this event. Read what John says at the end of his account. They had already decided to follow, and this sign backed up their decision.

Praying

Fill us up to the brim
with your Spirit, O Lord,
   (with hands horizontal like a water level, raise the level to the top of your head)
and use our lives
   (open up hands and extend them in offering)
for the good of the world.
   (trace large circle in the air with hands)
Amen.

Activities

The teaching is reinforced on the worksheet with an activity which matches different people with different reactions. There is also space to record discussion outcomes concerning the significance of this event. Instructions are included for making a 'black-and-white into colour' picture.

GOLD PANNERS

Aim: To look at how God's glory is revealed both at Cana and in our own lives.

Starter

Characters	Prospective bride and bridegroom, and the priest.
Bride	This must be the priest's house. Sure you want to go on with this?
Bridegroom	Yeah, why not? The pub isn't open yet.
Bride	P'raps he'll offer you a drink? *(Rings doorbell)*
Priest	Ah, good evening! Tracy and Martin, isn't it? Do come in.
Both	Thanks / OK. *(They sit on chairs)*
Priest	I'm sure you'd like a drink . . .
Bridegroom	*(Eagerly)* Oh yes, please!
Priest	Tea for both of you is it . . . with sugar?
Bridegroom	*(Disappointed)* Oh . . . er . . . yes, that will be great.
Bride	*(Whispers loudly)* Martin, behave yourself!
Priest	Does he always do what you tell him?
Bride	Heavens, no. If I tell him anything he's more likely to go and do the opposite!
Priest	What about that, Martin? Does she do what you tell her?
Bridegroom	Heck, no. She's really stubborn. It drives me mad!
Priest	Mmm, I see. And you two are thinking of getting married, are you?
Bride	Yes, that's right. I've seen a fantastic dress and it's all covered in . . .
Priest	How about you, Martin – how do you feel about getting married?
Bridegroom	Well, I don't mind either way, really, but it's a good excuse for a party, and she says her dad will be paying.
Priest	Mmm, I see. Do you think you two could cope with a lifetime together?

Bridegroom A lifetime? Cor, that's pretty steep, isn't it?

Bride A lifetime? Is that what you charge? Well, I think that's outrageous!

Bridegroom Come on, Tracy, let's get out of here. Lifetime, indeed! Anyone would think I loved her! *(They exit)*

Priest *(Shrugs shoulders and shakes head)*

A voice is heard: 'Your love, O Lord, reaches to the heavens, your faithfulness to the skies.' (Psalm 35:6)

Teaching

Why did Tracy and Martin not want to commit themselves to getting married? Suppose they had loved each other, what difference would that make? Human love can be very deep and beautiful. Humans can behave faithfully to one another – many marriages last happily for fifty years or more!

God has given us the ability to love like this, and his complete love and faithfulness are reflected in the good, lasting marriages and friendships we see around us.

Read the Isaiah passage together, to see something of God's nature, and then read the Gospel, with different people taking parts. What qualities of God expressed in the Isaiah reading can we see revealed in John's account of Jesus at the wedding? There is space on the worksheet to record ideas, and you may like to make a large version for display in church. Help them to see the event as a sign of God's glory, and not as a conjuring trick. When we are living in the Spirit it should show in our lives. Look at ways in which this might be true, using the Corinthians passage to help you.

Praying

Pray for one another and for any known to the group who are going through a difficult time. Use music and silence and something to help focus yourselves, such as a cross, to remind you of the extent of God's love for his people.

Activities

The worksheet will help to think through where we are with God, and where we would like to be. The rest of the time may be needed to talk through what it means to commit ourselves to Jesus. Those not ready for such a discussion can follow the instructions for making the fruit cup, ready to offer to people after the service.

THIRD SUNDAY OF THE YEAR

Thought for the day

The meaning of the scriptures is revealed to the people.

Reflection on the readings

Nehemiah 8:2-6, 8-10
Psalm 18
1 Corinthians 12:12-30
Luke 1:1-4; 4:14-21

Sometimes we may be reading a very familiar passage of scripture, yet for the first time it seems to shoot out at us with great significance and we realise with a shock that it is exactly what we needed to hear. When this happens it reminds us of the way the scriptures are much more than historical data and fine literature. They are also in-breathed with God's presence so that through them we can be given God's guidance.

As the law was read out to that ancient crowd in the square in front of the temple, we can imagine their emotions: sorrow and grief as it suddenly dawned on them how they had neglected their spiritual heritage, the yearning to put things right, and the joy that at last they were able to see things more clearly. It seems to be a hallmark of God's way of doing things that instead of condemnation, he gently brings us to see for ourselves what and where we are wrong, and gives with this insight a joy and excitement at the prospect of putting things right.

In the Gospel we see another congregation, gathered and attentive as the scriptures are read. But there is a difference, which Jesus must have been aware of even before he started his teaching. These people were his own people, the people he had grown up with, representative of the chosen people of Israel. They are privileged to be hearing the scriptures explained by the Word of God in person. And yet whether or not they were able to receive him and what he said would depend on where they were spiritually as they sat there that morning. Jesus cannot but reveal to us the truth, because that is his nature. If we are to recognise it as the truth, we need to make sure we are open and receptive.

The Church is a body of people, rich from its diversity of types and gifts, and strong when it recognises its unity in Christ. When as a body we are open and receptive, the life of Christ in us can speak out love and truth to the world. But wherever individual members lose their receptiveness to Christ, the whole body is seriously weakened.

Discussion starters

1. Why do you think the people were encouraged to go and spend the rest of the day celebrating? Where does true penitence turn into a wallowing in guilt?

2. What kind of atmosphere do you detect in the event described in today's Gospel? What might have blocked the people from 'hearing' what Jesus was saying?

All-stage talk

Begin by telling everyone you are going to drop a pin. Ask people to raise their hand if they hear it. (If the building is large, choose something slightly noisier to drop.) Point out how they all listened to be able to hear it. Today we are thinking about careful listening. Tell everyone you are going to drop the pin again, and this time ask them to notice what their bodies are doing to hear such a little sound. When you have dropped the pin, collect some of the things people have noticed. (These might include things like concentrating, waiting, being very still, cutting out our own noises, putting our best ear forward, turning our hearing aid up a bit.)

Today we are told that God is often revealed or shown to us through the scriptures – through the words in the Bible. (Hold a Bible and open it as you talk about it.) In our first reading we heard how all the people gathered in the square in front of the temple and had God's law read out clearly to them so they could really understand it. And when they heard it like this, they couldn't wait to start living the way they knew God wanted them to live. The reason they heard God's voice that day was because they were really trying to listen, like us trying to hear the pin drop.

When Jesus went to preach at his local synagogue he taught the people that the prophecy from Isaiah was coming true that very day. The ones who were listening as carefully as you listened for the pin dropping would have been very excited. Jesus was giving them a very strong clue about who he really was. And it isn't every day you have the promised Messiah turning out to be someone you grew up with!

The trouble is that lots of them weren't listening at all. And in our lives we are often so busy and preoccupied with things that don't really matter that we make too much noise to hear the still, small voice of God telling us really important things about what is right and what is wrong, and how we can live good lives, full of honest, loving behaviour.

God will always whisper what is good and true and loving to help us. We won't hear an actual voice because God can speak straight into our hearts and minds, so we will just know, suddenly, that what we are doing is very good or very bad, very thoughtful or rather selfish and unkind. Once we know, we can stop the wrong behaviour and change it. But we do need to get used to listening so we can hear God clearly.

All-age ideas

- Make a large card jigsaw of a body outline and a church. During the reading from Corinthians, have two groups of children working on these in the aisle so that the shapes are being built up visually in line with our understanding. The puzzles can be left on the floor so that people walk past (or over) them on their way to communion as one body.

- Act out the Gospel by having it fixed on a scroll. The Gospel reader reads the first section from the Bible as he walks to the lectern. A scroll is handed over and verses 17b to 20a are read from this. When it is handed back the reader takes up the Bible again and walks over to sit down for the rest of the passage.

Prayer of the Faithful

Celebrant
Let us still our bodies and our minds
as we pray together to the Father.

Reader
As we call to mind
that we are members of the worldwide Church,
we pray for those who are insulted
or persecuted for our shared faith.
We stand alongside them now.

Silence

Open our ears, Lord:
and teach us to listen to you.

We pray that all of us
who inhabit planet Earth in this age
may learn to hear again
and respond to God's voice of creative love.

Silence

Open our ears, Lord:
and teach us to listen to you.

We pray that wherever materialism
or stress or sorrow or sin
have deafened us to God's will,
we may be prompted to put things right.

Silence

Open our ears, Lord:
and teach us to listen to you.

We pray that our homes may be places
where the Lord is welcomed and recognised
through the good and the troubled times.

Silence

Open our ears, Lord:
and teach us to listen to you.

We pray for all who are ill, injured or sad.
May the Spirit show us how we can help,
and give them a real sense
of his comforting presence.

Silence

Open our ears, Lord:
and teach us to listen to you.

We remember those who have travelled through life
and now have gone through death into eternity.
We give thanks for their lives
and commend them to the Lord's safekeeping.
May he prepare us all, through our living, for eternal
    life.

Silence

Open our ears, Lord:
and teach us to listen to you.

We pray with Mary,
Mother of the Church:
Hail, Mary . . .

We make our own personal petitions
in silence, now,
to God our loving Father.

Silence

Celebrant
Father, we ask you to hear our prayers,
through Christ our Lord.
Amen.

TREASURE SEEKERS

Aim: For them to develop listening skills, both
physically and spiritually.

Starter

Listen for your name. Sit in a circle. Have a plate of
pieces of fruit and tell the children that one by one
they can choose a piece to eat. You will call their
name when it's their turn. For each one you can say
something like, 'Max, you can jump to choose a
piece of fruit now. Imogen, you can crawl to choose
a piece of fruit now.' Speaking our name alerts us
to listen, and God knows us by name.

Teaching

Give out percussion instruments (home-made
shakers will be fine) to everyone and have a quiet
bell yourself. Get everyone to play loudly, along
with a track from a praise tape. Stop everyone and
ask if anyone could hear the little bell. Play it on its
own so they know what to listen for and then get
everyone playing again, but listening out for the
bell. Now collect all the instruments in and give the
bell to a child to play while we all listen. Now it
sounds quite clear, but before, when we were all
making a noise, it was so quiet we could hardly
hear it.

Stand at one end of the room facing the wall,
and see if the children can creep up on you without
you hearing them.

Sit in the circle again and try passing the bell (or
a crackly, rustly bag) around the circle without it
making any noise at all. All these things develop
listening skills, both the attentiveness and concentration and also the body control. Praise the children
for their success as some will find this quite a challenge. Tell the children how God helps us to know
if something is right or wrong, and show this using
puppets. Just as a puppet is thinking aloud about
stealing something, or telling a lie or being unkind,
ring the little bell. The puppet realises that something is wrong, and changes his/her action.

Explain that God never forces us to make the right
choice (that's for us to decide) but he does let us
know what is right, to help us make the right choice.

Praying

Jesus, when you say
Stop! Think! Change! *(ring the bell three times)*
Help me to hear you *(hands on ears)*
and help me to do it. Amen. *(hands out, palms up)*

Activities

The worksheet helps the children to explore how
we hear best, both physically and spiritually. The
instruments can then be used to make a storm,
starting very quiet, building up and then dying
away into silence.

PEARL DIVERS

Aim: To see how God is revealed through the scriptures.

Starter

Who can it be? Sit in a circle. Start giving one piece of information about a particular child and continue down the clues until someone guesses who you are describing.

Teaching

Point out how in the game the words that were spoken gave everyone clues about the person being described. No one has ever seen God in this life, but we have been given plenty of good clues in the writings in the Bible. Look together at the passage from Isaiah. Who do they think it sounds as if it is describing? It does sound very like Jesus because he did those things in his life.

This prophecy of Isaiah was well known to the people in the town of Nazareth, where Jesus grew up. But at that time they had no idea who the prophet was talking about. They were in for quite a surprise one morning when they went to worship at their local synagogue.

Now act out the Gospel for today much as described in the All-age ideas, involving an attendant who gives you the scroll to read from. Make yourself thoroughly familiar with the text beforehand so that the other parts of the Gospel can be told informally. Have the words of the chorus to *God's Spirit is in my heart* displayed so that they can be read or sung afterwards:

> He sent me to give the Good News to the poor
> tell pris'ners that they are pris'ners no more,
> tell blind people that they can see
> and set the downtrodden free,
> and go tell ev'ryone
> the news that the kingdom of God has come
> and go tell ev'ryone
> the news that God's kingdom has come.

Talk together about how they might have felt if they had been there that morning and record their ideas on a sheet of paper headed: 'When Jesus preached this week I wondered/felt/thought . . .'. Then you can write their thoughts in thought bubbles.

Praying

Jesus, I know you always speak what is true.
Help me to listen
with my heart as well as my ears. Amen.

Activities

Make a group collage of today's Gospel, based on the picture drawn below. Give the children the appropriate sized pieces of paper to draw various people from the town and clothe them by cutting and sticking from a selection of different coloured and textured paper or fabric. All the characters are then assembled in the synagogue and Jesus can be holding a rolled scroll. The title for the collage is 'Today this scripture is fulfilled in your hearing'.

The worksheet looks at our need to listen so that when God is speaking to us through his word we are able to hear him.

GOLD PANNERS

Aim: To see how God's revelation of himself to us is linked with our readiness to listen.

Starter

Play a brief game of dodge ball, using a soft sponge ball if inside.

Teaching

Talk about what methods we use to switch off from something we don't want to hear (like pretending to be asleep, pretending not to have heard, or heard something different). God doesn't want to keep himself a secret, and is always showing us things that can help us get to know him better, but sometimes it's a bit like trying to get the ball through to the person in the middle – they keep turning away, and putting up barriers to stop themselves getting the message.

Read Luke 4:16-30 together, which includes the crowd's reaction to Jesus' teaching. Have different people taking various parts but ensure that the person who reads the part of Jesus is a sensitive reader; you may prefer to read this yourself, having prepared it well. Everyone can join in the crowd's words. Before you read it, ask them to be listening out for the barriers people were putting up against the truth.

After the reading talk over why the people first of all thought Jesus was wonderful and then turned against him. Draw out such things as: the difference between pride in a local hero, and faith in God; the craving for signs and wonders instead of goodness and truth; possessiveness – wanting to own and control Jesus; familiarity breeds contempt.

On a sheet of paper keep a record of the main ideas raised in the discussion. Show them a coin. If they think of this reaction as tails, we're now going to look at the heads reaction.

Turn to the Nehemiah reading and listen out for the contrasts. Both crowds are being shown new truths about God and his ways. How does this crowd react?

Record their ideas on the other side of the paper. Draw out such things as: when you come ready to listen you can hear; when the truth gets through to you it makes you want to change your life.

Praying

Use this song:

Open our eyes, Lord,
we want to see Jesus,
to reach out and touch him
and say that we love him.
Open our ears, Lord,
and teach us to listen,
open our eyes, Lord,
we want to see Jesus.

Robert Cull
© 1976 Maranatha! Music/CopyCare Ltd

Activities

Have plenty of Bibles available so that everyone becomes familiar with finding their way about. The worksheet provides space for the main discussion points to be recorded. Choose one of the events and act it out. Or split the group and have each group working on an acted version, and then performing to the others.

FOURTH SUNDAY OF THE YEAR

Thought for the day

As a prophet, Jesus' work is to proclaim the reign of God's love, not only to the Jewish people but to the whole world.

Reflection on the readings

Jeremiah 1:4-5, 17-19
Psalm 70
1 Corinthians 12:31-13:13
Luke 4:21-30

Jeremiah is commissioned by God to give a message the people will not want to hear. In order to encourage him, God reminds Jeremiah of the long-standing love he has for him – stretching right back to even before he was born. Being called to be a messenger for such a loving and faithful God helps brace Jeremiah for the hostility he is bound to face. There is a strong sense of God and Jeremiah working co-operatively here, and in that yoked work God promises that Jeremiah will be ultimately safe.

In the Gospel we find another prophet speaking out what he well knows will not be popular. This time it is Jesus himself, speaking in the synagogue of his home town, with familiar faces around him. They have heard on the grapevine that their familiar young carpenter has been seen performing astounding acts of healing in other towns, and now they're all waiting for him to perform here, for them. Looking round at the faces, Jesus sees not a longing to understand God better, or a recognition of their need for God, but more a cynical audience before a well-billed magic show. When Jesus starts pointing out from their history occasions when not the insiders but the outsiders received the blessing, they are, not surprisingly, angry and highly offended!

But Jesus knows that to have given these people what they wanted, rather than what they needed, would have been unloving, and unloving is never what Jesus does, since it is totally in opposition to God's character.

We can often behave like those people in the synagogue, thinking it our right and prerogative to have Jesus resourcing our plans and behaving as we think he ought to. We would prefer him to stick to the limits we ourselves impose. But to think in this way is to behave as mini-gods ourselves, controlling how and when Christ is convenient for us. The reality knocks away from under us such pompous pretensions and leaves us recognising our vulnerability and need of God, and entering a loving friendship with him, welcoming him and learning from him what real, wide, unlimited loving is all about.

Discussion starters

1. How wide and unlimited is our loving – both as individuals and as the Church?

2. How is this love different from the popularly understood commodity?

All-stage talk

Bring along some sentimental love music, red heart balloons and so on, and show them, explaining that in today's readings there is a lot about love.

The only trouble is, the love we've been hearing about doesn't sound much like all these audio-visual aids. The love we've heard about sounds more like this . . . Bring out a pair of rubber gloves, a bucket and mop and an apron. This love sounds much more like hard work, the kind of thing we need to roll up our sleeves to start on; the kind of thing that always needs doing, even though we did it yesterday and last week and twenty years ago.

We heard Jeremiah the prophet being reminded of the way God had always known and loved him, right from before he was born, and part of that love is going to be Jeremiah taking a message which is bound to make him very unpopular indeed. That's hard work love.

We heard Paul's letter describing love as always patient and always kind, never jealous, never taking offence. That sounds like hard work love, too.

And in the Gospel we find Jesus refusing to go along with what the people in his town wanted him to do because he knew it would lead them away from God, and not be helpful for them. He also knew that this would make the people angry and possibly violent towards him. So that was hard work love.

That means we have to ask: is hard work love actually worth all the effort? Why don't we just go for the sloppy, comfortable sort instead, and do what feels nice instead of putting ourselves out for people and risking our popularity or image?

The truth is that although the sloppy, indulgent sort of love feels nice for a while, it doesn't satisfy us deep down to our human roots, because we are made in the image of God, and God's nature is full of the expensive, costly loving. When we love this way it may be much more hard work, and it will almost certainly hurt, but it will satisfy us as the humans we were made to be, in every corner of our being.

All-age ideas

- Arrange the props for both sorts of love for people to see. With them put labels: 'LOVE?' and 'LOVE!'.

- Have a globe surrounded with flowers or votive candles, with the words between the candles: 'Let the whole world be filled with your love.'

Prayer of the Faithful

Celebrant
Let us pray to our loving and faithful God.

Reader
We pray that the Church may be noticeable by its
    loving;
that all Christians may be remarkable
for their caring and joyful serving
without restrictions or boundaries.

Silence

Loving Father:
hear our prayer.

We pray that through the power of love
conflicts may be resolved, injustices righted,
corruption cleansed and revenge dissolved,
for the world's healing.

Silence

Loving Father:
hear our prayer.

We pray that our homes may be training grounds
for the selfless loving which gives and forgives,
and never ends.

Silence

Loving Father:
hear our prayer.

We pray that fears may be calmed
and the anxious reassured;
that all in pain may be comforted
and restored to wholeness.

Silence

Loving Father:
hear our prayer.

We pray that through Christ's deathless love
those who have died may be forgiven
and brought to eternal life.

Silence

Loving Father:
hear our prayer.

Encouraged by Mary's example of love,
we join our prayers with hers:
Hail, Mary . . .

In the silence of God's attentive love,
we name those we know
who are in any particular need.

Silence

Celebrant
God our Father, hear these prayers;
give us all those qualities of faith, hope and love
which last for ever.
Through Christ our Lord.
Amen.

TREASURE SEEKERS

Aim: To look at what love is.

Starter

Have an 'I love it' face at one end of the room, an 'I hate it' face at the other, and an 'I don't really mind' face in the middle. You call out all sorts of different things – various foods, colours and things to do – and in each case the children run to the face which they agree with.

Teaching

Prepare a large red heart-shaped piece of paper folded like this so that you can open it up.

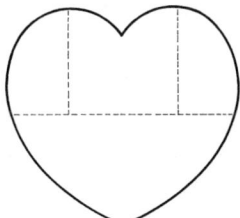

In our game there were some things we really loved, and some things we hated. In Treasure Seekers we are always saying that God loves us. We sing that God's love is so wide we can't get round it, so high we can't get over it and so low we can't get under it. (You might want to sing it now.) So what does that mean? What is God's wonderful love like? Here are some of the things the Bible tells us about love. (Open the heart and read the slips of paper which you have hidden inside:

* Love is kind.
* Love is never selfish.
* Love doesn't show off.
* Love cares for others.
* Love sees the good in people.
* Love is full of trust.
* Love goes on trying.
* Love doesn't get in a bad mood.
* Love lasts for ever.

That's how God loves each of us, and it makes God happy to see us loving one another like this as well.

Praying

Dear Father God
thank you for loving us.
Teach us to love one another.
Amen.

Activities

The children can do some loving act of kindness (like helping put the chairs away, or putting out the cups and biscuits for after Mass), and they can make the sheet into a sampler by threading coloured wool through the punched holes. (You may want to mount the sheets on thin card for extra strength. Punch inaccessible holes with a pencil, resting the sheet on Blu-Tack.)

PEARL DIVERS

Aim: To know the events of today's Gospel.

Starter

Riddles. Split into teams, give each team a bell or hooter, and ask some riddles. The first team to ring their bell and give the right answer gains a point. The winning team has a small prize. Choose riddles which you solve by looking at the question in a different way, like these:

* What has four wheels and flies? A dustcart.
* When is a door not a door? When it's ajar.
* What goes up when it comes down? An umbrella.
* What runs but cannot walk? Water.

Teaching

Those riddles only made sense once we started understanding them in a new way. Until then, they sounded like nonsense – to run yet not be able to walk; to be a door and yet not to be a door. Today we are going to find that Jesus is a rather like a riddle for the people in his home town to solve.

Two leaders or imported Gold Panners stand up and start a 'Have you heard about the miracles of healing Jesus has been doing?' conversation together about some of the healings they've heard about. They finish by saying they can't wait to see what happens when he comes home to Nazareth. Then they sit down.

Explain that Jesus came that weekend to his home town of Nazareth, and that Sabbath everyone crowded into the synagogue to hear him, and see what miracles he would do for them. Perhaps they were fed up that he hadn't started at his home town. They liked it when he told them the old prophecies were being fulfilled today, in their own synagogue. They all waited for some amazing signs and wonders to happen, because that was what they were expecting Jesus to do. As his home town, they thought he ought to make it extra special.

But Jesus didn't do anything spectacular at all. Instead he told them they were looking at him in the wrong way, and didn't understand what he was there for. Jesus wasn't there to do clever tricks, but to show God's love. If they could only see him as a local boy doing clever tricks, then they wouldn't get to see any of the wonderful signs of God's love! He even hinted that there were plenty of outsiders who would end up seeing more than them.

The two leaders or Gold Panners stand up again, talking angrily about the way Jesus had upset them that day, and how disappointed they were in him, even if he was a local lad. They remind each other of the way the men in their town had dragged Jesus out of the synagogue and thrown him out of the town. They end up folding their arms and both agreeing that it was disgraceful! Then they sit down.

What had Jesus done wrong? Nothing, except to tell them the truth, which they didn't want to hear. It wouldn't have helped them get to know God better if Jesus had done what they wanted and performed lots of miracles. Miracles are not magic tricks, and Jesus wasn't a clever magician. If the people didn't trust in God's love, they wouldn't be able to see it in action anyway. And neither will we.

Praying

Father God,
train us to want what you want;
to see as you see
and understand as you do.
Let your kingdom come and
your will be done on earth
as it is in heaven. Amen.

Activities

The sheet can be made into a model of the people angrily forcing Jesus out of the synagogue. They are also encouraged to think about times we try to push Jesus away because we don't want to hear what he is saying in our hearts.

GOLD PANNERS

Aim: To see Jesus as a prophet proclaiming the reign of God's love to the Jewish people and the whole world.

Starter

Set up dominoes and knock the first one so that the domino effect kicks in.

Teaching

With the dominoes, there was an impressive knock-on effect. Today we are going to look at how the life and teaching of Jesus was starting a great wave of spreading the good news, far beyond the Jewish people to those of all nations and times, including us.

First look at the Jeremiah reading, seeing how prophets are chosen and called to speak out God's message, even when that makes them extremely unpopular. They are to speak it out whether the people want to hear it or not. During the bad times they may well be given, God promises to stand by them and support them.

Now read today's Gospel, and notice any ways

Jesus is a prophet like Jeremiah. Is his message popular? Does that mean he doesn't speak it out? How do the people treat him? Look too at what Jesus' message was to the people of his home town. He was saying that God's blessing never was just for the chosen people.

Then read the passage from Corinthians to see what real love is all about. They can try reading it with Jesus' name in place of 'love' to see how Jesus showed such love in person.

Praying

Lord, the light of your love is shining,
in the midst of the darkness, shining;
Jesus, Light of the World, shine upon us,
set us free by the truth you now bring us,
shine on me, shine on me.

(From the song by Graham Kendrick,
© 1987 Make Way Music Ltd)

Activities

On the sheet they investigate what it is to be a prophet and why they are often unpopular, even though they are speaking out the words of the loving God. They can look up the Elijah and Elisha stories Jesus refers to, and there is a role-play to do which picks up on the Gospel events.

FIFTH SUNDAY OF THE YEAR

Thought for the day

God calls his people and commissions them.

Reflection on the readings

Isaiah 6:1-8
Psalm 137
1 Corinthians 15:1-11
Luke 5:1-11

We can be driving along the motorway without a care in the world until we glance at the petrol gauge and discover that we are about to run out of fuel. Suddenly we are anxiously watching the miles to the next service station, and at the first opportunity we drive in with great relief to sort things out. Similarly, it is only when we suddenly catch sight of God that the meanness of our lives sharpens into focus and we cannot wait to put things right. Before we noticed, we were quite happy to carry on as we were.

It is when Isaiah sees that vision of God in glory that he is suddenly aware of the lack of righteousness and integrity both in his own life and his society. It is when Simon sees the signs of God's power in the catch of fish that he feels completely unworthy to be in the company of Jesus.

At this point it is always God's nature to reach out and never to condemn. Isaiah has his guilt taken away by the angel's burning coal from the altar, and Jesus rescues Simon, telling him not to be afraid. Our God is full of compassion and mercy, and will never take advantage of us at moments of weakness or vulnerability. The realisation is necessary for restoration to happen but, the moment we see the problem, God helps and enables us to put things right.

Only after this does God commission us, involving us and working with our consent each step of the way. All three characters in our readings today – Isaiah, Paul and Simon – have been made so acutely aware of the need that they enthusiastically agree to work with God. I love this characteristic of God's; the way he almost gets us thinking his commission is our idea! Sometimes after prayer about something we will get a sudden and unexpected good idea which we can't wait to put into practice. It may well be that God was speaking silently into our hearts.

As a result of God's commissioning, the good news is spread. Those who have recently had their eyes opened are still excited by what they can see, and their excitement is infectious, so they are particularly effective at spreading the news.

Discussion starters

1. What do you think made Simon decide to follow Jesus?

2. What did Jesus mean when he said he would make Simon 'a fisher of men'?

All-stage talk

You will need a mirror. First do a spot of face-painting on a volunteer, writing their own name in mirror-writing across their face. Then show them their face in the mirror. They will be surprised at what they look like because it isn't their familiar face looking back at them. Yet it is their own named self they are looking at.

Whenever Jesus met up with people he seems to have been able to show them who they were; what they were really like. By the things he said, the stories he told, and by the signs and miracles he did, people were able to look at him and suddenly see something about themselves they hadn't realised before. Some suddenly realised that they were lovable and important, when they had always thought they were rubbish. Others suddenly saw that they were living very mean, selfish lives, and knew they wanted to change.

In the event we hear about today, Simon Peter has been fishing all night long without any success at all. It's possible that Jesus had watched them, and noticed how they carried on even when they were tired and disappointed. Perhaps Jesus brought that into his teaching, and the fishermen would have sat up on the beach and thought, 'This man really knows what it's like to be a fisherman like me, working all night with nothing to show for it!' So when Jesus suggested they try again, Simon was doubtful, but willing to give it a go. The huge catch of fish, coming suddenly after all that time they had worked in vain, must have given Simon a shock. It was a bit like looking in a mirror and seeing who he really was for the first time.

He saw that this man Jesus, who had been sitting in Simon's own fishing boat talking to the crowds, was different from anyone he had ever met before. His goodness, his wise teaching and his knowledge of where the fish were, all made Simon suddenly ashamed. We don't know what it was in Simon's life that went through his mind. It might have been some particular sin he still felt guilty about, or it might have been remembering all the general meanness and selfishness, or the bad temper he knew he had.

The important thing for us to look at is how Jesus helped him see himself, and then said, 'Don't be afraid, follow me.' That is what Jesus does with us today as well. So be ready for it. If something makes you suddenly see yourself and you don't like everything you see, Jesus will not be standing at your elbow, saying, 'There's no hope for you, then, is there? You might as well give up.' He will be there, speaking into your heart words of love and comfort and hope: 'Don't be afraid of what you really are. Come and follow me.'

All-age ideas

• For the Gospel have different voices for Simon and Jesus.

• Have a fishing net, sand and shells incorporated into the main flower arrangement, or make a boaty display with oars, life jackets, oilskins and waders at the entrance, with a prayer for those who work on the sea.

• Have music played as background to the reading from Isaiah which reflects the sense of overwhelming holiness and wonder of God. Begin with the music on its own, then lower the volume as the reading starts. The reader leaves longer spaces between sentences than usual and the music gives people time to reflect on the vision. Fade the music out during verse 7.

Prayer of the Faithful

Celebrant
Let us pray together in the presence of our God.

Reader
We pray for all who have been called
to be workers in God's harvest,
searching for the lost and loving them
into the kingdom.
We pray for those who teach God's love,
both by word and by the way they live.

Silence

Here I am, Lord:
ready for your service!

We pray for those in authority
and in positions of power,
that under their leadership
there may be mutual respect, integrity and justice.
We pray for discernment
to see where injustice needs righting
and when we need to speak out.

Silence

Here I am, Lord:
ready for your service!

We pray for families suffering poverty
or financial difficulties,
for families full of tension and disagreement,
and for families coping with grief or separation.
We pray for the extended families represented here.
We pray for better awareness
of how our behaviour affects others.

Silence

Here I am, Lord:
ready for your service!

We pray for those who have been working all night
and all who work long hours in poor conditions.
We pray for those who have no work
and feel rejected.
We pray for any resisting
what God is calling them into.

Silence

Here I am, Lord:
ready for your service!

We pray for those who have died
and those who grieve for the loss of their company.

We ask for the opportunity to prepare for death
by the way we live from now on.

Silence

Here I am, Lord:
ready for your service!

Remembering Mary's special vocation,
we join our prayer with hers:
Hail, Mary . . .

As God's stillness fills our hearts,
we pray for any needs
known to us personally.

Silence

Celebrant
Heavenly Father, hear us,
give us strength and dedication
to offer ourselves to do his will.
Through Christ our Lord.
Amen.

TREASURE SEEKERS

Aim: To introduce them to the story of the catch of fishes.

Starter

Have a fish-catching game, either using magnets on strings and paperclips on the fish, or a bazaar-stall fishing game with floating fish which are caught with hooks. The fish for the magnet game can either be made beforehand or cut out ready and then coloured by the children.

Teaching

Tell the story with the children acting it out as you go along. They can find their way to their boat in the dark, push their boat out, throw out the nets, sit and wait, pull in the nets and shake their heads when they find no fish, throw the nets out again, wait and yawn, pull the nets in, and repeat this until morning comes and they rub their eyes. They can shade their eyes to see all the crowds coming, beckon Jesus and help him into the boat, and sit on the sand to listen. Then they push the boat out again, throw in the nets, wait, and pull them in full of fish! Tell the children how Peter was amazed at what had happened, and a bit frightened by it. Jesus told him he didn't need to be afraid, and invited Peter to follow him. Peter said yes, and spent the rest of his life following Jesus and telling other people about him.

Praying

Sing this prayer to the tune of *One, two, three, four, five, once I caught a fish alive.*

One, two, three, four, five,
Thank you, God, that I'm alive!
Six, seven, eight, nine, ten,
Here I am to help you, then.
What job can I do?
Love God as he wants me to,
show his love each day
living life the loving way.

Activities

On the sheet the children create a collage picture of the story. You will need some scraps of net curtain or the net bags that oranges come in and some fish cut from shiny paper.

PEARL DIVERS

Aim: To see the stages that Simon Peter went through in this calling.

Starter

Pass it on. Sit in a circle and choose a leader. The leader does something (claps hands, crosses legs, winks, etc.) and this action is taken up by each person one by one, going clockwise round the circle. When it gets back to the leader, they start a new action for the next round. The point is that each person needs to be attentive to what the person sitting next to them is doing, and they then become the next in the chain of passing the message on.

Teaching

Beforehand prepare a film clapperboard to snap shut as signs with the following headings are displayed. (The titles in brackets are written on the reverse.)
1. The night shift
2. Simon helps out *(welcome Jesus)*
3. Time to listen *(listen to him)*
4. The Maker's instructions *(see him in action)*
5. I'm not good enough! *(recognise who he is)*
6. Follow me *(follow him)*

Go through the story as if the film is being made, narrating it, with the leaders and children acting it out.
1. The children act the setting-out and pulling-in of empty nets through the night.
2. The crowd arrives, and Simon Peter offers Jesus his boat to sit in.
3. Simon Peter sits on the sand with the crowd,

first busy with his nets and gradually listening more keenly. Give out an old net curtain for everyone to work on.
4. Jesus tells the fishermen to cast their nets again and they do so, with surprising and dramatic results.
5. Simon Peter reacts to the huge catch by realising Jesus' importance and his own lack of goodness.
6. Jesus shows Simon Peter that he knows what he is like and still wants him to work for the spreading of the kingdom of God. He calls him to follow and search for people instead of fish. Simon Peter follows him.

Display all the signs in order, then turn them over to show the titles in brackets. These lead on to the prayer time.

Praying

Give the children a set of five paper footprints, which they put down in a line in front of them. As you pray, move forward to each footprint in turn:

Like Simon Peter
I want to *welcome* you, Jesus,
listen to what you say,
see what you do,
get to *know* you better
and *follow* you all my life. Amen.

Activities

On the sheet there are instructions for making a fishes-and-shell mobile, based on today's prayer. You will need to have string, card, and a shell for each child. There is also a wordsearch to reinforce the teaching, and a picture to complete, which will give them the sense of things falling into place as Jesus enables us to see where we need to go next in life.

GOLD PANNERS

Aim: To explore how God commissions people.

Starter

In a circle, try to describe something which is hard to explain, such as a circle (without using your hands), a pair of scissors, a line, or an envelope. We will be looking at how two people were affected by things which amazed them.

Teaching

Look at the Isaiah passage, first explaining that Isaiah was trying to describe the impossible, but he has given us a sense of God's holiness which he was shown. Ask them to listen out for how this affected him. After the reading discuss how the vision made Isaiah feel, and what was done about it. Draw their attention to the way Isaiah's vision of God's perfect holiness gave him insight into the shallowness and lack of purity and truth in our lives, and this realisation enabled him to be forgiven and commissioned.

Now read the Luke passage together, with different voices for different parts. Again, ask them to listen out for how Peter was affected by seeing the signs of God's glory in the way Jesus behaved.

Praying

Look at the prayer of Richard of Chichester and see how the same steps follow on, in both passages and in our own lives. Then pray the words together:

O most merciful Redeemer,
friend and brother,
may I know you more clearly,
love you more dearly,
and follow you more nearly
day by day. Amen.

Activities

There is a game to play on the sheet to help the group explore what calling and commissioning meant for Isaiah and Peter, and what it means for us. You will need to prepare ten card fish with the following instructions on them:

1. Why did the angel touch Isaiah's lips with the burning coal from the altar? (Isaiah 6:7)

2. What were the angels calling to one another? (Isaiah 6:3)

3. Who did the Lord send to speak out his words? (Isaiah 6:8)

4. What did Simon Peter say when he saw the huge catch of fish? (Luke 5:8)

5. What did Jesus call Simon Peter to do? (Luke 5:10-11)

6. How were Simon Peter's partners affected by the catch? (Luke 5:10)

7. Find out how many people in the group know what job they want to do.

8. Find out when your group leader started to follow Jesus.

9. Tell the group how you think you would feel if Jesus called you to do his work.

10. Pray together for God's will for your lives to be made clear to you, and for courage to follow where Jesus leads you.

SIXTH SUNDAY OF THE YEAR

Thought for the day
The challenges and rewards of living by faith.

Reflection on the readings
Jeremiah 17:5-8
Psalm 1
1 Corinthians 15:12, 16-20
Luke 6:17, 20-26

It is always noticeable how much less you spend if for some reason you can't get out. Shops rely on our habit of browsing and getting what we don't particularly need. Several times an hour on radio and television we are persuaded to invest in all those things we cannot possibly live without, and the social pressure to wear or use or play with particular brand-name items is very strong. The young, and the insecure, are particularly vulnerable.

Such consumerism is a symptom of our trust in things and systems and wealth and power. We bank on all this bringing us happiness and fulfilment. And although the actual items change across the centuries, the basic problem is exactly the same now as it was in the days of Jeremiah. Through him God spoke to his people of the foolishness of living with our faith in things which cannot ever satisfy and which stunt our spiritual growth.

The lovely image of a strongly rooted tree near the water, so that its leaves are always green, shows up the blessings to the whole community, as well as the individual, that spring from right living, based on trust in God. Psalm 1 also reflects on this valuable fruitfulness of well-rooted lives.

Jesus' teaching in today's Gospel comes after the resentful anger of the teachers and Pharisees resulting from his healing on the Sabbath, and after the apostles have been chosen and called. Luke sets the beatitudes on a level place with a large crowd, and Jesus is looking at his disciples as he speaks. We can only guess at what was going through the minds of these people. They have given up their security and their earning potential, they have no idea where their next meal will be coming from, and they have glimpsed the hostility they are inviting by committing themselves to walking around with this leader.

Jesus speaks into their possible misgivings and natural concerns, reassuring them that although they have chosen poverty, insecurity, insult and rejection, they have indeed chosen wisely and bravely, and the rewards of living by faith are great and lasting. In contrast, those who cling to the material, intellectual or even religious security, which stunts their growth and anchors them to the ground, can never be swept up in the wind of the spirit and experience the fullness of joy God longs to provide.

The quantity of our possessions does need looking at, and we cannot sweep such teaching comfortably into the realm of attitudes towards our wealth and lifestyle. If we are really living by faith in God it is bound to affect our comfort. If we know we have given up anything or any relationship for the sake of living God's way, then today's Gospel is reassuring and comforting us that we have chosen well and in the long term the tears will be wiped away.

And if we discover that much of our happiness is linked with things, or systems, or other people's praise, then today's readings challenge us to choose the risky vulnerability of living instead by faith in God.

Discussion starters

1. How is our own society cursed, or damaged, by widespread trust in what people say, make and sell?

2. Are the beatitudes impractical and idealistic, or simply too challenging to accept?

All-stage talk

Beforehand gather a selection of brand-name items relevant to each age group in the congregation.

Begin by displaying each item and drawing attention to the brand name to impress people. Talk about how we are sometimes made to feel we have to have a particular thing in order to be thought normal or worth anything. Sometimes we are teased if we haven't got them. Sometimes we go out shopping to cheer ourselves up, thinking that having more will make us happy. Sometimes we spend money we can't afford to keep up with our friends or neighbours.

Put all the items into a carton labelled 'Very Important' and close the lid. Explain that Jesus turns our ideas of what is important upside down. As you say this, turn the carton upside down. Today we have heard Jesus telling the people that trust in what you can buy and possess is not the good thing the advertisements say it is, and these things don't give us long-term happiness at all.

So what does he offer instead?

Jesus says that we will be much happier if we trust in God rather than in things people say about us, and things people make and sell. Getting stuck in the 'wanting something else' mode or the 'everybody else does it' mode just ends up making us dissatisfied and greedy and selfish, which doesn't bring happiness to us or those we live with. But if we put our trust in God, all the riches of the kingdom of God will be ours. We'll enjoy the lovely and surprising ways God provides for our needs. We'll be able to see what is good and right, and want to work enthusiastically again instead of just going through the motions. We won't be frantically running to keep up with the latest fashion. We won't be so anxious about material things.

Jesus doesn't say we'll have lots of comforts or fame or money if we live like this. In fact he says we will run into insults and people will think we're crazy, and they will laugh at us and make life difficult for us. We can't say we haven't been warned!

But the rewards far outweigh the disadvantages. Putting our trust in God will enable us to live as free, contented and generous-hearted people – the kind of people we would, deep down, probably prefer to be.

All-age ideas

• Have a twin flower arrangement of a dry, dead branch set in sand, and a bonsai tree or a cluster of flowering pot plants, standing in a wide, shallow tray filled with water and a few pebbles. Have a quotation from Jeremiah or Psalm 1 beside the arrangement.

• Have a collection of actual items needed, rather than money, for a local project to help the homeless, for example.

Prayer of the Faithful

Celebrant
Knowing our need of God,
let us pray.

Reader
We bring to mind our Church
both here in (*name of town*) and throughout the world.
It is for right values and right priorities
that we pray, in all we decide and do.

Silence

Lord our God:
in you we put our trust.

We bring to mind all who lead and govern,
and all meetings where important decisions are made.
We pray that justice and mercy are upheld
in line with the Father's loving will.

Silence

Lord our God:
in you we put our trust.

We bring to mind our circle of family and friends
with whom we share the good
and the difficult times.
We pray for the grace to discern more readily
the good in each person
and the gifts they have to offer.

Silence

Lord our God:
in you we put our trust.

We bring to mind those caught up
in the frenetic pressures of life,
and those who are stressed to breaking point.
We pray for insight and courage to change things.

Silence

Lord our God:
in you we put our trust.

We bring to mind the dying,
especially those who are alone,
and we remember those we know who have died.
May they and we share
in the everlasting joy of God's presence.

Silence

Lord our God:
in you we put our trust.

We make our prayer with Mary,
whose trust in the Lord is our example:
Hail, Mary . . .

Together now in silence,
we pray our individual petitions
to our heavenly Father.

Silence

Celebrant
We commend all our cares
to the God who loves us as his children.
Through Christ our Lord.
Amen.

TREASURE SEEKERS

Aim: To know that we can trust God.

Starter

Chickens. The children run and peck around until
the mother hen clucks a danger warning. Whenever
that happens, the chickens stop what they are doing
and run to the safety of the mother hen (one of the
leaders on a rug). When she tells them the danger
is over, they can scatter again.

Teaching

Talk about how the chickens know they will be safe
with the mother hen. They can trust her to look
after them. Talk together about what happens if
they fall over and hurt themselves, and draw their
attention to the fact that because someone loves
them, they look after them. Talk about the way
they look after pets and the way they can look after
their mums and dads and grandparents with hugs
and helping them.

God looks after us all. He has given us a lovely
world to live in, with food for us to eat, and all the
things we need to make homes and clothes and
toys and cars. That's because he loves us.

Praying

When I am afraid
I will trust in you, O God.
I will take shelter under your wings.

(From Psalms 56 and 57)

Activities

On the worksheet there are instructions for making
a working model of chickens running to the safety
of the mother hen's wings. You will need string and
sticky tape, and may prefer to prepare the chicks
and hen in card.

PEARL DIVERS

Aim: To think about where we put our trust, and
whether this is the best place for it.

Starter

See I haven't got it! Use a soft ball or beanbag. The
children line up across one end of the room and a
child at the other end throws the ball into the centre
of the room before turning away from the other
children. The children run to collect the ball and
whoever has it tries not to show it. The child who
threw the ball can ask anyone to turn round and
eventually guesses who has it.

Teaching

First refer to the starter game. Ask the children who
were trying to decide who had the ball, if they felt
they could trust those who said they hadn't got it.
(No, they couldn't trust them because the game
meant they were hiding the truth.) What or whom
can we trust? Today we are going to look at some
teaching of Jesus. He was helping people see what
they really trusted in.

(Use the carpet tiles method to tell the story. Pictures needed are shown below.)

Luke tells us that Jesus had been on a mountainside praying all night long before choosing his twelve apostles. They had all agreed to leave their homes and jobs and set out with Jesus. That was a big thing to do, and a lot to give up. Ask the children what might have worried the apostles about their new life and give them some ideas. (Will there be enough to eat? Where will we sleep? Will people think I am stupid? Am I being stupid? Will it be dangerous? Will I be able to do it well enough?)

Jesus brought the apostles to a large level place, and lots of people came to hear what he said. Some of these people were his friends and followers, and some were people who didn't want to follow him because that would mean changing the way they lived and they were comfortable as they were.

First Jesus spoke to the ones who had given up their security to follow him. He told them that the choice they had made – to risk being poor and hungry and sad and insulted, in order to do what was right and good – was a choice that would bring them great rewards of happiness, happiness that would last for ever.

Then he spoke to those who still put all their trust in being rich and having lots of possessions, and doing only what would keep them popular. He told them that we can't get long-term happiness and security from things other people say and make and sell. This kind of richness doesn't last and will leave us poor in the end because it will make us greedy and selfish and never satisfied.

Praying

There is a real challenge to people of all ages in today's teaching, and it is important that we never force children to make decisions or feel they have to believe things they are not ready to. At the same time, it is very important that we give them all the opportunity to voice their love and commitment. Invite the children to join in this prayer having read it to them first. If they don't feel ready to pray it they needn't. Ask them simply to sit quietly so they allow others to pray.

Lord God,
I want to live by faith in you.
I understand that it may not be easy,
but I can see it is the best way to live.
Please show me how.
Thank you. Amen.

Activities

On the worksheet there are instructions for making a contrasting collage of living rooted in God and rooted in a dry place. The children also explore trust at different levels so they can begin to see the difference between enjoying what God has provided, and becoming so attached to something that it takes over our life and stops us moving on.

GOLD PANNERS

Aim: To be introduced to the beatitudes and explore their meaning.

Starter

Write the following items on separate pieces of card (have several sets if the group is larger) and have everyone discussing how to place them in order of importance in life.

Happiness

Having my own way

A job with power

Lots of money

Pleasing God

Good friends

Helping other people

Having children

Teaching

First set the reading in its context as Luke has arranged it, immediately after the choosing of the apostles and the growing hostility towards Jesus from the religious authorities. Ask some of the group to imagine they have just been chosen and have agreed to be apostles, with a dangerous and insecure future ahead of them. Ask others to imagine they have thought of following Jesus but decided it's too risky and they'd rather keep their money, security and friends. Now read the Gospel together, with a narrator and a different voice for Jesus.

Have a brainstorm of how the apostles feel, listening to what Jesus has been saying, and how the others feel.

Now read the passage from Jeremiah and see how it links up with what Jesus was teaching. What about us? Where do we stand?

Praying

This prayer voices our love and commitment to living in a very challenging way. Make it clear that if they do not feel able or ready to pray it they don't have to.

Father,
you showed us through Jesus
the best way to live.
I want to live that way.
I want to trust in you
instead of trusting in
money or possessions
or what other people say.
Please help me
and show me
whatever is holding me back. Amen.

Activities

The worksheet enables them to explore what Jesus' teaching involves in practical terms in their own lives. They can also make a display using words and pictures to show the teaching visually. This could be placed in church or on one of the notice-boards outside.

SEVENTH SUNDAY OF THE YEAR

Thought for the day

Jesus teaches us to love our enemies and forgive those who sin against us.

Reflection on the readings

1 Samuel 26:2, 7-9, 12-13, 22-23
Psalm 102
1 Corinthians 15:45-49
Luke 6:27-38

How we deal with our enemies is a real test of our spiritual strength. We may have actual enemies, or those who are against us, or simply those we don't like. Whatever wrong they do to us, however much they may hurt us – or we imagine they hurt us – and however strong our case may be, we must remember that all of us – friend or foe – are special in God's eyes. David was having a hard time with Saul and theirs was not a good relationship to say the least. But David respected the status of Saul in the Lord's eyes although his instinct (and certainly the instinct of Abishai) might have been to extract violent retribution.

So often we insist on carrying grudges, and they weigh us down. They imprison us and prevent us from knowing inner peace. In advising us to forgive those who sin against us, and to love our enemies, Jesus is actually setting us free from the chains we clank around with us, sometimes for years.

Jesus would not have been talking simply to a group of friends and sympathisers at this point. Among his hearers there were no doubt some who regarded Jesus as their enemy, so this teaching was very close to the bone. While your heart is filled with hurt and anger and hatred towards someone, the last thing you want to do is love and forgive them. It can be a real battleground as we wrestle with our rage and disappointment and frustration, and it is important that we don't pretend these feelings are not there. To squash such emotions deep down inside us and sit on them is in no way forgiveness. Yet neither are these very real emotions an excuse for permitting us to behave badly.

We do need to recognise and acknowledge them, asking for God's grace to transform what is going on inside us, and then face the battle which may be long and difficult. But if we really want God's will to be done in us then we are playing on the winning side, and victory over revenge, resentment and hatred will eventually come. That victory is a

cleansing and wonderfully refreshing desire to forgive. And it melts the hatred away.

Discussion starters

1. What stops us from putting down our grievances?
   What might Jesus say about this?

2. Does our present concern with the importance
   of self-assertion clash with Jesus' teaching on
   loving our enemies?

All-stage talk

Beforehand ask the children to make lots of paper
chains.

Remind everyone of what Jesus teaches us in
today's Gospel: to love our enemies and forgive those
who sin against us. How on earth are we supposed
to do it? Surely enemies are people you hate? Why
does Jesus tell us to love them, then?

Ask a volunteer to run and skip around a bit
and talk about how life can feel when we are
happy with ourselves, and everything is going well
for us. But sooner or later we get into a mood with
someone, someone upsets us and annoys us, someone else winds us up, someone makes our life a
real misery, someone lets us down and spoils our
plans, someone hurts a person we love, or someone
steals from us a close friend or a marriage partner,
or our dignity in old age. (At each suggestion,
drape a chain around the volunteer until s/he is
smothered in chains.) And if we haven't forgiven
these people who have sinned against us and hurt
us, we end up still carrying invisible chains which
weigh us down. The volunteer can walk around
bowed down with the heavy chains.

So when Jesus says to us, 'Love your enemies
and forgive those who wrong you', he knows it is
hard, but he also knows it will set us free to live
fully again. Every time we say (and really mean it)
'I forgive you for what you did', a chain drops off.
(Pull a chain off the volunteer.) Every time we
wrestle with our feelings of hate for someone and
ask God to help us sort things out, a chain drops
off. (Pull off another chain.) Pull off the remaining
chains, with everyone saying 'I forgive you!' for
each one.

Jesus doesn't like to see us weighed down with
heavy invisible chains of hate and resentment and
bitterness against people. He wants us to be free to
enjoy life, and he will always help us to do the forgiving. Forgiving is not easy; it's very hard work. If
you know there is someone you are finding it very
hard to forgive, ask God for the grace to forgive
and then work at the forgiving. Don't live with the
chains any more.

All-age ideas

- The very dramatic first reading can be acted out
  while being narrated. Saul lies asleep at the
  front of the church. David and Abishai creep up
  the aisle and take the spear, running off to the
  back, side or balcony, from where David shouts
  his words to the awakened Saul.

- A chant. Have the following words written on
  the weekly handout or on an OHP: 'Love your
  enemies. Do good to those who hate you. Pray
  for those who hurt you.' Very quietly the congregation recites these words, repeating them
  six times. Above this hushed chanting of Jesus'
  teaching, have three people, standing in different
  parts of the church, to call out their protests.
  They should leave enough space between each
  protest for the teaching to be heard through,
  and the chant should be the last thing left in
  people's minds.

  Here are the protests:

  1. 'But you can't expect me to forgive them!
     Not after what they've done!'

  2. 'It was terrible.
     It was unforgivable.
     How can I possibly love them now?'

  3. 'But they've ruined my whole life.
     Why should I forgive them?'

Prayer of the Faithful

Celebrant
God remembers our frailty;
let us pray to him now.

Reader
When conflicts threaten to disrupt our fellowship
in the church community,
may the Spirit help us to deal
with our frustrations and anger,
and give us the grace to forgive.

Silence

Father, may we love one another:
as you have loved us.

When the luggage we carry from the past
interferes with our capacity to cope with the present,
may the Spirit heal the damage from our memories
and transform our experiences for good.

Silence

Father, may we love one another:
as you have loved us.

When the differences in cultures
block our understanding of one another

and obstruct the peace process,
may the Spirit broaden our vision
to discern the common ground.

Silence

Father, may we love one another:
as you have loved us.

When the layers of resentment
have turned into rock,
may the Spirit dissolve them
with the rain of loving mercy.

Silence

Father, may we love one another:
as you have loved us.

As those we have known and loved
pass through the gate of death,
may the Lord have mercy on them,
and receive them into the joy of eternal life.

Silence

Father, may we love one another:
as you have loved us.

We join our prayers with those of Mary,
the Mother of our Lord:
Hail, Mary . . .

We pray in silence now
for our own petitions
to God our heavenly Father.

Silence

Celebrant
Father, accept these prayers;
may your love strengthen
and encourage us all.
Through Christ our Lord.
Amen.

TREASURE SEEKERS

Aim: To learn to make up when things go wrong.

Starter

Let the children draw on chalkboards and rub it all
out again. Or use the magic writer pads that enable
you to erase what you have drawn.

Teaching

Talk about and demonstrate how we can rub out
our mistakes on a chalkboard. Draw a nasty splodge
as you talk about someone being unkind. But then
they say, 'I'm sorry I was unkind.' If someone says

that to us we can say, 'That's OK. I forgive you!' As
you say it, rub out the splodge.

Jesus says, 'Forgive one another. Pray for those
who are unkind to you.' When we do this we are
rubbing out the unkindness and clearing the way
to start again.

Praying

Thank you, God,
for forgiving me.
Help me to forgive as well. Amen.

Activities

Help the children to make the two finger puppets
from the worksheet and fix them on their fingers,
so they can practise getting cross and making up
again. They can also colour and fold the model on
the sheet to see what a difference forgiveness makes.

PEARL DIVERS

Aim: To explore what it means to love enemies.

Starter

Play any quick softball or beanbag game in two
teams, so they experience working against one
another. In all these games each side is trying to
make it hard for the other. Point out that in the
game we are playing at being enemies.

Teaching

Sit everyone in a circle and pass a card round with
the word 'enemies' on it. As each person holds the
card they say, 'An enemy is someone who . . .' If
they don't wish to say anything they just pass the
card on. The rule is that only the person holding
the card can speak.

Draw all the ideas together, or record them on
paper. Then place a card which says 'Love your' in
front of the other card so they can see Jesus' teaching:
Love your enemies. Surely that can't be right? We've
just heard all these nasty things about enemies, and
here is Jesus telling us to love them. How on earth
can we do that? How can we love someone who's
always out to get us, and hates us?

Check in the Bible and find that it isn't a mistake;
it really says, 'love your enemies'. Read the passage
together.

Ask the children to make their faces full of hate
and bitterness. Get them to notice how hard the
muscles have to work to do it. It's better and
healthier for us not to make a habit of hating and
sulking if we're upset, and God knows that. Perhaps
they can remember seeing some older people's

faces. If we are always thinking life isn't fair, and we hate and resent people, it will show in our faces as we get older. But if we get used to forgiving quickly, and putting the resentment down, that will show in our faces instead. It's right and it's sensible to take Jesus' teaching seriously, even though it is hard to do.

Have the three words of the teaching written on three balloons and learn the teaching off by heart by saying it several times, popping one balloon each time.

Praying

Forgive us our trespasses
as we forgive those
who trespass against us. Amen.

Activities

On the worksheet there are instructions for making a card and envelope to give to someone with whom they need to make up or strengthen a good relationship. The teaching is also reinforced with a code activity.

GOLD PANNERS

Aim: To look at the practical implications of loving and forgiving enemies.

Starter

In groups of two or three, have an argument using only strings of numbers to speak with. This takes away the embarrassment of having to think of actual words, but all the emotions can be heard loud and clear.

Teaching

Ask them to imagine that they are meeting some people who beat them up and left them for dead many years ago. What would they want to say to them now?

Read the passage from 1 Samuel and see how David's behaviour compares with their own feelings. Point out that God can always transform ugly situations so that some good comes from them, especially if we invite him into our hurt to work there.

Now read the passage from Luke's Gospel. What is the difference between loving your enemies and being a doormat and letting people walk all over you?

You could also read them an extract from the writing of Corrie Ten Boom who has much to say about forgiveness.

Praying

This week's prayer is one that was found near a child's body in Ravensbruck Women's Concentration Camp.

Lord, remember not only
the men and women of good will,
but also those of evil will.
But do not remember all the suffering
they have inflicted upon us;
remember the fruits we have borne,
thanks to this suffering:
our comradeship, our loyalty, our humility,
our courage, our generosity,
the greatness of heart which has grown out of all this;
and when they come to judgement,
let all the fruits we have borne
be their forgiveness.

Activities

The sheet includes a sketch to act out, and space to record practical ideas for living in a forgiving way in various situations. Also, give out recycled cards for them to use to get in touch with someone they have lost contact with, or with whom there needs to be some healing of conflict.

EIGHTH SUNDAY OF THE YEAR

Thought for the day

What we think important flows out in the way we speak.

Reflection on the readings

Ecclesiasticus 27:4-7
Psalm 91
1 Corinthians 15:54-58
Luke 6:39-45

The teaching of Jesus in today's Gospel picks up on the wisdom and good sense of those people-watchers who observe human behaviour candidly, think it all over, and learn from it. When we read the passage from Ecclesiasticus it rings true with what we, too, have observed. A clay pot may look fine, but the firing will make any defects dramatically plain; and the way people speak certainly does betray what they feel. How often the words of an apology actually show clearly not sorrow but resentment, anger and disdain. Blind people, relying heavily on aural clues, are often particularly quick at discerning how integrated a person's speech is in terms of content and delivery; the agendas we may try to hide come out in our voices, whether we like it or not.

Real integrity also shows. And it is this which is at the heart of Jesus' teaching. Hypocrisy seems to have grated with Jesus more than anything, since he longs for us to be honest before God, and honest with ourselves as well as with those around us. The temptation for us all is to put off the hard work of integrity and cheat instead, by pretending we have it, and acting as the kind of person we think we ought to be. This may deceive some for a while, but sooner or later we'll be discovered, and God is never taken in for a moment.

Religious people are particularly prone to this, since they feel increasingly embarrassed by their true, messy hearts, and the time it is taking to be renewed and purified, so they try to speed up the process. Also, the shame of being what they really are can't always be faced, and then the self-deception takes over. Today we are being invited to face what we are really like, and recognise that the purity and integrity we would like will only come by standing before God in all the mess of our reality, allowing his love to transform us from the heart outwards.

Discussion starters

1. Why does Jesus find hypocrisy so disturbing?

2. How can we help one another in our parish community to develop the kind of personal integrity Jesus taught?

All-stage talk

Beforehand arrange for two volunteers to say they are sorry – one sounding not at all interested or bothered, and the other angry and resentful, rather than sorry. Start by telling everyone that you are going to test their powers of detection in a short experiment. Introduce your team, and ask everyone to listen to what is *really* being said by each of them. Now point out to the first person something they've done which is very thoughtless or unkind, such as not feeding the rabbit for two days, or wiping their filthy hands on a clean towel without washing first. The person says they're sorry. But can people detect what they are *really* saying? (Such as 'Do you really think I care about that?' or 'So what?')

Now say the same thing to the other helper, and they also say their 'sorry'. But what are they *really* saying? (Such as 'You're always getting at me and I've had enough of it' or 'Good – I'm glad I did it and upset you because I don't like you'.)

In the Gospel today Jesus is teaching us that God can see what we really mean, whatever we actually say, and it saddens him to see us pretending to be good when we're really being quite selfish, cruel, deceitful, unfaithful or bullying. We can't get away with pretending to God, and often we can't get away with pretending to other people either.

Jesus says we're a bit like fruit trees. If we're rotten trees, then that will show in our rotten fruit. If our hearts are lying and selfish, then what we say and do will show that up, whether we are Christians or not, and whether we go to Mass each week or not. As far as God is concerned, we are to be honest about what we are really like, and when we don't like what we see in ourselves, God will help us to change.

All-age ideas

• As a penitential rite, try using *Come, Spirit, come, prise open my heart*, the words and music for which can be found on page 214. This can be sung by a single voice, or a small group of singers, or even said if there are no singers, giving everyone the space to reflect on areas in their own hearts where openness and healing are needed.

• Try this sketch. Have a sign up with the doctor's name on it and the doctor wearing a stethoscope. A patient walks in with wads of cotton wool plastered over his eyes so that he can barely see. He gropes around, bumping into the wall, and finds his way to the chair, with the doctor guiding him, something like this:

Doc   Ah, good morning, Mr Henning! Do take a seat . . . no, that's the table . . . the seat's over to the right a bit.

Patient All right, all right, I know where I'm going. What do you think I am . . . blind or something?

Doc   Now, how can I help you?

Patient Help me? How on earth would you be able to help me? Anyone would think there was something wrong with me!

Doc   Er . . . Perhaps I could examine your eyes?

Patient (*jumping up*) Oh no, you don't! I've heard about people like you. As if I'd trust my eyes to your interfering fingers. They're my own eyes, aren't they?

Doc   Well, yes, of course, but . . .

Patient There you are, then, my eyes are my own private business, thanks very much. Now, why don't you get a move on and

Teaching

Talk about why cartoons are funny – the way they over-emphasise a point and make us notice it. Jesus sometimes used the cartoon technique in his teaching.

Read today's Gospel, looking out for the cartoons, and talk these over, together with what they are getting at. A cartoonist among you may like to put them in visual format. Now look at the reading from Ecclesiasticus, noticing where Jesus has used these examples from Scripture to base his teaching on. Do they agree with the writer that a person's conversation shows up what they're really like? Is it possible to deceive clients/potential buyers of your product? Can we hear in a person's voice whether they are being honest to themselves? Why is God never deceived?

Finally read the passage from Corinthians, particularly looking at the last verse with its message of encouragement and hope. It's true that we get it wrong, and God has lots of work to do on us still, but as long as we recognise this honestly and humbly, the work can go on.

Praying

Faithful God, we can trust you
as the people we really are,
still with much to learn about loving,
but ready to spend the rest of our lives
as your disciples. Amen.

Activities

On the sheet there is space to draw a cartoon to illustrate Jesus' teaching, and to record some of the glaring areas of hypocrisy they have recognised, in the world, in the Church and in themselves.

NINTH SUNDAY OF THE YEAR

Thought for the day

The good news we have been given is not just for us, but to pass on to the rest of the world.

Reflection on the readings

1 Kings 8:41-43
Psalm 116
Galatians 1:1-2, 6-10
Luke 7:1-10

When Jesus commissioned his apostles to go out and make disciples of all nations, he was not breaking with Jewish tradition but taking it one stage further. There had always been the understanding amongst God's chosen people that eventually through them the whole earth would be blessed, and all nations would come to realise that the God of Israel was the one and only God.

We see that in Psalm 116 today, and in the fervent prayer of King Solomon. These writings from the Old Testament assume that the truth is for everyone to share.

In the letter to the Church in Galatia it is clear that Paul has been putting into practice the command of Jesus to preach the good news to all nations. He had founded this church community during his first missionary journey, and encouraged the pagans to accept the sovereignty of the living God in their lives. Now he is finding that some of them are being persuaded that in order to become proper Christians they must also be brought under the Jewish Law. Passionately Paul writes to prevent the new freedom in Christ from being clawed back into the past confines of the legalistic traditions of Judaism.

In contrast, we find the army officer, who is not even Jewish, displaying a degree of faith that Jesus finds amazing.

Today's readings raise questions for us about who we should be evangelising, and what expectations we should have concerning rules and traditions, in view of where the unchurched are coming from. What shines out clearly is that outsiders are best persuaded of the truth about God by the behaviour of his followers and the amount of access they allow him into their lives.

Discussion starters

1. Where should we stand as a church on the question of proclaiming the Gospel to those of other faiths?

2. Do we sometimes expect unchurched newcomers to faith to take on habits and traditions which confuse them, or run contrary to their culture?

All-stage talk

Bring with you a newspaper, a TV remote control, a mobile phone, an airmail letter and, if possible, a trumpeter (failing a real one, a recorded version will do nicely).

Begin by picking up the newspaper and reading out a few headlines. Talk about this being one of the ways we use to get other people to hear our news. People used to use a town crier. (You could ask a loud-voiced volunteer to demonstrate. The news they bellow is written on a piece of paper: 'There is only one real God. He made us and he loves us!') Pick up the remote control and explain that now we don't have to shout so loud because we invite the town criers into our homes and sit them in the corner to tell us the latest news. We can even switch them off!

Another thing people used was a trumpeter. (Have this demonstrated briefly.) That got people's attention so they would listen to what you were saying. Now we have this to get people's attention, and get them listening to us. (Demonstrate the mobile phone.) People used to send their news by pigeons, and now we send it on a metal bird. (Show the airmail letter.)

What has stayed the same all through the years is that people always want to pass on their news. And today we are being told that the news the town crier shouted to us (they can do it again) is such good news, not just for us but for everyone, that we need to make sure we pass it on. Like honey or peanut butter, we are not to keep the good news to ourselves, but spread it!

We can tell people about God's love by behaving in a kind and loving way, by being generous with our time and money, by praying for our friends and for difficult situations, by living by God's rules, and by bringing our faith into the conversation instead of only mentioning it among our church friends. And who knows, God may also call some of you to tell the good news as newspaper reporters, in government, on television or as a famous sports star. However you do it, do it!

All-age ideas

- Have the items used in the talk arranged in front of the altar with the sign: 'The Lord is God! (Don't keep the faith, spread it.)'

- Have a clapping message passed all around the church: 'The real God loves you, pass it on.' As you say it you do these claps: clap your own hands, right with your partner, your own again, left with your partner, clap your sides, clap your own hands and then both hands with your partner. When someone has clapped it with you, you find someone else to do it with until eventually everyone has caught the message.

Prayer of the Faithful

Celebrant
We have gathered here today
in the company of the true God.
Let us pray to him now.

Reader
We pray for the Lord's blessing and anointing
on all involved with mission and outreach,
both here and abroad, among children and adults,
as they commit themselves
to spreading the good news.

Silence

You are the living God:
let your will be done in us.

We pray for all who have influence and authority,
through their political standing, fame or wealth;
speak into their hearts of righteousness and justice,
integrity and compassion.

Silence

You are the living God:
let your will be done in us.

We pray that we may take seriously
our responsibilities for nurturing our children
and those who do not yet know God's love.
May our living be transformed to reveal that love.

Silence

You are the living God:
let your will be done in us.

We call to mind those in need
of comfort and reassurance,
all in pain and mental anguish.
We pray for the lapsed and the doubting
and those who need the good news this week.

Silence

You are the living God:
let your will be done in us.

We pray for those who have recently died
and those on that last journey now.
May we all be brought safely to heaven.

Silence

You are the living God:
let your will be done in us.

With Mary, Mother of Jesus,
let us pray:
Hail, Mary . . .

In silence, we pray our individual petitions
to the Lord of all.

Silence

Celebrant
Heavenly Father, we ask you to hear our prayers,
through Christ our Lord.
Amen.

TREASURE SEEKERS

Aim: To learn how to start spreading the good news.

Starter

Sit in a circle and pass the parcel. Put a Christian sticker in each layer, and a Bible story book in the middle.

Teaching

Talk about the way they have been passing the parcel on, so everyone gets a turn, and how good they were at that. Now we're going to pass our news on to each other, but we don't need to put it in a parcel. We can speak our news and everyone will be able to hear it at once. Have a sharing news session, making sure the children listen to each other by passing a 'talking shell/stone' around. Only the one holding this can speak.

Tell the children that you have a piece of very good news you want to pass on to them. Holding the talking stone/shell tell them that you have found out that God is real and that he loves us all. Following Jesus makes you very happy and helps you live a good life. Ask if any of them know that piece of good news as well.

Tell the children that there are quite a lot of people who don't know this good news yet, and they need people to tell them. What can we do about that?

Write their ideas down. It doesn't matter that they can't read them; they know adults write things down that are important, and will pick up on the truth that their ideas are being taken seriously.

Praying

Lord Jesus,
I am sad that some people
don't know you yet.
Please bless them
and send someone
to tell them about you.
Amen.

Activities

This will lead on from the ideas the children have. You may be scribing messages to go with their drawings that can be copied and given to Baptism families, or people being married in your church. You may be making posters to be put up where the slimming and line-dancing classes are held. You may be taping their messages. Have an assortment of materials at the ready.

The worksheet has a 'message delivery' activity, an outline to use for messages, and a 'matching people with message' puzzle.

PEARL DIVERS

Aim: To understand the meaning of Jewish, Gentile and Christian, and to look at who can be what.

Starter

Have an alphabetical list of all the different names of the children, so that those in the same family or sharing the same surname will be listed together. Talk briefly about where some of these names come from originally. Then play some music with everyone dancing and moving around until you call out a surname, or a letter. Only the members of these families can keep on moving; the others must freeze until you call another name out.

Teaching

Explain that we are members of our family because we were born or adopted into it, and that when we read about the Jewish people in the Bible, it means people who were born as members of the Jewish race which could be traced back to Abraham. No one else could be Jewish, and God chose the Jewish people to work through. Through them all the other nations would eventually be brought to know God's saving love. Jesus was born into a Jewish family, so he was Jewish. Anyone who isn't Jewish by birth is called a Gentile, and as we often hear about Gentiles in the Bible as well, it's a good idea to know about them.

Have two hoops labelled 'Jewish' and 'Gentile' and some names written on small cards. As a group, work out which names should go in which hoop. (Suggestions for names: Abraham, Goliath, Joseph, Moses, Pharaoh, Jesus, Mary, Peter, Paul, St Francis and the names of some of the children.)

Now take the hoops and names away and replace them with one hoop labelled 'Christian – a follower of Christ'. Scatter around the hoop cards with these categories written on them: women, men, boys, girls, people with black skin, people with pink skin, people who go to (West Leigh) school, people who support (an approved) football club, people who support (a rival) football club, Jewish people, Gentile people, old people, rich people, poor people. Ask them to put in the hoop those they think can be Christians and leave outside those who can't. Draw them to the realisation that everybody can be a follower of Jesus Christ, and the good news of God's love is for everybody everywhere to enjoy.

Praying

Dear Jesus,
we pray for those
who have not heard of you
and do not know you.
Give us the opportunity
to share the good news
with someone today. Amen.

Activities

The worksheet encourages them to look at how they can spread the good news, and gives examples of people who have been called to tell others the Gospel even though it put them in danger.

GOLD PANNERS

Aim: To look at the contrast between the centurion and the situation among the Galatians.

Starter

Bring in an assortment of junk mail (preferably unopened). Get the group to open and sort it according to things they would immediately throw out, those they may consider, and those they would definitely use or become involved with.

Teaching

First read the passage from 1 Kings 8, where King Solomon is praying. Establish what his attitude was to the Gentile world. Help them see that the hope is there for all nations to come to know God. Then find out what had happened to the people in Galatia. Fill in the background of how they had heard the good news in the first place and discuss whether the Jewish Christians were right or misguided in insisting on the new Christians also having to accept the Jewish Law. Compare their attitude with that of King Solomon.

Now read the passage from Luke 7, with different people taking the parts. What amazed Jesus about this man? How does this fit in with King Solomon's prayer?

Explain how we all have choices to make all the time in our lives. We make them just going through the mail, deciding what offers we consider are worth looking into and which are not. When anyone hears about God, and his love for us shown in Jesus, they have a decision to make. Are they going to take the good news on board in their life, or are they going

to dismiss it and reject God's offer of new and fulfilled life?

But they can't make a decision like that unless they know the good news properly. And how will they know it unless someone tells them?

Praying

Lord God, we bring before you all those we meet
who are not yet in a position
to make a well-informed decision
about your offer of a new life.
We offer you ourselves to speak and live through,
so that they may come to know and love you. Amen.

Activities

On the worksheet there is space to keep track of the discussion, and places to pray in and for to prepare them for the purposes of God. Any of their ideas for parish outreach might be passed on to the Parish Pastoral Council.

TENTH SUNDAY OF THE YEAR

Thought for the day

Our God is full of compassion; he hears our crying and it is his nature to rescue us.

Reflection on the readings

1 Kings 17:17-24
Psalm 29
Galatians 1:11-19
Luke 7:11-17

Look at a picture of any person's face and you will see that one side speaks more of the hope and happiness and the other side more of the pain and suffering they have known. Although there is widespread expectation that we should be happy in life, the truth is that life is always a mixture of light and deep shadow, and our calling as humans is not so much to be happy as to be real.

God reaches down into our deep shadows and feels with us in the grieving and emptiness there. We see examples of that practical compassion in the readings from Kings and from Luke.

As God's close friend, Elijah has a love for people, which is poured out in prayer as he pleads for the child's life. Love is like a channel that cuts through any situation and allows God's healing to happen. Even those who have not received physical healing witness to the way that, through the prayers of faithful people, God has healed their anxiety or their attitude, and enabled them to face their suffering courageously. Many sense that they are being 'carried through' a difficult time.

When Jesus sees the heartbroken widow, with her dead son being carried out of the house, we are told he is filled with compassion, and it is out of this loving that he acts, speaking right into death and calling the young man back, for a while longer, into earthly life with his mother.

In a sense God calls all his people out of death. He calls us into the possibility of a life in which we are no longer living to the old rules of selfishness, but are freed to walk tall in the light and life of God's loving.

Discussion starters

1. In today's readings, how important was the willingness to co-operate? What can we learn from this?

2. What is the point of praying for those who are ill or dying?

All-stage talk

Bring with you a pair of balance scales. These can be either a heavy-duty kitchen type or a children's educational toy. You could even use a small portable seesaw and have two children to demonstrate it. It's the balancing of weights that matters.

Demonstrate the scales/seesaw with the help of some children, reminding everyone of the way the scales are balanced when there is the same weight both sides. Sometimes our lives can feel like a seesaw or a pair of scales. We might be really happy, and everything is going well, and our team is winning, and we passed our driving test on the eighth attempt, and our operation was successful, and someone has just changed our nappy and fed us. However old or young we are, we all know what it feels like to have the 'joy' side of the scales full up.

Other times we may feel that everything is against us. Our best friend is moving away to another town, our team has lost for the third time running, the washing machine floods the kitchen, and you fall over and graze your knees. Sometimes the pain is so deep that we can hardly bear it – like when someone we love dies, or we are suddenly let down by someone we thought we could trust, or we are faced with serious illness. We all know what it feels like to have the 'sadness' side of the scales full up.

We heard today about the way God looked after a widow and her son through Elijah. And we heard about another widow, beside herself with grief, whose dead son was brought to life by Jesus and given back to her.

So does it look as if our God is only interested in us when the happy side of our scales is full to bursting? No, it proclaims loud and clear that our God is tenderly interested in us all the time, during those terrible times of sadness we sometimes have to go through, as well as the times of great joy we dance through. And that is because he really loves us.

All-age ideas

- Have different voices to read the story of Elijah.

- Show slides or acetates of faces from all over the world which focus our compassion on the greed, poverty, pain, violence, vulnerability and loneliness of many. This can be done in silence or with music suggested by the young people. They are particularly good at putting together pictures and music with sensitivity. If slides and OHPs are not suitable for your church, have the pictures mounted and carried around the church, or fixed on the walls, and encourage the congregation to move around and pray.

Prayer of the Faithful

Celebrant
Let us bring to the God who loves us
our prayers and concerns for the Church
and the world.

Reader
May the God of compassion
take our hearts of stone
and give us feeling hearts,
so that we as the Church
may be more responsive
to the needs and sorrows around us.

Silence

God of love:
show us the Way.

May the God of wisdom
teach all in authority,
inspire those who lead,
protect each nation from evil,
and further each right decision.

Silence

God of love:
show us the Way.

May the God of tenderness
dwell in our homes
through all the times of joy
and all the heartaches and sadness,
teaching us to show one another
the love he shows to us.

Silence

God of love:
show us the Way.

May the God of wholeness
speak into the despair and loneliness
of all who struggle with life and its troubles;
to reassure, affirm and encourage them,
and alert us to ways we can help.

Silence

God of love:
show us the Way.

May the God of peace
be with the dying,
and welcome those who have died in faith
into the full life of the kingdom.

Silence

God of love:
show us the Way.

We make our prayer with Mary,
Mother of our risen Lord:
Hail, Mary . . .

We know our Father is listening;
in silence we bring to him
our own particular needs or burdens.

Silence

Celebrant
God our Father, hear our prayer
and help us to do your will.
Through Christ our Lord.
Amen.

TREASURE SEEKERS

Aim: To get to know the story of the widow at Nain.

Starter

Sad and happy. Make a smiley face for one end of the room and a sad face for the other end. The children find a space in the middle. The leader calls out situations, and if it's something that makes them sad they run to the sad face; if happy, to the happy face. Situations may be eating chocolate, playing with friends, your pet being ill, going on holiday, having a tummy ache, and getting an invitation to a party.

Teaching

Bring the wall labels down and lay them on the floor together, back to back. Today we are going to hear about someone who started off being very sad (show this side) and Jesus helped to make her very happy (show the happy side.)

Tell the story, making sure the children understand what a widow is (otherwise they may assume you are talking about a window). When you tell them about her son dying, ask them how the mother was feeling, and show the sad face. How did Jesus know she was so sad? Let them add these details to the story. Take your time over telling them how Jesus raised the young man to life, pausing for a moment after he has said, 'Young man, get up'. When Jesus gives the young man back to his mother, look at the sad face again. Did the mother feel sad now? Change the face to match her joy.

Praying

Lord Jesus,
we pray for people who are sad.
Please help them to be happy again. Amen.

Activities

Make masks using paper plates with the eyes already cut out. They draw a happy face on one side and a sad one on the other.

PEARL DIVERS

Aim: To know that God is tenderly interested in us in the heartbreak as well as the happy times.

Starter

Using a long bamboo cane balanced across two people's hands, play 'higher and higher', with the children taking turns to jump over the ever-increasing height. (Make sure the cane will fall as soon as it's touched, so that no one gets hurt.)

Teaching

In that high-jump exercise we were finding our limits. We discovered how high we could jump and what was just too much for us at the moment until we grow taller. Sometimes life can feel a bit like the high jump, when we are expected to do harder and harder things, and cope with bigger and bigger hurts, until we feel we can't cope with much more.

Today we have two amazing examples of how much God loves and cares for us in the sad times of our lives, as well as when everything is going well. One event is from the Old Testament, long before Jesus had been born, and the other is from the New Testament, when Jesus was walking about on earth. Introduce two women, who can be leaders or volunteers brought in specially. They are dressed in costume, or at least with cloths over their heads. You are going to interview them both.

First introduce the widow of Zarephath, and interview her so that the story of her great sadness and anger are brought out because of her son's illness and death, as well as the amazing way God showed his love through Elijah. (Make sure you are both very familiar with the whole story as told in 1 Kings 17, and talk together in a relaxed and natural way.)

Then turn to the other woman, also a widow, and interview her in the same way, bringing out her great sorrow and fears for the future, and the love shown to her through the way Jesus speaks to her and to her son. Then ask both women what the experience has taught them about God. The widow of Zarephath can say how it has helped her to know that this God (whom she didn't know before) seems to be completely faithful and loving. The widow of Nain can say how it has helped her to know that God must be interested in ordinary people and their troubles, and want to help them. He must be even more powerful than death.

Thank the two visitors and invite them to stay for the rest of Pearl Divers this morning.

Praying

Lord, whenever we pray,
you are listening.
Whenever we are crying,
you share in our sadness,
and whenever we are happy,
you share in our joy.
Your love always surrounds us.
Amen.

Activities

On a world map find out where Zarephath is. (It's midway between Tyre and Sidon, on the Mediterranean coast.) The worksheet encourages them to sympathise with both widows, and this can lead on to praying for those in the news at the moment who must be very sad.

GOLD PANNERS

Aim: To look at how God's compassion is revealed, and how that challenges our behaviour.

Starter

Divide into two teams, give everyone a Bible and see which team can find these verses first. They are all references to God's love and compassion. The Bible references: Psalm 102:8; Psalm 114:5-6; Isaiah 54:10; Jonah 4:2; Matthew 9:36; Mark 1:41; 2 Corinthians 1:3-4; Titus 3:4-8.

Teaching

First read the story from 1 Kings 17:17-24. You can do this with a narrator and others acting it out, or using different voices. The factfile on the worksheet may be useful to start discussion about this story. Then look at the Luke passage, with another widow and another son being brought back to life. Draw their attention to what initiated the healing in each case – great compassion for the grieving mother.

Use the worksheet to see how the Psalms reflect on this compassionate, rescuing quality of our God, and let these lead on to a straight look at whether the church, universally and in our particular area, is doing what it is called to do as the body of Christ.

Praying

Use the Psalms, particularly Psalm 29:

I will exalt you, O Lord,
for you lifted me out of the depths
and did not let my enemies gloat over me.
Lord, my God, I called to you for help
and you healed me.
Lord my God, I will give you thanks for ever.

Activities

The worksheet gives a chart to fill in about future action, having looked at the areas of need locally. Pray for these situations, and any good ideas can be put into practice.

ELEVENTH SUNDAY OF THE YEAR

Thought for the day

God has the authority and the desire to forgive our sins completely and set us free from guilt.

Reflection on the readings

2 Samuel 12:7-10, 13
Psalm 31
Galatians 2:16, 19-21
Luke 7:36-8:3

Most of the time it is not so much a falling into sin as a sliding into sin that happens. David was not the kind of person to stick one of his men deliberately in the front line to have him out of the way. We slip gradually towards committing the terrible wrongs by not paying attention to the top of the slide – sins of pride, greed, laziness and self-indulgence, for instance – which if unchecked will start us sliding further and further into wrong values and wrong behaviour.

Since the slide is often so gradual, we may not notice what is happening, and our readings today show us some examples of the ways God does his best to draw our attention to what needs putting right. Being in the position of God's spokesperson at such times is an unenviable job, but a very necessary one. We may well prefer to wriggle out of the responsibility with the excuse that we don't want to be judgemental. But to avoid alerting someone to a downward slide in their lives is actually unloving behaviour. Provided we ensure that we do it in love, and without being judgemental, it is one of the kindest acts we can do.

Once our attention is drawn to the wrong we have done, or the wrong attitudes we have allowed to become habits, we are faced with a choice. Since it is never pleasant to be faced with criticism, and we have probably put considerable energy into persuading ourselves that our behaviour and attitudes are justifiable, we may wish to go on the defensive, and reject what we have been shown. If we choose that route God is unable to put things right for us.

If, on the other hand, we are honest enough to see some truth in what has been said, we can take that great and difficult step of breaking down our defences before God and acknowledging that we need him to sort things out. God is the only one with the authority to forgive sin completely, and he is very good at it. The other thing about him is that he loves doing it, and will help us as much as possible.

The only way of crawling back to the top of the slide is recognising and acknowledging before God what is wrong, taking full responsibility for it, and expressing our shame and sorrow – our desire to stop and change. It is those who have known the incredible release and joy of God's forgiveness in large measure who have great love for the one who has let them out of their prison.

Discussion starters

1. How tolerant should we be of wrong attitudes and behaviour among those in our church community; what balance do we need to achieve between expressing God's loving acceptance and upholding right values?

2. What is, or what would you like to see, in place in our churches for helping us deal with sin?

All-stage talk

During the week collect a few well-known parish voices on tape, perhaps from choir practice or children's liturgy. If you can have some photographs taken at such things, these can be displayed as people come into church. (See All-age ideas.) You will also need a length of string with a Lego person tied on one end, and a pair of scissors.

Begin by playing the tape and letting people experience the 'Good heavens, that's me!' factor. Remind everyone of how you feel when a raffle ticket is called and you suddenly realise it's the same as the number staring at you from your own hand, or when you catch sight of yourself unexpectedly in a mirror when you're out shopping.

David and Simon were both given that shock in our readings today. They had all done wrong, and yet hadn't really recognised it. Now, suddenly, they are shown the truth about themselves, and it isn't a pretty sight.

Like them, we don't always know when we've

done wrong or sinned. We might have had a little tug of conscience but quickly stamped it out so we could go on doing what we wanted to be doing! If you're in doubt, think to yourself, 'Am I happy for God to see me saying this, or doing this, or thinking this?' And if you're not happy with God seeing how you behave at school, or with particular people, or at work, or at your club, then the way you are behaving is probably wrong, and you need to change it.

Sometimes we will need to point out gently to one another where we are wrong. That's all part of loving one another and helping one another to live God's way.

Show the piece of string with a Lego person tied on the end. Explain that whenever we fall into sin, we cut ourselves off from God (cut the string and let the person drop). God longs to put things right, but he can't, unless we call out to him and say, 'I've fallen down! I'm sorry!' As soon as we turn to God like that, and ask him to forgive us, he ties us on again so we're not cut off any more. And the funny thing is we end up closer, if anything, because being forgiven is so wonderful that it makes us love God more than ever.

All-age ideas

- The Gospel story is an excellent one to act out, with different people speaking their parts, either reading them or studying the text first and saying the words.

- Have a sheet of paper with the shape of a cross cut out of it, and fix it on to a mirror, so the effect is of a cross made out of a mirror. This can be used at the Penitential Rite, to remind people that Jesus' love will reflect back to us the state of our inner selves, just as a mirror shows us our outer appearance.

Prayer of the Faithful

Celebrant
Knowing your love for us, Holy God,
we have come before you to pray together.

Reader
We pray for all who have the care of souls,
and are entrusted with helping others to repentance
and giving them good counsel.
We pray for those called to speak God's values,
whatever the danger and regardless of popularity.

Silence

Work in us, Lord:
work in us for good.

We pray for those who refuse
to allow injustice or evil to go unchallenged;
for all who are under pressure
to behave wrongly
or keep quiet about something
they know to be wrong.

Silence

Work in us, Lord:
work in us for good.

We pray for more loving forgiveness
in all our relationships,
for more self-knowledge,
the grace to recognise where we are in the wrong,
and the courage to seek God's forgiveness.

Silence

Work in us, Lord:
work in us for good.

We pray for all imprisoned by guilt, resentment,
bitterness and self-pity,
that they may come to know
the relief of being forgiven.
We pray for all innocent victims,
that their scars may be completely healed.

Silence

Work in us, Lord:
work in us for good.

We pray for those who have died
unprepared to meet the Lord,
and for all who have died in faith.
May the Lord have mercy on us all.

Silence

Work in us, Lord:
work in us for good.

We make our prayer with Mary,
who listened in loving obedience to God:
Hail, Mary . . .

We pray in silence,
making our own petitions
to God our heavenly Father.

Silence

Celebrant
Father, we ask you to hear our prayers
through your Son, Christ our Lord.
Amen.

TREASURE SEEKERS

Aim: To know that God loves us and forgives us.

Starter

Have a number of sorting-out games, such as getting different shapes into the right holes, sorting out a Happy Families set of cards into families, and tidying a muddle of a cupboard or dressing-up box.

Teaching

Talk about what a good job we did of sorting those things out and putting things right again. Whenever we do that we're being like God, because God loves putting things right and sorting out the messes we make in our lives. Let's look at the sort of things God puts right.

Using toys or puppets, have them acting out various situations where someone is behaving wrongly. For instance, one toy can be greedy and take all the cakes, so there aren't enough for the others; there may be two being nasty to a third, and leaving them out all the time; 'Mum' may leave the children playing, and one keeps kicking or saying nasty things to the other. Vary the situations to suit your group. At the end of each situation let the children say what the wrong behaviour was, and think how they should have behaved. (This may be fun to find out!)

Talk about how we all behave badly sometimes, and the good thing is that, as soon as we realise we have done wrong, we can say 'I'm sorry' to God and 'I'm sorry' to the people we have upset. And then it can be put right straight away so we can get on with enjoying life again.

Praying

Thank you, Jesus,
for showing me
when I was being unkind.
I'm sorry I did it.
Thank you for forgiving me!

Activities

On the worksheet there are examples of unkind and selfish behaviour for the children to talk about, together with an activity to put right what is wrong. Even young children need to be taught about these things. It is important that the teaching is matched with friendly, trustworthy leaders and a secure, loving church environment. The children are invited to think of an area where they know they find it hard to behave well, and draw them doing it God's way. The process of drawing the

right behaviour is positive reinforcement and will help develop good self-esteem.

PEARL DIVERS

Aim: To know that God can help us face up to our sin as well as forgive and set us free.

Starter

Sit in a circle. Each person in turn says three things about someone in the circle (only positives allowed), and everyone guesses who it is. Each person can only be described once, which means that everyone gets a turn to be described. Or play 'Stuck in the mud', which is a kind of 'tag'. When caught, you stand with arms and legs apart, stuck in the mud, unless someone crawls between your legs to set you free again.

Teaching

Set up the circle as if you are all guests at a meal, with a tablecloth, and plates of things to eat, which are handed round as you tell the children about a meal Jesus was invited to at a grand house belonging to a Pharisee called Simon. Simon thought of himself as a good person, something of an expert where God was concerned. At the meal something happened which Jesus used to help Simon see himself as not very loving or forgiving.

As you explain about the woman coming in, bring out some perfumed oil and rub a little in the palms of your hands so that the children can smell the fragrance as you speak.

Continue relating how Simon was indignant about this and thought Jesus should know what kind of bad woman this was, if he really was a prophet. When you tell the story Jesus told Simon, invite the children to answer the question before telling them what Simon (rather grudgingly) answered. Then finish by telling how Jesus used this story to help Simon understand himself better and give him the opportunity to put things right with God. God never makes us do things against our will, but he does all he can to help us choose what is right.

Praying

Talk about our need to recognise and admit to God the times when we let him down by our unloving, selfish behaviour, knowing that he is able to forgive us.

Lord God,
thank you for helping me do good today,
when I . . .

I am sorry that I let you down
and hurt others
when I . . .
Please forgive me
and help me put it right.
Thank you, Lord God,
for forgiving me!

Activities

On the worksheet there are instructions for making a 'soul mirror'; each child will need either a small hand mirror or shiny mirror paper. There is also an activity to reinforce the teaching and encourage discussion about the Gospel.

GOLD PANNERS

Aim: To know that we can slip into sin gradually, and to see how God draws our attention to where we are so as to set us free.

Starter

Who is it? One person describes another by saying what they would be if they were a car, an animal and a colour. The others guess who it is. This only works well if everyone knows each other and they are relaxed with each other. If your group isn't like this, get everyone to make a quick sketch of one another and enjoy the results.

Teaching

Point out that, for some of us, our identity, either in description or sketch, came as quite a shock or a surprise. We hadn't seen ourselves like that before! Today we are going to look at some people who had become blind to their need of forgiveness, and had it pointed out to them.

First have a dramatised reading of the passage from Luke 7, looking out for someone being shown where they are and what they are really like. Was Simon surprised by what Jesus showed him? What choice has Simon to make in his life now?

Talk about the importance of training ourselves to check our attitudes and behaviour, not against the standards of our friends or what society expects, but against the measure of God's love for us and his commands to love God and love one another.

Praying

Happy is the person
whose sins are forgiven,
whose wrongs are pardoned.
When I kept things to myself,

I felt weak deep inside me.
Then I confessed my sins to you.
I didn't hide my guilt.
And you forgave my sin.
You are my hiding place.
You protect me from my troubles.
You fill me with songs of salvation! Amen.

(From Psalm 31)

Activities

On the worksheet there is a short sketch like an inner conversation which is interrupted by an outside voice making the truth clear. Spend some time, with quiet music playing, thinking over the things in our lives that do need God's healing forgiveness, bringing them before God and being given a lighted candle each as the words from the Baptism service are said:

Leader   Receive this light to show
that you have passed
from darkness to light.

All   Shine as a light in the world
to the glory of God the Father.

TWELFTH SUNDAY OF THE YEAR

Thought for the day
Following Christ means daily taking up our cross.

Reflection on the readings
Zechariah 12:10-11
Psalm 62
Galatians 3:26-29
Luke 9:18-24

Is Christ's willingness to become totally vulnerable some kind of madness? The idea of a vulnerable, suffering Saviour looks at first sight to be a complete contradiction in terms, and yet in reality it points to such depth of truth and wisdom that our human spirit rings with the resonance of it. We know it, rather than understand it, to be true.

We know it in wise and mature people whose suffering has enabled them to become agents of healing, compassion and forgiveness. We know it in the extraordinary way we find ourselves able to minister to others in our weakness more than in our strength. Supremely we know it in the living Jesus, entering into each bleak landscape of human misery and pain, and transforming it. Only a suffering Saviour could do this. It is through Christ's wounds that we are healed; through his persistent loving forgiveness in the face of ultimate evil that he wins the victory over death and sin.

The prophecies of the Old Testament had gradually focused on the necessity for the Saviour to be an innocent suffering servant, through whom the whole world could be saved. And immediately Peter has voiced the disciples' realisation of who he is, Jesus lays out before them the necessary, agonising path he is to walk as the Christ of God.

In the light of all this, being a follower of Jesus takes on new significance and a disturbing but unavoidable challenge. We are not going to be following merely a valuable set of principles, or the example of a kind and loving person. We are going to have to follow him also in his willingness to lay down his life, loving and forgiving persistently through whatever pain and suffering comes our way, whatever unfairness gets thrown at us, however our bodies or emotions are insulted, beaten or abused. That is some calling, and it takes some courage to follow Christ resolutely into such a future.

Yet it can be no other way. Part of the deal is the recognition that of ourselves we are unable to take it on, and equally that we are not required to do it in our own strength. Following Christ involves taking on Christ's life, which itself enables us to follow him through that intense darkness and watch it exploding into light as we tread the path with him.

Discussion starters

1. How does today's Gospel challenge us as individual Christians and as the Church?

2. What evidence have you seen in your experience of human life which bears out Christ's pronouncement that anyone who wants to save his life will lose it, but anyone who loses his life for Christ's sake will save it?

All-stage talk

Ask two people to come out and stand at least three metres apart. Ask one of the people to walk down to reach the other. Was there any problem with that? (Hopefully not.) Now ask both people to get to you, only this time with one condition – they mustn't move. Can they do it? (No, it's impossible.) If they want to get across to reach you they will have to go on a journey to do it. Is the journey easy or difficult? (They can try it to find out.) They probably did that with no trouble at all.

But suppose the journey is made very difficult?

(Tie all four ankles together with a scarf and walk away from them.) Can they get to you now? (Let them try.) As they are moving along, explain that they can certainly do it, but only with quite a struggle.

Stop them half-way and explain that being crucified was like a terrible journey that Jesus had to make to rescue us. In the middle of his journey people shouted at him to come down from the cross and save himself from the suffering.

Ask the people if they would be capable of untying the scarf and walking freely. (Presumably they could.) So could Jesus have come down from the cross and avoided all that suffering? In which case, why didn't he? He did it because he knew that there wasn't any other way to rescue us apart from accepting all the chains of our sin and carrying them for us, even though it made his journey so difficult. Instead of opting out, he chose to carry on (the volunteers can carry on as well) until the journey of rescue was finished, so we can all be set free. (Untie the legs of the volunteers.) And as followers of Christ, we are called to follow him in the kind of loving which led to that terrible journey – the loving which doesn't take the selfish or easy way out, but carries on loving and forgiving however difficult it is.

All-age ideas

• Play some haunting, sad music either to surround the first reading as a background to it, or played afterwards as a reflection upon it.

• At the offering of the gifts invite everyone to recommit themselves to following Christ, marking their foreheads with the sign of the cross.

Prayer of the Faithful

Celebrant
As followers of Christ, let us pray.

Reader
When following Christ brings danger,
weariness or suffering,
we pray for courage and strength.

Silence

In the shadow of your wings:
we shall be in safety.

When we watch the violence and selfishness
of a bewildered and fearful world,
we know our desperate need for peace.
May Christ's peace transform our world.

Silence

In the shadow of your wings:
we shall be in safety.

When we struggle in our relationships
and ache for those we love,
we pray for guidance, forgiveness
and the grace to go on forgiving.

Silence

In the shadow of your wings:
we shall be in safety.

We pray that into all the suffering, pain and hunger
which cries out from our humanity,
Christ will bring the refreshment of his healing love.

Silence

In the shadow of your wings:
we shall be in safety.

When those we know and love meet death,
and we must let them go,
may they be welcomed into the kingdom
of the Father's eternal peace.

Silence

In the shadow of your wings:
we shall be in safety.

We pray with Mary,
who shared her Son's sorrows:
Hail, Mary . . .

In silence now,
we share with God our Father
our personal burdens, joys and sorrows.

Silence

Celebrant
Father, hear our prayers;
we ask for mercy,
encouragement and support.
Through Christ our Lord.
Amen.

TREASURE SEEKERS

Aim: To help the children see that often things need
to be broken before they can be used.

Starter

Break open a new pack of modelling clay while the
children watch, and give them each a chunk to
model with.

Teaching

You will need some cooking chocolate, shredded
wheat, bowls and spoons for mixing, and cake cases.

Also a pan of hot water over which to melt the
chocolate. Explain that you are going to make some
chocolate cakes. Pretend to make these by stirring
the unopened packets together. Then, as you all
share in the breaking of the chocolate and the wheat,
talk about how this has to happen so that they can
be made into something even better.

As everyone shares in stirring the wheat into
the melted chocolate, point out how the chocolate
has to stop being separate squares so it can become
warm and melted, ready to join with the wheat and
make delicious cakes.

Sometimes we have to give up having a toy all
to ourselves, so we can share with someone as
friends. Sometimes we have to give up doing what
we want to do so that we can let someone else have
some fun as well as us.

Giving up what we want to make someone else
happy is all part of loving, and every time we do it
we get a bit better at it. Whenever we are being
loving we are following Jesus.

Praying

Jesus, you have called me to follow you,
and that's what I want to do.
I'm learning all about loving
because loving is what you do,
and I am following you!

Activities

On the sheet there are pictures of some people
following Jesus in different ways. Look at them
together and talk about them. How is each person
learning to follow Jesus in love? Then they can
draw a picture of themselves following Jesus by
doing a job God likes them to do. This may be any
kind of caring, thoughtful or unselfish behaviour.

PEARL DIVERS

Aim: To help them understand how brokenness and
dying are necessary for new life.

Starter

Unpack a fresh wad of modelling clay and break it
up, sharing it among everyone so they can make
something with it. Display the models and remind
everyone how necessary it was to break the beautifully packaged modelling clay in order to make all
these creative new things with it.

Teaching

Read to the children the story of the crucifixion
from a children's Bible version (such as *The road to*

the cross from the Palm Tree series, or an excerpt from *Donkeys' glory* by Nan Goodall) or show one of the children's video versions. (Think carefully about what you use, as it is important that you choose something suitable for your particular group.)

Explain how Jesus knew that all this was bound to happen to him, and he didn't try and escape from it, even though it scared him. He did it because he knew it was the only way to save us – through going on and on loving and forgiving right through everything.

All the violence and pain directed towards Jesus is difficult for them to cope with, and it may help them to see how beans have to break apart to allow new growth. Bring along to show them a jar with germinated beans between damp blotting paper and the glass, so that they can see how the bean needs to be broken before new life can come from it.

Jesus said that anyone wanting to be his follower would have to be prepared to give themselves up like this. Draw a capital I on a large sheet. When we cross out selfishness (cross out the capital I) what shape does it make? The shape of Jesus' cross.

Praying

Jesus, your unselfish loving
led you to the pain of the cross.
Thank you for loving us that much.
Help us to follow you
in unselfish loving
even if it hurts. Amen.

Activities

On the sheet there are instructions for planting their own beans in jars (they will need a jar each, damp blotting paper or cotton wadding, and beans), and there is a picture of the crucifixion for them to colour and mount the prayer on.

GOLD PANNERS

Aim: To look at the implications of taking discipleship seriously.

Starter

Bring along some holiday brochures and in pairs or threes work out the best bargain holiday in terms of value for money.

Teaching

With anything we plan to buy, we probably do a bit of research to make sure we know what's involved, what hidden costs there are and so on. Today we are going to look at what it really costs to be a follower of Jesus.

First we look at what the cost was for Jesus as the Christ, or Messiah. Read the prophecy from Zechariah, one of many prophecies pointing to a Saviour who innocently suffers in order to save. Jesus would have known these prophecies, and he saw his suffering as inevitable. Read today's Gospel, up to verse 22, noticing how, as soon as the disciples identify him, he spells out what this will mean.

Now look at the implications for us as followers of Jesus. Read the rest of today's Gospel and talk over what this means. Look at how following Jesus in selfless love is bound to result in some kind of suffering. Why does Jesus suggest that this giving away of ourselves actually brings us lasting life? How does that fit in with his own death? How did that bring life?

Praying

May I know thee more clearly
love thee more dearly
and follow thee more nearly
day by day. Amen.

(From the Prayer of St Richard of Chichester)

Activities

On the sheet they are encouraged to think through the cost of discipleship as well as the rewards of it, and what it means to take up our cross every day. They also explore the ways different groups of people were trying to make sense of Jesus during his life on earth, and how they think of him now.

THIRTEENTH SUNDAY OF THE YEAR

Thought for the day

When we are called to follow Jesus, that means total commitment, with no half-measures.

Reflection on the readings

1 Kings 19:16, 19-21
Psalm 15
Galatians 5:1, 13-18
Luke 9:51-62

The reading from Kings describes Elisha's calling to be Elijah's servant and disciple. Later, he would be his successor. The cloak is an important sign of authority and acceptance, and Elisha will later take up the mantle, with all the commitment that this involves.

In the reading from Luke other people are called to follow Jesus, and not everyone is prepared to do this. Others enthusiastically offer to come with him, and Jesus has to dampen their enthusiasm somewhat by bringing them down to earth, and making them count the cost of the commitment before they decide. The practical living arrangements, for instance, and probable lack of home comforts, need to be looked squarely in the face before the choice is made.

It is not everyone's calling to wander with Jesus around the countryside, preaching and healing the sick. Equally valid is the ministry of those chatting the good news among their own people in their own towns and villages, and of all those living by God's values in commerce and industry. What binds all these people together, though, is the decision made to commitment.

In the baptismal promises the Church continues to place people on the spot. What commitment to Christ entails is stated clearly, so there may be no misunderstanding, and the candidates are free to choose whether to commit themselves or not. But, having made the choice, there is no getting away from the fact that they are committed to living differently.

As Paul explains to the Galatians, it is for *our* freedom that Christ has set us free, and to settle back into former sin patterns will only enslave us. Living as committed Christians we need to check constantly that we are still walking in step with the Spirit. Paul gives us a whole list of examples to check our behaviour against, so that we can adjust our direction accordingly.

Discussion starters

1. Does our discipleship apply only on Sundays, or are we consciously living as followers of Christ throughout the week?

2. What is the difference between a Christian and a person with a loving and generous nature who isn't a committed Christian?

All-stage talk

You will need someone who can do gymnastics or dance. Ask them to prepare a sequence of moves which need total commitment in order to work, such as somersaults and cartwheels, pirouettes and arabesques.

Begin by asking the gymnasts or dancers to perform their demonstration. Briefly interview them, thanking them and asking whether they could do these things first time, or whether they had to practise. Draw attention to the commitment that has to be given to anything you want to do really well. You can't 'half do' some of those moves, or you'd probably fall flat on your face.

As Christians we are called to that same kind of commitment. We can't 'half do' it. When we commit ourselves to following Christ, it's going to affect the way we talk, the way we behave with our friends and our enemies, the way we spend our time and our money. It's going to affect all our thinking and the choices we make. So it's a bit like deciding to do a double somersault, or a triple pirouette – it takes a lot of dedication and courage to launch off.

Imagine if you were just launching yourself into a triple somersault and all your strength suddenly wasn't there. You'd certainly notice it was missing! In fact, you wouldn't be able to do any of those clever moves without strength.

In our Christian life, God's Holy Spirit is the strength. It enables us to do those triple somersaults of caring love for those we don't much like, and the double pirouettes of co-operating when all we want is our own way. Real loving is very hard work, and it takes lots of dedication. With God's strength we can do it, and then we will be moving freely and beautifully through life, in the way God called us to, and knows will make us, and others, truly happy.

All-age ideas

- In a time of prayer, ask various groups of people to stand so that the others can pray for them in their ministry – all those, for instance, who are involved with learning, teaching and education, those in industry and commerce, those caring for children, those who have time during the day to pray, and those whose sporting or leisure activities bring them into contact with people who don't know Jesus.

- Have a display with a list on one side of good works, or things in the parish that need to be done. On the other half, list excuses why they can't be done. Next to this have a list of the things Jesus did, and list of the excuses he might have used, but didn't, not to do them.

Prayer of the Faithful

Celebrant
Holy God, you have called us
to meet and pray together,
and here we are.

Reader
We pray for those called
to lay and ordained ministry in the Church,

and for those at present testing their vocation.
We lay before the Lord the work that needs doing here
and ask him to provide people to do it.

Silence

We ask in Jesus' name:
give us grace to discern your answer.

We pray for those called to serve
in positions of authority and influence;
for all leaders to see true greatness as service
and true strength as humility.

Silence

We ask in Jesus' name:
give us grace to discern your answer.

We pray for those called to marriage,
and those called to the single life,
for parents and grandparents,
sons and daughters,
for acceptance of what we cannot change
and strength to live the Christian life
in our present situation.

Silence

We ask in Jesus' name:
give us grace to discern your answer.

We pray for those whose lives
are full of disappointment,
disillusion and discontent;
for all who struggle with great perseverance
in difficult circumstances.
We pray for strength, encouragement and direction.

Silence

We ask in Jesus' name:
give us grace to discern your answer.

We pray for those called, through death,
into eternal life
and freedom from all their pain and suffering.
May they receive mercy
and be welcomed into the kingdom.

Silence

We ask in Jesus' name:
give us grace to discern your answer.

We make our prayer with Mary,
who committed herself fully to God's will:
Hail, Mary . . .

In loving silence, now,
we make our private petitions.

Silence

Celebrant
Lord and heavenly Father,
as we commit our lives afresh
to your service,
we ask you to hear our prayers.
Through Christ our Lord.
Amen.

TREASURE SEEKERS

Aim: To understand that we are called to follow Jesus.

Starter

A 'you-do-as-I-do' story. Here is one example. The actions are mostly obvious.

'I'll tell you a story. This story is new,
  so you listen carefully and do as I do.
This is Tom Thumb and this is his house.
These are his windows (*hands make glasses at eyes*)
  and this is Squeaky, his mouse (*your little finger*).
Early one morning the sun began to shine.
Squeaky mouse sat up in bed and counted up to nine.
One, two, three, four, five, six, seven, eight, nine!
(*in a squeaky voice*)
Then he took a great big jump and landed on Tom's bed (*your left hand*).
He quickly ran right up Tom's arm and landed on his head.
Squeaky pulled Tom's hair, Squeaky pulled Tom's nose,
till in the end Tom Thumb jumped up and put on all his clothes.
Then they sat down to breakfast and ate some crusty bread.
And when all that was over, Tom Thumb said . . .'
(*back to the beginning*)

Teaching

Have several chairs in a line, and prepare beforehand card church windows, door and tower clock as shown below.

By name, ask a particular child to sit on one of the chairs and hold a window. Continue to call by name for particular jobs until you have a complete church. Point out that you called them all to do particular jobs, and in doing them the children have become a church.

Jesus calls his followers to jobs that only we can do, and when we agree, and start doing them, we all become the Church of God. This Church isn't really a building, is it – it's a group of people. And that's what the Church is – a group of people called to do God's work in the world.

Praying

Jesus, you have called me
to follow you,
and here I am!
Lead on, Jesus,
I'm right behind you. Amen.

Activities

Have a look at the pictures of some jobs people have been called to and talk about them, and people you know who do such jobs. Then they can draw a picture of themselves doing a job that God likes them to do. This may be any kind of caring, thoughtful behaviour.

PEARL DIVERS

Aim: To get to know the story of Elisha responding to Elijah's call.

Starter

What's my line? In turn the children mime a job, and everyone has to guess what it is. The one who guesses correctly does the next mime, or you can work round the group circle.

Teaching

Prepare the different pictures for the story on card. Suggestions are given below.

Then tell the story using carpet tiles on the floor and move the pictures around as you talk.

Praying

Lord God, here I am,
ready to do
whatever you need me to.
And, Lord, prepare me now
for what you would like me to do
in the future. Amen.

Activities

The worksheet explores the nature of vocation, with quotations from people in varied ministries. Talk through with the children the ministry they have in places no one but them can reach, such as in their families and friendships, in their playground and at their clubs. Jesus likes to use us where we are.

GOLD PANNERS

Aim: To look at the nature of vocation and commitment.

Starter

Spin the tray. Sit in a wide circle. One person spins a tray in the middle and leaves it, calling someone's name as they go. This person has to try and get to the tray before it falls to the ground.

Teaching

Put a rolled-up cloak on display and alert everyone to look out for the significance of this as you read the account of Elijah calling Elisha. Afterwards jot their suggestions down.

Look next at the Gospel reading, pointing out the way the Samaritans are too tied up with their political details to accept Jesus, and James and John are over-enthusiastic to protect Jesus from insult.

Some enthusiastic would-be followers have to be reminded to count the real cost of being a disciple, and other hesitant ones have to be reminded to get their priorities right and be ready as soon as they are called.

It's worth pointing out that since God knows our circumstances really well, there is no way Jesus would have called them if they were not in a position to come, so their remarks must have been side-stepping the responsibility. God's timing is always perfect, and you will get to know that when he says, 'Now!' that's the best time to act.

Finally read the passage from Galatians, preferably from *The Message* version, as this expresses it so helpfully in language the young people will be able to relate to. Having been called by God, the ongoing commitment is essential, to ensure that we don't get slack and drift away from our calling.

Praying

Your ways, O God, are holy.
What god is so great as our God?
You are the God who performs miracles;
you display your power among the peoples.

Activities

The worksheet helps them look at what God's calling is like, and the discussion can lead on to creating a display for the church about vocation. Bring with you pictures of people with different jobs within your local church, select verses from the readings to write out, and write prayers for those already involved and those needed in the parish.

FOURTEENTH SUNDAY OF THE YEAR

Thought for the day

In Christ we become a new creation.

Reflection on the readings

Isaiah 66:10-14
Psalm 65
Galatians 6:14-18
Luke 10:1-12, 17-20

After all the trauma of exile, God's people have had to wrestle with their sense of disorientation and confusion. They have had to face up to taking responsibilty for what has happened, and now the prophet offers them the hope of being comforted and fed and cared for like a young child. God can give us all that 'fresh as a young child' sensation, as we allow him to make us new creations, born of the Spirit. Paul, writing to the Galatians, sees that a constant battle is going on between our sinful nature and our spiritual nature, and inspires us to go for the better deal of the spiritual nature, which brings joy and lasts for eternity. It is bringing people to enjoy this new creation which is the whole point of our ministry, says Paul, and the religious traditions and habits matter only in so far as they help to make us aware of our need of God's nursing and bathing. The really important thing is being made new.

And there are so many tired and disillusioned souls, all struggling to save themselves, and suspecting their frenetic attempts are actually doomed to failure, if they dared stop for a minute and look. Jesus sees it as a huge harvest, ripe for gathering, but with far too few workers; and people remain trapped in their distracted existence as a result of meeting no one able to offer them the freedom of God's new life.

So today offers us both great hope and a great challenge. Who are the workers to be?

Discussion starters

1. What are the workers in the harvest setting out to do, and why are they needed?

2. How can we best enable others to discover what it means to be made a new creation in Christ?

All-stage talk

Beforehand write out clearly on different colours of paper, six or twelve (depending on numbers of children expected) healings that may well have taken place when the seventy were sent out. (For example, a blind woman got her sight back; two children were dying of a disease, and now they're playing outside; a young man can now walk again; a boy who stuttered can now speak clearly; a family feud has been sorted out.) Give these to different adults to hold in different places around the church when the talk begins. Also give each adult some food to give the children who come to them. Some will be given a sweet each, some a bun each, and some a piece of dry bread.

Begin by reminding everyone that Jesus sent out seventy of his disciples in pairs, to different towns and villages. Let them suggest some reasons for the disciples being sent in pairs. (Friendly; supportive; safer.) So you are going to send people out around the church in pairs, on a mission to find a notice the same colour as the slip of paper you give each pair.

Before they go, tell them to be careful, travel light, not stop to speak to strangers on the way, eat what they're given, say 'Peace be with you' to the person holding their colour, and tell them the kingdom is very near. Get the pairs to repeat the instructions. As they go off around the church, some people can try to make some of the older ones talk on their way. As they reach their paper, the adult there can remind them of their message, if necessary, and give them their food and the notice. The pairs return to you and you can enthuse with them over all the wonderful things that have happened.

Thank them for all their hard work, and tell everyone about Jesus wanting everyone to be restored and like a new person. But we're still short of workers in this harvest of people. We need to pray that God will send more workers. And we need to make ourselves available, in case it's us he can use!

All-age ideas

- Have a flower arrangement like a cornfield, with wheat and grasses, poppies and cornflowers, and have a scythe beside the arrangement with the words from Luke: 'Ask the Lord of the harvest to send out workers into his harvest field.'

- As a background to, or reflection upon, the first reading, have some gentle nursery music played, possibly from a music box.

Prayer of the Faithful

Celebrant
Let us bring our cares and concerns
before the God who loves us.

Reader
We pray for more workers
to gather in the harvest of the kingdom;
for our churches to be places of welcome
and wholesome spiritual nurture.

Silence

Use us, Lord:
in the building of your kingdom.

We pray for our nation and the nations of the world;
for an upholding of godly principles and just laws,
for reconciliation, peace and mutual co-operation.

Silence

Use us, Lord:
in the building of your kingdom.

We pray for those among our families and friends
who have no idea of the new life the Lord offers;
we pray for them to discover him
so they may share the joy of living in his love.

Silence

Use us, Lord:
in the building of your kingdom.

We pray for those who are suffering,
for those disfigured by disease or accidents,
for the lonely, the confused and the outcasts.

Silence

Use us, Lord:
in the building of your kingdom.

We pray for the dying, and their loved ones,
for those who have passed through death,
and the families and friends who miss them.
May they be surrounded
by the Father's everlasting love.

Silence

Use us, Lord:
in the building of your kingdom.

We pray now with Mary,
serene Mother of our Lord:
Hail, Mary . . .

God our Father loves us;
in silence we pray
our personal petitions to him now.

Silence

Celebrant
Father, knowing that you alone
have the words of eternal life,
we lay our prayers before you.
Through Christ our Lord.
Amen.

TREASURE SEEKERS

Aim: To know the importance of spreading the good news of God's love.

Starter

Bring with you some postcards you have received from friends on holiday. Show these round, talking together about how nice it is when you hear good news from people who love you enough to let you know about it.

Teaching

Begin by having a time of good news sharing with the group. Then show them a cross (or a number of different ones, from necklace size to a church size one). All these show us the best good news of all –

that Jesus is alive and loves us. And we can be good messengers, passing that good news on to the people we meet. We can tell them with our voices and show them by the way we live our lives.

Praying

Lord Jesus, I pray for the people
who do not know you yet
and do not realise that you love us all.
I'd like to be a messenger
and tell them the good news.
Amen.

Activities

On the sheet there is a postcard to make, colour and send with some good news on it. Each child will need a stamp.

PEARL DIVERS

Aim: To hear about the seventy being sent out by Jesus.

Starter

Send people out in pairs with matchboxes, on a mission to collect six different things which fit in their box. Show one another the results when everyone gets back. You can make this a timed activity if your schedule is tight.

Teaching

First fill in the background to this mission. Jesus began by doing the teaching and healing all over the local area, training his followers or disciples as he went. Jesus realises that there are huge numbers of people all ready to hear the good news, but only a few people to teach them. He talks about it as being like a huge harvest of people, ripe to gather in, but with very few workers to do it. So now he spreads the net wider, by sending out seventy-two of his trained followers. As this is quite a large number to visualise, have seventy-two paper people cut out and spread them all over the floor in the middle of the circle. Let a few children put them into pairs, because Jesus sent these people out in pairs. They can discuss the advantages of this.

Jesus gathered this crowd of people together and gave them their instructions. Have these written out on a large sheet of paper or length of wallpaper:

1. Be careful.
2. Travel light.
3. Don't waste time chatting on the way.
4. 'Peace to this house!'
5. Eat what you are given.
6. Heal the sick in body and mind.
7. Tell them the kingdom of God is very close to them.

Use the instruction list on the worksheet with its picture symbols as you tell the children what happened, and how excited they were when they got back because of the many ways God had blessed their work.

Praying

Lord, so many people
have no idea of how happy they could be
with you at the centre of their life.
Please send us lots more workers
into this harvest,
to let the people know about you
and bring them safely into your kingdom.

Activities

Using the cut-out people and a large sheet of paper, make a collage picture of this mission, sticking on the children's drawings of roads, villages, trees and the people hearing the good news everywhere, and being healed. The worksheet has a copy of the list of instructions given to the seventy-two.

GOLD PANNERS

Aim: To explore the mission of the seventy-two, and the implications of being made a new creation in Christ.

Starter

Have packs of playing cards available, and in pairs build houses of cards. Admire one another's results before they collapse.

Teaching

With the card houses we have been doing some delicate and painstaking building work. Explain how God works carefully and painstakingly with us in making us a new creation. It takes patience, gentleness and a very steady hand!

You also have to start at the beginning, rather than half-way up. In the Old Testament reading it sounds as if a baby is being cared for and fed. (Place down a feeding bottle, baby's bath towel and baby clothes.) Read together the passage from Isaiah 66 and explain how this was like a new, fresh start for the people of Israel after all they had been through. God was going to make them new, treating them gently and carefully like newborn children.

Now read the passage from Galatians. We find that we can't fool God. If we come saying we want to be made new, when really we're only going through the motions and are not prepared to change or alter anything in us, then God's not interested. What he's interested in is people genuinely wanting to be made new. When that happens he's there like a shot, helping us to change things we'd never have thought we could, and setting us free from bad habits and wrong attitudes of a lifetime.

Finally read about the seventy-two people sent out by Jesus in twos, to bring this good news to anyone who would listen. Look at how Jesus reacts when they get back – he is so thrilled by what's been going on through these amateurs; it's been like a battleground, as Satan has lost hold of lots of people. And there are still loads of people who haven't grasped what Jesus is offering. Lots more workers are still needed.

Praying

Lord, we pray for those who are still resisting you.
Give them courage to relax in your company
and allow your life to fill them
and bring them peace and joy.

Activities

Give everyone a lump of clay. Put on some music and, as you mould the lump into a new creation, think of God moulding you and other people you care for into the new and fulfilling life God has in mind.

FIFTEENTH SUNDAY OF THE YEAR

Thought for the day

Straighten your lives out and live by God's standards of love.

Reflection on the readings

Deuteronomy 30:10-14
Psalm 68
Colossians 1:15-20
Luke 10:25-37

It is in today's Psalm that God's standards of loving are clearly and beautifully stated. These precepts of defending the cause of the poor and oppressed, upholding right judgement and caring for those in need, are like a strong heartbeat pulsing underneath the events and stories of the other readings.

In the reading from Luke, Jesus faces opposition. The seventy-two have recently arrived back, and there has no doubt been an angry backlash from those towns denounced by Jesus for their refusal to receive the message brought to them. The law expert is smugly deprecating as he leads Jesus into a trap, which Jesus neatly sidesteps, dropping the man in instead. Perhaps he was hoping for Jesus to agree that 'neighbour' only refers to those within the law – such as the denounced Capernaum, for instance?

The story Jesus gives by way of an answer forces him to look with God's measure, or plumb line, at attitudes and assumptions which need a thorough overhaul. The right words may still be in place, so that love for God and neighbour can be glibly quoted, but the spirit of those words has dried up inside and left only the empty shell.

In contrast, Paul, full of thankfulness at the lush growth of the Christians at Colossae, rejoices in Jesus as the wonderful revelation of God's own love. As the Samaritan stretched out in love to his neighbour, so God stretches out to us in Christ.

Discussion starters

1. Why does human nature so often react to God's light as something to be deflected or shut out?

2. What should we do if we find God pointing out an error or sin in our life?

All-stage talk

Bring with you an egg cup, a whole egg in its shell, and a boiled egg which someone has eaten, so that just the shell is left, with a spoon hole at one end. Put this into the egg cup upside down so that it looks like a complete egg ready to eat. You will also need an egg spoon.

Begin by talking about those times you've desperately needed help, like missing the bus when you're already a bit late, or being caught in a downpour on your way to school, and you're hoping one of your friends will happen to drive past and see you. Perhaps the man who had been mugged in Jesus' story felt a bit like that, if he was still able to think after the beating-up he'd been given. Perhaps in the daze of his injuries he heard each set of footsteps coming nearer, and hoped that now he'd get some help. But no, the footsteps quickened up when they got nearer and then went off into the distance again. And the man still lay there, unable to move.

Perhaps he had almost given up hope when the Samaritan, a foreigner, stopped and came to peer at him to see what was wrong. Perhaps, as he swayed in and out of consciousness, he was half aware of being carefully given first aid, of being comforted and reassured that he was going to be all right. Those are good things to feel and hear, when you're in great need. You have no power at such times to make anyone care for you, so all you can do is rely on other people choosing to treat you well.

And that's what we're being taught today: that as Christians we are people called to treat others well, whether we're told to or not, whether anyone sees us or not, whether we want to or not. Why? Simply because our God says that this is the right and good way to live.

The man in today's Gospel, to whom Jesus told his 'good neighbour' story, could recite the rules he was supposed to live by off by heart: 'Love the Lord your God with all your heart and with all your soul and with all your strength and with all your mind. And love your neighbour as yourself.' But for him and for lots of others, those words are like this boiled egg. It looks wonderful and full of goodness. But if I start to dig into it (do that) with my spoon, I find that all the inside is missing, and there's nothing of any goodness there at all.

We must be brave and dig into the words we sing and pray together today, and look at what we find inside. Perhaps there will be rich meaning, and you will know that the words your mouth says are backed up with the way you live. Perhaps you will find the words are just a shell, and your life doesn't back them up at all. If so, come to God today and ask him to fill the shell with new meaning. He can do that, and he's waiting for you to ask.

All-age ideas

- Print out the first reading so that everyone can join in with the questions in it, which you print in bold. (Who will . . .?) Have a narrator and Moses to read the rest of the passage.

- Have a group acting out the story of the good Samaritan, but make sure the first section – the conversation with the expert in the Law – is included in the acting.

Prayer of the Faithful

Celebrant
Let us pray to God,
knowing we can trust him.

Reader
We pray that as Christians we may take to heart
the need to walk the talk,
and live out what we profess.

We pray that nothing may get so important to us
that it pushes God's values aside.

Silence

Father:
let only your will be done.

We pray that those in authority and power
do not lose touch with the needs of those they serve,
so that the poor and oppressed and vulnerable
are always given value and respect.

Silence

Father:
let only your will be done.

We pray for those in our families
whom we love and have hurt or upset;
we pray too for those who have hurt or upset us,
and ask for God's reconciliation and healing.

Silence

Father:
let only your will be done.

We pray for those who have lost hope
of being rescued, noticed or valued;
for the complacent who cannot see their poverty,
for the prejudiced who mistake blindness for sight.

Silence

Father:
let only your will be done.

We pray for our loved ones
who have reached the moment of death;
we give thanks for the example of their lives
and commend them all to God's safekeeping.

Silence

Father:
let only your will be done.

Mary's example teaches us
the power of loving response;
with her we make our prayer:
Hail, Mary . . .

In the silence of God's stillness,
we name any we know
who especially need our prayer.

Silence

Celebrant
Lord God of love,
we offer you these prayers,
through Christ our Lord.
Amen.

TREASURE SEEKERS

Aim: To know the parable of the good neighbour.

Starter

Have a free play session with games such as dressing-up, which encourage the children to play together as well as alongside each other.

Teaching

Tell the story of the good neighbour, involving the children as the characters and helping them act it out. Teach them the summary of the Law to the tune of *London's burning*:

You shall love the
> *(hands on heart)*

Lord your God with
> *(point upwards)*

all your heart and
> *(hands on heart)*

all your mind and
> *(hold head with hands)*

all your strength! All your strength!
> *(show biceps)*

And love your neighbour,
and love your neighbour.
> *(arms round one another's shoulders)*

Praying

Lord Jesus,
with my lips
I can tell you I love you.
With my life
I will show you I love you! Amen.

Activities

The worksheet encourages the children to look at the way people look after others, and there is a picture to finish and colour of the mugged man in the story being looked after by the good Samaritan. Help the children to talk about ways they can be good neighbours.

PEARL DIVERS

Aim: To know the story and context of 'The Good Samaritan'.

Starter

Sit in a circle and first ask everyone to find out the favourite colour or food of the person on their left. Now go round the circle with each person introducing their neighbour – 'This is Charlie and his favourite colour is dark metallic green.'

Teaching

Read verse 25 from the Gospel, and ask the children what they think Jesus might have said. Explain that he didn't actually give the expert an answer, but another question. (Read verse 26.) Remind the children of what it does say in the Law as the two 'life rules' – have it written up so you can all read it out together: 'Love the Lord your God with all your heart and with all your soul and with all your mind, and love your neighbour as yourself.'

Now ask a child to read Jesus' reply in verse 28. Explain that the expert didn't feel it should be as simple as that ('experts' often like things to be very complicated) and, also, the experts didn't much like the way Jesus was mixing with all the wrong sort of people.

So Jesus told them a story to teach them that loving our neighbour is more than being nice to those we happen to like.

Tell the story, drawing it as you go on a blackboard with coloured chalks. The drawings don't need to be grand, but will help the children focus, and the simpler the drawings are, the more their imaginations can work.

At the end of the story, read the question Jesus asked (verse 36). The expert had to admit that it was the unliked foreigner who had actually been living by God's law of loving care.

Praying

Lord God,
help me to notice
when other people need my help,
and remind me to do
what I can to help them. Amen.

Activities

On the sheet there are pictures of the story to which they add various things, and also some space to write in the names of their own neighbours, so they can pray for them. They can try measuring up their own lives against the summary of the Law, so that they begin to understand that loving sometimes involves doing things we may not want to do at all.

GOLD PANNERS

Aim: To look at the Gospel with its challenge of living God's way.

Starter

Choices. One person goes outside and the others decide which is the 'right' chair to sit on. When the person comes in they have to choose the chair they think is right. If it's the wrong one they get tipped off. If it's the right one they get a sweet.

Teaching

In the starter activity we were having to choose 'blind', so there was no way we could be sure we'd chosen right. But God doesn't leave us to choose blindly; he has made the choices very clear. If we live to please ourselves and indulge all our wants and fancies, we will be choosing destruction and death, and history has proved that true. If we live to please God, in a way marked by love for God and neighbour, we will be choosing fulfilment and life – both for us as individuals and for our society.

Now read the passage from Luke 10, and see how this story Jesus tells allows the expert in the Law to see more clearly that he can choose which direction he wants his life to go. We are not told what decision he made.

Finally read Colossians for the good news of what happens when we do choose life.

Praying

Lord, it's hard
to please you and love others
when our selfishness
shouts at us to look after Number One
and get our own way.
Make our love for you so strong
that we really want to think of others
rather than indulging
our own wants and plans. Amen.

Activities

They look up and write in the summary of the Law (from the Gospel and Deuteronomy 6:5), and explore how this relates to practical, everyday situations. They can either discuss these or act them out in role-play.

SIXTEENTH SUNDAY OF THE YEAR

Thought for the day

Attentive listening is all part of serving.

Reflection on the readings

Genesis 18:1-10
Psalm 14
Colossians 1:24-28
Luke 10:38-42

Today's first reading is an account in Genesis of Abraham looking after his unexpected guests with dedicated and generous hospitality. It is a warm and affectionate image which shows up how attentively Abraham and Sarah care for the needs of the three visitors; a gracious harmony of listening and serving. The practical story is heavy with the mystery of God, as these strangers are somehow the Lord appearing to Abraham and giving him the promise of a son, unlikely as that appears to be in view of their age and many childless years.

In the passage from Colossians, Paul is writing after the resurrection of Christ, and can delight in the way God's mysterious nature has in Christ been made clear to the whole world. God's revealed nature in Christ turns out to be not a conquering national king, but an attentive servant, seeing the very serving as a great honour.

In Martha and Mary we find both the attentive listening and the serving, but not yet in the total harmony which gives meaning to both.

In Jesus' own ministry we are given many examples of the balance between listening and doing; regularly in the night, or very early dawn, Jesus is out on his own, deep in prayer. These times of holy listening seem to energise him for the day ahead and enable the doing. Both are vital. For us, too, the challenge is to listen so attentively that we may serve more cheerfully and reverently, not with resentment or stress, but in the joy of knowing that we are serving God by our open-hearted serving of others.

Discussion starters

1. Are individual lives reflected in the way a society develops? Do our small sparks of Christian living affect society? Do our slips of behaviour matter to society?

2. Paul talks of his exhausting labour of love in spreading the Gospel. What Martha/Mary balance should we be aiming for as Christians?

All-stage talk

Beforehand make a pair of large card ears, about 30 centimetres high, and a pair of large card hands, about the same size.

Start by asking for two volunteers, one of whom holds the ears to the side of her head, and the other who has the hands fixed to her own hands with large rubber bands. Remind everyone of the two people in the Gospel for today, both very good friends of Jesus. Their names were Martha and Mary and they were sisters. Jesus often went round to the home where they lived with their brother Lazarus, and they all enjoyed one another's company.

(Alice) is like a cartoon picture of Mary, because what she liked to do was sit and listen to Jesus and she could listen to him for hours. She probably liked listening to all sorts of people, and may have been the kind of person people could talk easily to because they could see she was interested in them. Mary's idea of cooking a meal was probably beans on toast, and she probably didn't notice the dust creeping up until she could write in it.

(Laura) is like a cartoon picture of Martha, because what she liked best was doing things for people and making sure they had clean shirts and well-balanced meals. Her idea of cooking a meal would be something like roast chicken with all the trimmings. If you wanted something done, you'd ask Martha.

Now people sometimes get upset by today's Gospel because they think Jesus is saying that everyone ought to spend their time listening like Mary, and that busy, practical people like Martha aren't somehow as good. But, of course, Jesus isn't saying that at all. His own life was full of work and activity, travelling, preaching, teaching and healing, and none of that would have got done if he hadn't been a doer.

But he also spent hours late at night, or early in the morning on his own with God, talking things over and quietly listening. And he knew that this was a really important part of the doing. He knew we need to keep the right balance between input (the ears) and output (the hands). On that particular visit to Martha and Mary's house, the listening was more important than the doing. What we all have to do is notice when we need to listen, and be ready to stop what we're doing and listen.

All of us need to set aside a quiet time to be with God morning and night, every day. It doesn't have to be long, but it has to be there. If we neglect that, our ability to discern right behaviour will start to slip, and we risk sliding into the kind of life that hurts God so much. Spending time quietly with God is not an optional extra for people with time on their hands, it's an absolute necessity, as well as being refreshing, rejuvenating and problem solving! (If there is a parish or diocesan retreat planned this year you can mention that as well.)

All-age ideas

- Have the first reading acted out while being narrated, with the three visitors walking up the aisle, and Abraham and Sarah welcoming them and providing thoroughly for their needs.

- Ask people to hold first their ears and then their hands as you pray for God's blessing on everyone's listening and activity in the week ahead.

Prayer of the Faithful

Celebrant
Our God is always ready to listen.
Let us pray to him now.

Reader
We pray to the Lord
that he may continue to pour out his gifts
on the Church,
so that many may be saved
and our faith may grow strong
and bear much fruit.

Silence

God of Love:
we put our trust in you.

We pray to the Lord
that he may look with mercy
on the conflicts of our world;
that we may realign our values and goals
until they are in line with his will,
and our laws and expectations
reflect his justice and love.

Silence

God of Love:
we put our trust in you.

We pray to the Lord
that he may bless our homes and families
and all our neighbours and friends;
may we listen to one another with full attention,
and recognise one another's gifts.

Silence

God of Love:
we put our trust in you.

We pray to the Lord
that he may encourage the hesitant,
curb the overpowering,
heal the sick, refresh the exhausted,

soften the hardened hearts,
open the eyes of the complacent,
and comfort all who are sad.

Silence

God of Love:
we put our trust in you.

We pray to the Lord
that he may welcome into eternity
all those who have died in faith;
may we in our turn share with them
the joy of living in his peace for ever.

Silence

God of Love:
we put our trust in you.

We pray with Mary,
who was the first to welcome Jesus:
Hail, Mary . . .

In the silence of God's attentive love,
we pray our private petitions.

Silence

Celebrant
God our Father, hear our prayer;
we ask you to help us fix our lives on you.
Through Christ our Lord.
Amen.

TREASURE SEEKERS

Aim: To look at the value of listening.

Starter

Play this game in which they have to listen carefully to the instructions. You give them an instruction of where to move to, followed by the way to do it, such as: 'Go to the front wall as aeroplanes; go to the back wall as window cleaners.'

Teaching

Get everyone to find their ears, and talk about what they are for. Try covering and uncovering ears to hear the effect, notice how loud it sounds if you rub your own ear, but if someone else does it to theirs you can hardly hear it at all. Enjoy the gift of hearing and listening that God has given us, and share your favourite sounds. Think about what sounds you hear when you first wake up.

Then do some exercises to train your listening. Sit very still and listen to all the sounds around for a minute, then share what you heard. Whisper something very quietly and see if you can hear it (it might be something funny, or an instruction to touch their toes with their hair). Have a 'news time', with everyone listening carefully to whoever is speaking.

Tell the children about the way all the grown-ups and children used to come out and listen to Jesus, because they found what he said so helpful.

Praying

Thank you, God,
for my ears to listen with.
Help me to get really good at listening
to you and to other people. Amen.

Activities

Have a tape of different sounds and see if the children can guess what they are. On the worksheet there are objects drawn for which they can make the sounds, and the picture of a park encourages them to imagine what sounds they would hear if they were in that place.

PEARL DIVERS

Aim: To look at the importance of listening to God.

Starter

Sit in a circle, with one blindfolded person in the centre. Another person creeps round the outside of the circle with a jangly set of keys. The blindfolded person points to where the person has got to. If they are right they take the keys and a new person is blindfolded.

Teaching

Begin with a sketch to express the busy nature of our lives. It will need to be prepared beforehand using one or two of the children. An alarm clock rings and the children dash in with dressing-gowns and teddies. They pretend to eat their breakfast really quickly, and grab books and pencil-case for school. They dash back in for lunch-boxes, and out, back for football kit or equivalent, and out, back for swimming gear, and out, back for violin or equivalent, and out, back to sit and watch television and eat something, and out, in wearing dressing-gowns and teddies again, and out.

Talk about what the children do on each day of the week and how nice it is to be able to do all these things, but how important it is to stop and spend quiet times every day with God. Have the children acting out the Martha and Mary story, bringing out the need to get the listening times right so that all the practical doing falls properly into place.

Praying

Here I am, Lord.
I have come to spend some time with you,
to sit at your feet and be quiet with you.

Activities

There are instructions on the worksheet for making a prayer corner for their bedroom, to be used as a reminder for daily prayer and a focus for them. There is also a prayer pattern using a hand drawing, which can be cut out and stuck on to the prayer corner.

GOLD PANNERS

Aim: To look at the harmony between attentiveness to Christ and working in his service.

Starter

Try some balancing acts, such as loads being carried on heads, some exercises which involve standing on one leg, and circus skills like spinning plastic plates on bamboo sticks, or finding the exact fulcrum on a cane which has bags of different weights at either end.

Teaching

As we know from trying to skate or ride a bike, it's very important to get the balance right. In our lives we need to get the balance right between listening attentively to God and to one another, and being actively involved in the serving of God and one another.

Look first at the Gospel, and talk over the problem here. Make it clear that Jesus is *not* telling us as Christians to do no practical helping, and just sit around in church all the time. Practical serving is vital (Jesus did lots of that) but, if it is to be without resentment or bullying, it all has to grow out of the attentive listening.

Now read the passage from Genesis, noticing the pleased and attentive way Abraham and Sarah care for their guests and serve them. In what sense are we always serving Christ when we humbly and lovingly serve other people? (See Matthew 25:31-46 – the sheep and goats story.)

Praying

God himself is my help.
The Lord upholds my life.
I will offer you a willing sacrifice;
I will praise your name, O Lord,
for its goodness.

(From Psalm 53)

Activities

On the sheet they explore what attentive listening to God means, and how it leads on to active serving. They are encouraged to put this into practice in the parish, noticing needs and responding to them.

SEVENTEENTH SUNDAY OF THE YEAR

Thought for the day

Keep asking for God's Spirit and he will keep pouring out his blessing on you.

Reflection on the readings

Genesis 18:20-32
Psalm 137
Colossians 2:12-24
Luke 11:1-13

It is not God's will that anyone should be lost; God longs for all of us to be saved. Each one of the inhabitants of Sodom and Gomorrah was part of God's loving creation, and made in his image. Each person in Israel was known and loved. Those in every generation, who deliberately turn away and feed their selfish nature until they can no longer hear God's prompting, are all cherished and of God's making.

Today's readings remind us of that immense parental tenderness that God has for us. He creates us full of potential and watches over our spiritual growth, ready to bathe us in his light, and drench us in his Spirit. The tragedy is that we so often refuse to let him give us the gifts necessary for our growth.

In the Genesis reading we are given this lovely example of the close relationship shared by Abraham with his God. He is full of respect, and perfectly understands the justice of the threatened destruction, but he feels with his God's love the terrible sadness of waste, and pleads for mercy on behalf of those cities. How his pleading must have made God's heart sing, for here was a man loving in the broad and generous way he longed to see in all his creation.

The passage from Paul's letter to the Colossians urges his readers to let their growth in faith continue to flourish in Christ so that their lives overflow with thankfulness. It is not a question of everything happening at the beginning of our journey when we first commit ourselves. To grow, and to remain in close fellowship with God, we need constant filling up, feeding and guiding on a daily basis. The Bible, prayer and communion are gifts provided for us to use, and without taking God up on these gifts, our spiritual growth will weaken and become stunted.

In the Gospel for today, the disciples ask Jesus to teach them to pray, and the guidelines they are given have been valued by Christians of all denominations and traditions through the centuries. Luke links this teaching on prayer with a whole passage encouraging us to ask for what we need, and ask persistently. God will never force himself on anyone; he waits for us to invite him into our lives, and that is why it is so vital that we do ask and seek and knock at the door.

If we look at many of his acts of healing, we find Jesus often gets people to state what they want; that is part of the healing because God likes to work in partnership with us, not as a take-over bid. So he wants us to wake up each morning and ask that the kingdom may come, that we may have our daily needs provided – both physical and spiritual – and that we may have our sins forgiven and be guided safely through temptation. That way we shall be actively seeking the God who made us and loves us, and has ready all the gifts we need to bear fruit.

Discussion starters

1. Do we assume God to be more tolerant of wrong than he really is, or doubt that he can really be as forgiving as he is?

2. How would you help someone to understand God's character when they've prayed for something faithfully and it hasn't materialised?

All-stage talk

Bring along some strips of bedding plants, or a packet of seeds and a flourishing plant of the same or similar variety.

Proudly show the results of your horticultural exploits, and talk about what your hopes are for the seed or the tiny bedding plants. You don't really want them to stay as they are because, although the pictures on the labels show wonderful flowers or fruit, at present they are only dry dusty things, or boring leafy things, in spite of your recent planting efforts. What you are hoping is that they will eventually grow and flourish, until they flower and fruit as you know they can if all goes well.

That's how God feels about us. When he plants us into life, he knows we have lots of potential, lots of good possibilities. Since he loves us, he really hopes that we will grow, spiritually as well as in our bodies. He doesn't want us to stay the same as when we first begin in our Christian life, because he knows that if all goes well we shall one day be full of flowers and fruit that will help the world.

If I want my little plants to grow I will have to give them things like water and food, and make sure I give them plenty of light. And, being plants, they will just sit there and let me give them the things they need to grow nicely. I also need to talk to them!

God wants to give us lots of things to make us grow. He wants to drench us in his Spirit, warm us with the light of his love, and feed us with his word and in communion. He also wants to talk to us! But because we are humans, and not plants, we sometimes turn away from his light, and put up huge umbrellas against the rain of his Spirit, and refuse to let him feed us, and block our ears to stop ourselves hearing what he says. And when that happens, we stop growing and we wilt and weaken, and we never get to bear any fruit.

Today God is saying to us, 'Let me give you the gifts you need to grow as Christians; keep asking me for them, keep looking for me, and I promise that you will receive everything you need to grow into strong, healthy plants with beautiful flowers and fruit.'

All-age ideas

- Use the Lord's Prayer from Luke today.

- Decorate a door with flowers around it and a notice on it from Luke 11:9.

Prayer of the Faithful

Celebrant
Heavenly Father, as you have taught us,
through Jesus,
we come to you in prayer.

Reader
We pray for all who uphold and teach the faith,
for young Christians in schools and universities,
for Christians witnessing to their faith at work,
for all in danger of persecution.
We pray for strength and courage.

Silence

In all things, Father:
let your will be done.

We pray for discernment and wisdom
as we strive for international co-operation
in managing the world's resources;
for perseverance as we work
towards peace and reconciliation.

Silence

In all things, Father:
let your will be done.

We pray for the good sense
in our family and community life
that knows the difference
between generosity and indulgence,
between lenience and neglect of responsibility.

Silence

In all things, Father:
let your will be done.

We pray for all victims of abuse and tyranny,
for all who suffer long-term effects
of torture, war or disease;
we pray for the grace to forgive,
and for healing of body, mind and spirit.

Silence

In all things, Father:
let your will be done.

We pray for those who have died,
and particularly for those
who have no one to mourn their going;
for those who have died unnoticed.
We pray that they may rest in peace for ever.

Silence

In all things, Father:
let your will be done.

Mary's response prepared the way
for our salvation;
we make our prayer with her:
Hail, Mary . . .

In silence filled with love,
we name our particular prayer burdens.

Silence

Celebrant
God our Father,
rejoicing in your tenderness and compassion,
we bring these prayers before you.
Through Christ our Lord.
Amen.

TREASURE SEEKERS

Aim: To know that we can ask God for things, and
seek him.

Starter

Play hide and seek, either with people, or hunting
for a shoe.

Teaching

Talk about asking for things from our parents. If
you asked for some bread, would they give you a
stone? If you asked for fish and chips, would they give
you snake and chips? If you asked for an egg, would
they give you a scorpion? You can laugh together over
these, and they will see that although they might look
a bit alike, their parents would give them what was
good for them, not something that was bad for
them. Why? Because their parents love them.

Explain that one day Jesus was teaching the
people to pray, and he looked at how good parents
are at giving good gifts to the children they love.
Well, he said, it's just the same only more so with
God. He is a very loving parent to all his children,
and we can trust him never to give us anything
that would be bad for us.

Jesus wants us to ask him about things, and to
ask for his help, and to ask for the things we need.
If we ask for something that might not be best for
us at the moment, he will probably say, 'No' or
'Not yet'. As we learn to ask for things that he
wants for us as well, we shall find that he often
says, 'Yes, I'd like that too.' He might even ask our
help in getting things done.

Praying

Our Father in heaven,
please give us
all we need today. Amen.

Activities

On the worksheet there are activities to reinforce
the asking, seeking and knocking. They can also
make a model of an opening and closing door.

PEARL DIVERS

Aim: To look at the meaning of the Lord's prayer.

Starter

Play a game of hide and seek, or sardines, or look
for a hidden object, with clues of 'hotter' or 'colder'
only being given if they are asked for.

Teaching

Jesus often used to go off on his own to talk things
over with his Father in heaven and listen to his
Father's advice. Sometimes they would just be quiet
in one another's company. These times helped
Jesus have the wisdom and energy he needed to do
his work, as we mentioned last week.

His followers could see how useful those times were to Jesus, and they wanted to do it themselves but they didn't know how to. So they asked Jesus to teach them all how to pray. And this is what Jesus suggested they did.

1. Remember that God is your Father in heaven, and that he is holy.
2. Ask for the kingdom of God to come, and God's will to be done.
3. Ask for enough to eat and for your needs for the day.
4. Ask God to forgive your sins, just as you have forgiven people who have upset you.
5. Ask God to lead you safely through temptation and out of evil.

Have them written up on separate cards, and answer any questions about each one as you go along. Jumble them up and invite a couple of children to put them in the right order again. Then have someone reading each one out, and a pause for everyone to do what the card says. Introducing them to the meaning like this, before the traditional words, will prevent understanding being blocked by familiar but undigested words.

Now see if any of them know the traditional form of this teaching, known as the Lord's Prayer. Teach them these actions to do as they say it, to make sure they are praying, and not just reciting some instructions.

Our Father,
who art in heaven,
hallowed be thy name;
thy kingdom come; (LOOK DOWN)
thy will be done on earth
as it is in heaven. (LOOK UP)
Give us this day our daily bread; (CUP HANDS)
and forgive us our trespasses
as we forgive those
who trespass against us;
and lead us not into temptation,
but deliver us from evil.
Amen.

Praying

Use the Lord's Prayer with actions.

Activities

The instructions are written on the sheet so that they can be coloured, decorated and stuck on to the prayer corner made last week. There is also an activity looking at giving and gifts.

GOLD PANNERS

Aim: To know that God wants to save us and see us grow as Christians.

Starter

Tip out a pile of bits and pieces, and get everyone picking out the sweets from among the muddle.

Teaching

Explain about Sodom and Gomorrah in the Genesis passage. Here is an example of things getting so bad that the whole society is heading for destruction. But someone is prepared to plead for these people. Using different voices read the conversation with God and Abraham. Abraham was loving like God loves – wanting to save people. We put some effort into simply untangling the sweets. Since we are so precious to God, he puts in huge effort to sort us out.

Now look at the passage from Luke, and the way Jesus teaches his disciples about prayer. Go through each phrase, making sure the meaning is clear, and then read the section on asking. Does Jesus mean we can ask and receive anything we want? Why does he sometimes say 'No' or 'Not yet'? Why does he want us to ask?

When we enrol on a course, we couldn't at that stage take and pass the final exam. But the hope is that if we go to all the classes and do the work we're given, we'll end up confident to take the exam and pass it. When we commit ourselves as Christians, that's also like a beginning, and we'll only develop and bear spiritual fruit if we take advantage of the teaching and feeding God provides for us. We need to ask God for it, and go on asking and receiving.

Praying

Use the version of the Lord's Prayer in Luke's gospel.

Activities

There are instructions on the worksheet for making a prayer trail in the church or grounds which can become a resource for the whole parish.

EIGHTEENTH SUNDAY OF THE YEAR

Thought for the day

True richness is not material wealth; true security is not a financial matter.

Reflection on the readings

Ecclesiastes 1:2; 2:21-23
Psalm 94
Colossians 3:1-5, 9-11
Luke 12:13-21

Our culture runs on consumerism, and one of the side-effects of that is an encouragement of greed and increase in the daily temptation through the media to us that security, happiness and peace of mind come from possessions and self-indulgence. It is a myth which has enough truth in it to be dangerous. It undoubtedly helps to have enough to live on, but the wisdom of Mr Micawber holds true, all the same: living within our means is happiness where finances are concerned, and sixpence over that is misery! Many know the misery of accumulated debts resulting from the pressure to live beyond our means and spend what we actually haven't got.

It is a short step from being told that we haven't got something to believing we need (rather than want) it, especially if we can see others who already have it. The 'if only's set in, with their accompanying sense of discontent and resentment. Equally dangerous is the possession of financial 'security' which can kid us that we have no need of God, so that we shut down our spiritual antennae and grow increasingly oblivious to the needs of others and the glaring inequalities. The preoccupation with protecting what we own is good news for the insurance and home security firms, but bad news for the soul.

Today's readings point out the foolishness of living in this way, and the wisdom of living with our security in the eternal things. Now that Christ has given us a new life, our insurance – or perhaps I should say 'assurance' – is kept with Christ in heaven. The whole yardstick of life is changed, and our time here recognised as only the first part of our full and lasting life. When we really grasp the implications of what Jesus has done for us, it is bound to alter our outlook on what is important to possess and what is of only minimal value.

It is not so much a question of giving away our possessions as changing our attitude to them and recognising them for what they are – pleasant comforts to thank God for, but lent to us to use, as good stewards, and in no way altering our real wealth and security.

Discussion starters

1. Is it possible to live in our culture without becoming materialistic?

2. How can we help people see the value of this longer-lasting spiritual wealth? And do we still need convincing ourselves?

All-stage talk

You will need the packing boxes for various consumables, such as a computer, electronic game, microwave, brand-name shoes, or luxury biscuits. You will also need such things as a CD, gardening and teenage magazines, and a film carton. Choose the items to suit the interests of the people in your congregation, and have enough for one person to hold all at once with great difficulty. Finally, you need a pocket Bible and a tiny spray of flowers.

Remind everyone of the story Jesus told us in the Gospel today, about the farmer who thought that having a bumper harvest, and therefore a financial windfall, meant total security, so that he could just do as he liked and take no care of his soul. His greed had made him foolish. As it happened, he was going to die and face God that very night, and he wasn't in the least prepared for death.

Ask for a volunteer to help you explain something. Explain how all the advertisements tell us that if we get a particular brand of yoghurt or car or shampoo, everyone will like us and fancy us, and we'll be really happy. Sometimes we get taken in by this lie, and start wanting to have things so we'll be safer or happier or better liked.

Go through the things we like to get, piling the packages into the arms of the volunteer as you talk. When they are completely loaded up, and have no hands left to hold anything else, point out the problem with all this 'having' being important to us. It means that when Jesus offers us his Word and his Love (offer the Bible and flowers), we simply haven't room to take it, and we turn it down, because our minds are too full of what we've got and what we want, and how we're going to hang on to what we've got.

And that is a tragedy that lasts not just for a few years but for ever. We need to put down our wanting and having, so that we can take the really important wealth that God offers us. (The volunteer is helped to unload, so they can hold the Bible and flowers.) These are the things which will make us content and happy and secure, whether we have all the other good things or not.

All-age ideas

- Have a flower arrangement in a cash box. Or have buttercups and daisies in a simple and generous arrangement.

- Use the short sketch from the Boulders programme.

  A I've got a new bike with 36 gears.
  B Well I need a new bike with 36 gears. I'll ask my parents.
  C Why shouldn't I steal a decent bike? I'll never have the money to buy one.

  A I'm going to Florida again this year.
  B We might go to Florida if I can persuade Mum to work more hours.
  C It's not fair. Everybody else goes to Florida. We stay with Nan at Clacton.

  A I am a rich, complacent fool.
  B I am an envious fool.
  C I am a resentful fool.

  A, B, C And we're all trapped by money!

Prayer of the Faithful

Celebrant
Let us pray to God our Father,
knowing that we are all precious to him.

Reader
We pray for all those who give
to support the work of the Church;
may the Lord bless our giving,
guide our spending,
and help us to value the true wealth
of his abundant love.

Silence

The Lord is our shepherd:
there is nothing we shall want.

We pray for the world's economy;
for fair management and distribution of resources;
for fair trade and just wages;
for greater awareness and concern about injustice;
for a commitment to our responsibilities
as planet-sharers and earth-dwellers.

Silence

The Lord is our shepherd:
there is nothing we shall want.

We pray for all parents with young children;
may they be blessed and guided in their parenting;
we pray for families in debt;
for those whose homes have been repossessed,

and those whose financial security
makes them forgetful of God's love.

Silence

The Lord is our shepherd:
there is nothing we shall want.

We pray for those who are burdened
with financial worries
and all who struggle to make ends meet,
all over the world;
we pray for the emotionally and spiritually bankrupt,
and those who do not yet know God's love for them.

Silence

The Lord is our shepherd:
there is nothing we shall want.

We pray for those who have died,
and those on that last journey at this moment;
for a merciful judgement
and the everlasting joy of heaven.

Silence

The Lord is our shepherd:
there is nothing we shall want.

We pray with Mary,
who knew the true value of all things:
Hail, Mary . . .

In the silence of our hearts,
we bring to our heavenly Father
our needs and concerns.

Silence

Celebrant
Lord our God,
acknowledging your greatness,
we ask you to accept these prayers,
through Christ our Lord.
Amen.

TREASURE SEEKERS

Aim: To know that God looks after us like a loving parent looks after a young child.

Starter

If you have a parent who would be willing to bath a baby with the children there, that would be lovely. Or play a matching parents and babies game. Give each child the picture of an animal, and they have to go round the room looking for the baby picture that matches their adult animal.

Teaching

Talk about the different ways in which the people who love us look after us. On the worksheet there are some pictures to start you off. Tell them how God said to his people, 'I love you like that!' Teach them this song, sung to the tune of 'Three blind mice' and putting in all the children's names.

God loves Oliver.
God loves Louise.
God loves Jordan.
God loves Daisy.
He knows when they're friendly
and when they get mad,
he knows when they're happy
and when they are sad,
if they help each other it makes him feel glad,
'cos God loves us!

Praying

Dear Jesus,
your love makes me rich.
Thank you for giving me
so much love to love with!

Activities

The worksheet gets the children thinking of three people they love, and drawing what they would like to give them if they could give them anything at all. This will help them to pray for their three people, and help develop their ability to think in out-giving mode. If you have a garden or outside area they can gather some small flowers (daisies, buttercups, dandelions and bindweed are fine) and make a posy of them in wet cotton wool and foil to take into church and lay as thank-offerings in front of the altar. They can take their flowers home with them afterwards.

PEARL DIVERS

Aim: To look at real lasting wealth.

Starter

My aunt went to Paris. Sit in a circle. The first person says, 'My aunt went to Paris and she bought a . . .' They name something and mime it at the same time. The next person has to say this item followed by their own, and so on.

Teaching

Have a tape recording of excerpts from several current TV advertisements, and they can guess what item is being advertised. Point out that the fact we know these means that the adverts are working. Although this is good for the company who makes the chocolate or car, it can encourage us to be greedy, and discontented.

Show the children a timeline with 'Now' at the left end, an ongoing arrow at the right end and a point marked 'Death' about a third of the way along the line. Remind the children that our new life in Christ doesn't stop at death, but goes on for ever in heaven. The bit on earth here is only quite a short section of our whole life.

Lots of people put their trust in money and things, rather than in God. They forget that these can only last up to death, at the very most. If they've spent no time getting the long-lasting spiritual treasure, then they're going to have to spend an awfully long time without anything.

Tell the story of the rich fool, using the script below.

Music from Beethoven's *Pastoral Symphony* fades in.

Narrator	There was once a rich man who had a very good harvest.
	(Sound of running)
Slave	Master! Master!
Rich man	*(Snoring; wakes up)* Oh! Yes – what is it, slave?
Slave	Master, we've filled all the barns with the crops but there's still lots more left to store.
Rich man	*(Laughs)* Well, well! Such a good harvest that there's no room to store my crops, eh? Now what can I do about that, I wonder.
Slave	Perhaps you could give some away?
Rich man	What! Good heavens, no! I know what I'll do. Slave – start pulling the barns down.
Slave	Pull them down, Master? B . . . b . . . but we've only just filled them up.
Rich man	Then empty them, you fool! We're going to build *enormous* barns – enough to hold all my grain.
Slave	Very well, Master; your wish is my command. *(Runs off. His voice is heard in the distance)* Come on, lads, get busy. All the grain is to be moved.
Other slaves	*(Groaning)* Oh no! What on earth for? After all that work, etc.

(Sounds of workers pouring grain fades into music. Music fades into building sounds.)

Slave driver Come on there, stop wasting time.
(Sound of whip)

Rich man Ah, good, the new barns are splendid! Keep up the good work. *(Music fades in)* Now I've got so much grain I can enjoy myself for years to come. I think I'll start with a feast. No more worries for me! *(Sounds of eating and drinking)*
(Cymbal, or saucepan lids)

God Fool! Fool! *(Cymbal)*

Rich man *(Flustered)* Eh? Oh, my goodness, who said that?
(Cymbal)

God I, God, tell you that you are a fool! This very night you are going to die. What use will your hoard of grain be to you then? *(Cymbal)* What use will your hoard of grain be to you then?
(Music fades in to finish)

Narrator So the man saw that getting rich did not make him safe and secure.

Praying

Thank you, Father,
for showing us a new way to live,
trusting in your love
and building treasure in heaven.

Activities

On the worksheet there is an activity to help them weigh up the better bargain: being rich or being loved – being happy because you've just bought a CD or being happy because you know God loves you? Try making the script into a radio play, with sound effects. It could then be used for a parish performance, or study day.

GOLD PANNERS

Aim: To explore what is real wealth.

Starter

On a long roll of wallpaper, stick a line of objects from magazines and catalogues. Split people into pairs and one of each pair looks at the line of objects as it is pulled past them (as on a game show). Then they have to tell their partner all the things they can remember, with the partner writing them down. Both get a Smartie or a penny for each object remembered.

Teaching

Read the Gospel for today, putting in sound effects and having different voices. Notice what had happened just before Jesus told the rich fool story, and that will help them get at what the parable is about. Use the shields on the worksheet to record ideas about the different things people use to protect themselves and make them feel safe and secure. Matching the 'sell-by date' of each with the timeline will draw them to see the limited value of some things and the good, lasting value of others.

Once again this week we are reminded of God's steadfast love and faithfulness, and his longing for us all to be rescued.

Praying

Lord, loving you
makes me happy and free.
No money can buy that.
Your offer is a complete bargain –
thank you for giving me
what I could never earn. Amen.

Activities

There is a short script on the worksheet to try, and this could be done in church. Accompanying cartoon sketches can be drawn on a flip chart or blackboard, or on acetates if you have an OHP.

NINETEENTH SUNDAY OF THE YEAR

Thought for the day

Have faith in God, and get yourself ready to meet him.

Reflection on the readings

Wisdom 18:6-9
Psalm 32
Hebrews 11:1-2, 8-19
Luke 12:32-48

The Gospel reading for today begins with such an affectionate reassurance. It is God's good pleasure and delight to give us the kingdom; everything is in hand, and nothing can ever tear us apart from the God who loves us. The only way separation can happen is by us choosing to walk away ourselves. So our God has us safe and expectant, knowing that there are great things in store for us both in this world and the next, even though we cannot see them.

And that is the faith God looks for in his people: believing the hope as a fact and trusting that what God has promised will indeed happen. The reading from Hebrews recalls the extraordinary faith of Abraham, God's close friend, in the way he was prepared to launch out into the unknown on many occasions, simply because God told him to. Not only did he believe that God had authority which asked for obedience; he also knew that God's responsible, caring nature would ensure that placing himself in the hands of his Lord was a sensible and safe thing to do.

So Abraham's faith determined how he lived. That always happens; you cannot trust the one true God and go on behaving with corruption, deceit, injustice or self-glory which you know to be totally alien to his nature. But it is, of course, perfectly possible to pretend you have faith, and go through the rituals of words and worship, while your eyes stoically avoid God's gaze, and your life proclaims that you actually despise the one you claim to worship.

It was exactly this which so wounded the heart of God about the people of Israel, to whom Isaiah was sent. How could God accept their offerings when they were living a lie? Hypocrisy and corruption creep up on us insidiously, minor detail by minor detail, so that we end up fooling ourselves that wrong is right. Sometimes we can fool others, too. But God we do not fool, and his reaction is to try to shake us out of the lie we are in, because he hates us being there and knows it causes all kinds of stress, whether we recognise that or not.

Having faith means looking seriously at the God we claim to believe in, and checking that our lives, in every aspect, in secret and in the open, are lined up with those qualities of truth, love, integrity and right action which are hallmarks of God and his friends.

Discussion starters

1. Why are we often more ready to check our standards against other people we know than against the nature of God, as shown to us in the person of Jesus?

2. Has your faith in God ever forced you to take decisions which you found very difficult? Was it worth it?

All-stage talk

You will need a pair of swimming flippers. Have ready a couple of large freezer labels with the words 'I believe in God' written on them.

Ask for a volunteer to walk up and down the church, so that everyone can see the way this person normally walks. Now give them the flippers to wear. As they are being put on, explain that today's readings teach us about how our faith in God affects the way we live. Remind them of Abraham and the way he was ready to get up and go when God asked him to, even though he didn't know exactly how the move would work out. He trusted God to want the best for him, and had faith that God would look after him.

Now that the volunteer is wearing flippers, is he going to walk in the same way as before? Well, let's see. As the person walks up and down, point out that we can all see the effect the flippers are having on the walking – it's a very distinctive flipper walk!

Put the freezer labels on the flippers, explaining that when we decide to walk with faith in God, that is going to affect the way we walk through life. It will give us a very distinctive faith walk. The readings today tell us the kind of things to expect. We will be stopping doing what is wrong and learning to do what is right. We will be noticing the needs of those around us and in our world, and making sure we help out with our time and prayers and money. We will be building up treasure in heaven by our loving kindness, patience, honesty, thoughtfulness and self-control.

All-age ideas

- The parables in the Gospel can be mimed while it is being read.

- In a flower arrangement express the idea of treasure by the container chosen, and have treasure items included in the arrangement. Have the text of Luke 12:34 beside it.

Prayer of the Faithful

Celebrant
As God's beloved children,
let us come to him and open our hearts to him.

Reader
The Father knows both our gifts as a congregation
and the needs of those in this parish;
we ask him to bless our ministry in this place,
to strengthen and encourage all Church leaders
and to deepen our faith and sure hope.

Silence

Lord our God:
we believe and trust in you.

We pray that the Father may heal our nation
and all the nations
of what is in the past and still corrodes the present,
so that we may build on good foundations
and learn to govern ourselves with honesty,
respect for one another and sensitivity to needs.

Silence

Lord our God:
we believe and trust in you.

We pray that the Father may be present
in the daily living of our homes
and in all our relationships,
and make us more trustworthy in our friendships,
and strengthen our resolve to live our faith in action.

Silence

Lord our God:
we believe and trust in you.

We call to mind all whose capacity to trust
has been damaged;
for those who are victims of injustice or corruption;
for the very young and the very old,
the frail, the vulnerable and the bereaved.

Silence

Lord our God:
we believe and trust in you.

We remember those
who have completed their earthly life in faith
and have now seen the Lord face to face.
May they know the peace of eternity;
we too look forward to sharing that life of joy.

Silence

Lord our God:
we believe and trust in you.

We make our prayer with Mary,
who was ever watchful in God's service:
Hail, Mary . . .

We pray in silence
to God, who knows our needs.

Silence

Celebrant
God our Father, accept our prayers;
as we learn to trust more in your promise,
may we grow to be more like Christ
and reflect the radiance of his love.
Through the same Christ, our Lord.
Amen.

TREASURE SEEKERS

Aim: To know that God can be trusted.

Starter

Play 'Simon says'. Point out that we had to make sure we only listened to Simon's instructions. We knew if we did that we wouldn't get it wrong.

Teaching

Bring a clock along, with the time an hour fast. Bring one of those pop-up toys which you press down and they suddenly surprise you by popping up before you expected.

As you start, pretend to have just noticed the time on the clock and the time gives you a shock – it's already time we were in church! Then you check with your watch and are very relieved that the clock must be wrong. You know you can trust your watch because you checked that against the television just before you came out.

Talk about there being some things you get to know you can trust, and other things let you down. Share stories about car breakdowns, toys that break, and so on.

We can trust God because he doesn't have 'off' days or go into a sulk. He doesn't move away just when you're getting to know him, and he doesn't go away on holiday. He doesn't have times when you can't get in touch with him. He's always there for us and always fair and loving. So we can trust God with all our fears and our hopes and dreams, all the things that upset us and all the things we're looking forward to. We can trust him with our secrets. He will stay our friend right through to when we're grown up, right to when we get old and even when we've died – he'll still be our friend. By the time we die we will have got to know and love him very well, and he will welcome us into heaven to enjoy being with him for ever.

Praying

Dear Jesus,
it's good to know
I can always trust you.
You are always there for me.
Thank you!

Activities

If you can borrow a parachute, you can play some games which build trust and co-operation – working together to make a ball bounce high, and creating a 'mushroom' shape and running underneath it one by one. Or help one another to complete a floor jigsaw. The worksheet gives them space to create a composite picture of themselves and their life, putting in such things as their favourite colours and animals, pastimes and people.

PEARL DIVERS

Aim: To know the importance of keeping ready.

Starter

'What's the time, Mr Wolf?' or a similar 'creeping-up' kind of game. Talk about the way you had to keep alert because you didn't know exactly when you were going to have to run, or when Mr Wolf would turn round.

Teaching

Remind the children that after Jesus died and rose again he went to live in heaven. (Let them tell you, if they know.) But one day he will come back, and he hopes that we'll still be watchful and ready for him when he comes.

How do people keep themselves prepared for helping at accidents? They learn first aid and they practise so they don't forget. How do we make sure we're prepared for a cycling test? We learn how to cycle safely and then practise. What about being prepared for Jesus – how can we do that? It's the same; we need to learn how to live his way and then keep practising. Point out that they are all learning week by week when they come to Pearl Divers, and when they read the Bible. They practise all through the week, doing their praying, and choosing how to behave. Sometimes we get it wrong, but the important thing is to keep trying.

Get some of the children to act out the parables of the master finding the faithful servants and waiting on them for a change, and the burglars not being able to rob the house because the owner is being very tiresome and keeping watch.

Praying

Lord Jesus,
I want you to find me
watching faithfully
when you come again.

Activities

On the worksheet there is a picture to colour of fire-fighters getting ready to rush to a fire. The quiz linked to it can be used to start discussion about our spiritual readiness. There is a cartoon to draw to reinforce the teaching, and an activity which requires Bibles so they can look up the Luke references.

GOLD PANNERS

Aim: To explore how to live our faith in readiness.

Starter

Any team game where the team members have to be ready to run as soon as the previous person gets back to base.

Teaching

Read Luke 12:39-40 and refer to the worksheet so they can have their burglar conversations in pairs. Then read the whole of the Luke Gospel passage, making a note of the verses which are full of encouragement and hope, and the ones which ring warning bells. There is space to record this on the sheet.

Then read the Hebrews passage, with Abraham's example of living by faith, and in the light of what you have discovered from the other readings, think about any corruption or injustices in society which need sorting out.

Praying

We wait in hope for the Lord;
he is our help and our shield.
In him our hearts rejoice,
for we trust in his holy name.
May your unfailing love rest upon us, O Lord,
even as we put our hope in you.

(From Psalm 32)

Activities

Any wrongs that have been noticed can be addressed by writing letters to those concerned.

TWENTIETH SUNDAY OF THE YEAR

Thought for the day

When we fix our eyes on Jesus our lives will reflect his nature.

Reflection on the readings

Jeremiah 38:4-6, 8-10
Psalm 39
Hebrews 12:1-4
Luke 12:49-53

Many parents have high hopes for their children.

Musical toys are given encouragingly to offspring who start singing in tune before they can talk. Balls to kick around are bought partly for fun and partly to foster any latent talent. Financial sacrifices are made for children showing potential in particular sports or arts. It would be cynical to think that all this is 'pushy parent syndrome'; mostly it shows the natural pride and delight of parents in the children they love.

God, too, has high hopes for the children he loves. He delights in our progress, and looks out for the seeds of gifts he has given us to blossom; he loves to watch us using these gifts for the good of the world. Today we sense God's sadness as he looks for the good and wholesome we are capable of as his creation, and finds instead destructive selfishness, bloodshed and cries of distress. We all know the aching disappointment of an attempt which has failed, in spite of the lavish care we have invested in it. Sadly we have to recognise that sometimes our behaviour, both collectively and individually, disappoints our parent God.

Such behaviour and attitudes are a waste of our life. The writer of the letter to the Hebrews urges us to get rid of everything that hinders and entangles us, so that we can run the race more easily and comfortably. And the best way of doing that is by keeping our sights fixed on Jesus. It is noticeable throughout history that whenever people have done this they have been enabled to bring about great good, both within the Church and in society. It is when their eyes swivel round to fix on other things that corruption, distortion of truth, and injustice start taking over. Rather like bindweed, they can look attractive, but throttle the life out of whatever they climb over. And the roots need to be totally eradicated to prevent strong regrowth. Jesus warns his followers that the path of righting deep-rooted wrong will not be straightforward or without radical disturbance and upheaval, not only in individuals, but also in families and nations and church communities.

Discussion starters

1. Why do we prefer to run cluttered when it would obviously be easier to be free?

2. If God is a God of peace, why is Jesus promising conflict?

All-stage talk

Beforehand prepare a number of heavy carrier bags and a rucksack, and have a sack or strong dustbin bag. Label the bags 'I want my own way', 'It isn't fair', 'So what?', 'I'll never forgive them' and 'No one will notice'. Also bring the local school's PE kit.

Begin by showing everyone the PE kit and draw from them what it is, who wears it, and why we do PE dressed like this instead of in our best clothes, or in bridesmaids' dresses, or Mickey Mouse suits. Establish that it's more practical and comfortable to wear light clothes like this which don't get in the way of our running and jumping.

Refer to the letter to the Hebrew Christians in which following Jesus through our lives is said to be a bit like running a race: we need to look where we're going. That means keeping our eyes on Jesus and his way of living. This will keep us on the right track in our own lives, reminding us to be honest instead of telling lies, thinking of other people's needs instead of just wanting our own way, and sharing our ideas and fears with God instead of ignoring him most of the time.

But often we run our Christian life in very unsuitable clothes. At this point ask for a volunteer, and load them up with all the bags, explaining what each represents, and how we weigh ourselves down with all this luggage. As you hand over the sack for them to stand in, point out how difficult we make it for ourselves by hanging on to all these attitudes which make Christian living extra hard. The volunteer can try running to prove the point.

Today we are being given a useful tip for Christian living: get rid of all these unhelpful habits (name them as you take them from the volunteer), so that we are free to run God's race-track uncluttered and 'light'. Then we can concentrate on Jesus, and learn to live his way – the way of love.

All-age ideas

• Have a display, linked with a flower arrangement, of a PE kit or an athlete's running kit and trophy.

• Collect newspaper pictures and headlines from the week which direct people to pray for the needs of our world. These are held, or fixed on pew ends, the floor, pillars and doors, and people are invited to walk slowly around the church building, being the Church in action as they pray for the concerns they see. The choir or music group will help people's prayer if they sing something like O Lord, hear my prayer (Taizé) while people are quietly moving around the church praying either silently or in small groups.

Prayer of the Faithful

Celebrant
God is close to us as we pray.
He is attentive to us now.

Reader
Whenever the Lord weeps over our harshness, may his tears melt our hearts of stone.

Whenever he grieves over our double standards,
may we be shocked into honesty again.
May he make us receptive to his teaching,
willing to take risks
and eager to run with our eyes fixed on him.

Silence

Lead us, Lord:
to walk in your ways.

Whenever the news overwhelms us,
may the Lord nudge us to fervent prayer.
Wherever leaders meet to negotiate peace,
may he be present at the conference table.
May he breathe his values into our thinking,
tear down the divisive barriers
and renew us to lead the world into loving.

Silence

Lead us, Lord:
to walk in your ways.

We pray that whenever tempers are frayed
and patience is wearing thin,
the Spirit may give us space
to collect ourselves and try again.
Whenever the demands of family and friends
remind us of our limitations,
may the Spirit minister graciously
through our weakness
and teach us the humility of apologising.

Silence

Lead us, Lord:
to walk in your ways.

Whenever people are enveloped by pain
or desolate grief or total exhaustion,
may the Spirit bring refreshment and peace,
tranquillity and hope,
and wherever the grip of the past
prevents free movement into the future,
bring release and healing.

Silence

Lead us, Lord:
to walk in your ways.

We pray for the dying,
especially those who are fearful and distressed;
may they be comforted and reassured
on that last journey.
May those who care for them
and those who mourn their going be blessed.

Silence

Lead us, Lord:
to walk in your ways.

We make our prayer with Mary,
Mother of our Saviour:
Hail, Mary . . .

Trustingly we pray in silence
to God our Father,
who considers each one of us special.

Silence

Celebrant
Loving Father, hear our prayers,
through Christ our Lord.
Amen.

TREASURE SEEKERS

Aim: To learn that God likes us and wants the best
for us.

Starter

Pass the parcel. Make sure everyone has a turn (if
necessary, have several parcels with several small
groups). Each layer contains a freezer label with
'I'm special' written on it. Eventually every child is
wearing one.

Teaching

Pass round a flower each for the children to hold,
and talk together about what it is like – what its
petals and leaves look like, what it smells and feels
like, and so on. Marvel over all the care that God
has taken in bringing a flower like this into being.

Now pass round something else to enjoy and
notice, such as feathers, stones or vegetables. Again
draw their attention to all the care God has taken
over these things.

Collect everything in and say we've got another
collection of beautiful, amazing things God has
made. Get everyone to stand up in the circle and
hold hands. At the moment they are making a sort
of chain, but they aren't daisies. At the moment
they are quiet, but they can speak. What – or who –
can they be? It's us!

Sit everyone down and go round the group
picking out one nice thing about everyone, and
then enthuse together over the loving care God has
taken over each one of us. No wonder God likes us
and thinks us all very special.

Praying

Thank you, God,
for making me
and knowing me
and liking me.
It's special being special!

Activities

Make finger-print pictures, using shallow trays of paint and hand-washing bowls between colours. Some suggestions for making their prints into people and objects are given on the worksheet.

PEARL DIVERS

Aim: To learn about fixing our eyes on Jesus and running the race unhindered.

Starter

Loads of fun. This team game involves the first team member running up to a point, collecting a heavy bag and lugging it back to the team. The second team member lugs it back, dumps it and runs back. The next collects it, and so on. The team with most luggage journeys logged in the time allocated wins.

Teaching

Point out how much everyone was slowed down by the weight of the luggage, and also how much easier it is to run to the right place if we look where we're going.

Bring out an envelope (stamped and franked) and explain how some of the early Christian leaders wrote letters to keep in touch with the churches. The Bible has collected some of these old letters, written nearly two thousand years ago, so that we can still read them today. So this letter (not the actual envelope, though!) has been around a very long time. We're not even sure who wrote it, but it's got such useful hints in it that it's well worth reading.

Take out the letter, and read the first introductory section to Hebrews, followed by the *International Children's Bible* (New Century) version of today's reading. Draw attention to how it fits in with what we found in our game, about running light and fixing our eyes on Jesus.

Talk about people who can't enjoy what they've got because they're always wishing they had something better or different, and it turns them into unhappy moaners. God wants them to be free of the 'wanting' so they can enjoy life whatever they have or haven't got.

Talk about people who want to boss their friends around all the time, and end up without friends or with people scared of them. Their bossiness and bullying is like a heavy bag they're carrying, and it stops them really enjoying life. God wants them to put it down so they can play with other children and be happy.

If we are carrying any habits like moaning or bossiness, or keeping an enemy or winding someone

up all the time, the writer of this letter from the Roman world is saying, 'Why don't you put that down today, and fix your eyes on Jesus, so you can live free and happy?'

Praying

Lord Jesus,
I'm going to run the race
with my eyes
fixed on you.
And if I get cluttered
with silly or bad habits,
please remind me
to put them down
so I can run free.

Activities

On the worksheet there are instructions for making a race game. It requires two fridge magnets for each child.

GOLD PANNERS

Aim: To recognise that following Jesus may well bring us into conflict.

Starter

Any game with goals and two sides playing against one another, such as football, netball, basketball or non-contact rugby.

Teaching

Draw attention to the way we kept the goal in sight as we aimed for it, and how we met opposition as we got involved in the game.

Read the passage from Hebrews, followed by today's Gospel from Luke, and see how these readings pick up on the importance of looking where you're going spiritually, putting aside any distractions or clutter as we concentrate on Jesus, and also the inevitability of conflict. This will probably increase as we get more committed to following Jesus, just as the opposition in our game was less if we stood around on the edge of the action, but became more intense if we were setting up the possibility of a goal.

Don't side-step the question of evil and Satan's dislike of Christian commitment. It is most important that our young people recognise the nature of the battle and are prepared for it. We aren't in the business of scaremongering or demon-spotting, but evil is a reality they are familiar with, and today's readings provide a good opportunity for exploring this area.

Praying

I waited, I waited for the Lord
and he stooped down to me;
he heard my cry.

(From Psalm 39)

Activities

Put together a short article for the magazine or handout which gives the congregation some idea of the areas of conflict resulting from following Jesus which the young people regularly face. Or this can be designed, with pictures and border designs, so as to be photocopied and given out for prayer support.

TWENTY-FIRST SUNDAY OF THE YEAR

Thought for the day

At the great and final gathering-in, it will be a question of each person's chosen life direction, and each response to the way of God.

Reflection on the readings

Isaiah 66:18-21
Psalm 116
Hebrews 12:5-7, 11-13
Luke 13:22-30

The prophecy from Isaiah reminds the people of Israel that through their nation the entire world will be blessed. From a chosen individual – Abraham – and his family, through the nation of his descendants and on outwards to embrace the whole of creation, God's saving plan moves forward, and the inference is that God is more than happy to include all kinds of present 'outsiders'. For the people of Israel, there is the choice either to rejoice with their God in such an amazing harvest, or to see it as a threat to their own identity and special calling.

The reading from Hebrews faces up to the fact that useful disciplining is invariably unpleasant at the time, and any of the Jewish people who are feeling disciplined can actually be comforted by the truth that if God didn't care so much about them, he wouldn't bother to correct them. The very chastising is a mark of his love for them, and for us. We so easily protest against any hardships, and sometimes fail to see how they can be a wonderfully valuable learning experience.

In today's Gospel, Jesus is concerned to make it quite clear that no one can assume they have a pre-booked seat as far as eternal life is concerned. We cannot earn that, either through effort or through birth, because the truth is that none of us is worthy to receive eternal life, and the only way we can be a part of it is through Jesus. He is the only worthy one, and we share eternity on the merits of his total love. Whether or not we are recognisable as people found in Christ will depend on the way we have chosen to live, each second of our time here.

Discussion starters

1. Are we still trying to earn a place in the eternity of God's heaven?

2. How can we make sure that God recognises us in order to welcome us into eternal life as true followers of Christ?

All-stage talk

Beforehand collect four shoe boxes, and in one of them place a pair of binoculars.

Ask a volunteer who wears glasses to help you with the talk. Ask her to stand where most people can see her, and put four chairs around her, not quite near enough for her to touch. Blindfold the volunteer, or ask her to keep her eyes shut. On each of the chairs place a box, and in the box containing binoculars also place her glasses. Turn the volunteer to face an empty box.

Point out how (Helen) needs her glasses, and life is very difficult for her because we've taken away her glasses and even covered her eyes! We may sometimes feel that God has done this to us – when everything we hoped for or felt sure of suddenly seems taken away. Or perhaps our best friend moves away, or there are rows at home, and suddenly we don't know exactly where we are or which way to turn. Perhaps we feel let down by God.

Today's readings tell us that God doesn't let us down. Ever. Sometimes he draws back from us a little to encourage us to walk in faith – like when we encourage our children to walk or cycle by moving away from them.

Sometimes the hardest times we have are the times we learn most or get closest to trusting God our loving Father. The secret is to turn in the right direction, because God is the One who has both power and inclination to help. His motive is ardent love for his precious child. If we turn any other way and walk in that direction, we will face emptiness and disappointment. (Help Helen to turn in each wrong direction, open the shoe box and not find her glasses.) But if we turn in God's direction and walk his ways (turn Helen the right way), then we will find fulfilment, just as Helen has found her glasses. And it's often far more than we would have dared hope. Helen has actually found more than just her glasses – there's binoculars here as well, so she can see much further than usual!

All-age ideas

- The Isaiah passage works well read chorally, with voices of different tones – low, medium and high. Work through copies of the passage, experimenting with what combination of voices best brings out the meaning and the poetry. Aim to emphasise the sense of a great gathering in of all the nations.

- Have large letters – N, S, E and W – fixed on the appropriate walls or on the floor of the church.

Prayer of the Faithful

Celebrant
Trusting not in ourselves but in God's mercy, let us pray.

Reader
That in all the decisions and activities of the church, we may be slow to rush ahead of God's guiding yet quick to follow where he leads.

Silence

In you, O Lord:
we place our trust.

That in all the hardships and dangers of life, in all the crises, conflicts and injustices, we may keep clear-sighted and attentive to God's will.

Silence

In you, O Lord:
we place our trust.

That with our friends, neighbours and loved ones, and those we are tempted to despise or dismiss, we may have many opportunities for loving service.

Silence

In you, O Lord:
we place our trust.

That in those who live fearfully, God may breathe his peace, and on those who are ill and frail, he may place healing hands.

Silence

In you, O Lord:
we place our trust.

That God's comfort may surround all who are dying unrecognised or unnoticed, and that all who die in God's friendship may be welcomed into eternity with him.

Silence

In you, O Lord:
we place our trust.

We join our prayers with those of Mary, our spiritual Mother:
Hail, Mary . . .

Confident in God's welcoming love, we pray in silence now, for our own particular needs and concerns.

Silence

Celebrant
God our Father, accept these prayers, through Christ our Lord.
Amen.

TREASURE SEEKERS

Aim: To know that God teaches us to love, and looks after us when we make mistakes.

Starter

Share each other's stories of times when we have been frightened or scared, and what helped us to be brave.

Teaching

Sometimes we have to do things which are frightening or which hurt. Some people don't like taking medicine, but we know we have to take it if we are ill, so that we get better. We have injections (which aren't much fun) because they are good for us and stop us getting ill. Sometimes our mums and dads make us sit still and quiet so that the other people in the family can watch a programme they like.

All through our lives we are learning, and sometimes the learning gives us bumps and bruises (like when we fall off our bikes or graze our knees).

God has given us a whole lifetime to spend, with a wonderful world to live in, and our job is to learn how to love. We start learning this as soon as we are born and we go on learning it till we die. And sometimes it hurts. But our God is always there with us, helping us learn, and comforting us when we make mistakes. It is God who teaches us how to love, and every time you find yourself not wanting to be kind and helpful and thoughtful,

TWENTY-FIRST SUNDAY OF THE YEAR 165

that's when you are being given your practice to do. It is hard to be loving when we don't want to be, and we need all the practice we can get.

Praying

Lord God, thank you for loving us
and giving us such a good world to live in.
Teach us how to live good and loving lives.
Amen.

Activities

On the sheet they can recognise objects based on the clues which leaders read out to them, and they can play a 'Bingo' type game, looking in a picture for people being given practice in loving. When they spot some forgiving or sharing going on, they place a counter or a card shape over the square until all six counters are on the picture, making the Jesus sign of love – a cross.

PEARL DIVERS

Aim: To be introduced to Jesus' teaching about the narrow door, and the way to eternal life.

Starter

Give out needles and thread, and see who is the fastest at threading a needle. Now try with wool and see if anyone can manage it. Or they could try squashing a sleeping bag into its sack.

Teaching

Beforehand prepare a narrow gateway, perhaps from two chairs with tall cardboard against them, or two leaders standing back to back. You'll also need some bulky parcels such as rolled sleeping bags, huge balloons, large cartons tied with string and so on.

Explain that Jesus was always wanting to help people understand about the important things like life and death, and why we are alive, and what happens when we die. All humans wonder about these things. Jesus could see that some people obviously thought they were definitely going to be OK when they died because they were Jewish and part of God's chosen people. Jesus wanted to show them that we can't earn a place in heaven by working hard, and we can't buy a ticket for it either. This is how Jesus explained it.

He said that getting to heaven is rather like having to go through a very narrow gate. We've just been finding out how hard it is to get a thick piece of

wool through a narrow needle, and a huge sleeping bag through the narrow opening of its sack.

Load a volunteer up with all the bulky parcels and explain that our problem with getting through a narrow gate is all the baggage we carry with us. We carry bags of 'I want', parcels of 'doubt', sacks of 'I've got to be better than anyone else' and boxes of 'I love me'. (The volunteer can demonstrate how hard it is to get through the narrow gate with this lot.)

What Jesus was saying was that entering the everlasting happiness of heaven is like going through a narrow gate because we just can't take any of this luggage with us. All God wants is for us to be ourselves, honestly and humbly trusting Jesus. Then it doesn't matter that the gate is narrow, because we're not trying to get our cool image through with us, or any of the other things. None of us deserves a place in heaven; we can only receive it as a free gift from the Jesus we know and love. And he will give us that gift when he recognises us.

Praying

Lord Jesus, I want you to recognise me
as one of your followers.
Give me the courage to follow you
and learn from you about real loving.
Amen.

Activities

On the sheet there is a wordsearch for keywords of today's teaching, and a model to make of the narrow gate. The children will need soft modelling clay (like plasticine) to make the person and all the bags.

GOLD PANNERS

Aim: To look at Jesus' criteria for entering the eternity of heaven.

Starter

The group gets itself into a line in order, according to different criteria, so it will probably change each time: 1. shoe size, 2. height, 3. age, 4. how much television watched yesterday, 5. colour of hair (dark to light).

Teaching

In that exercise they might have sometimes been first in the order, and last at other times. It all depends what the order is based on. In today's readings we are looking at the pecking order for eternal life and how it turns out to be a bit different from what some people think.

First read the Isaiah prophecy, putting it in its context of the returned exiled people of Israel, who were beginning to understand that God's plans for saving the world were wider than bringing them out of slavery in Egypt, and were going to include all nations. It must have felt a bit like the coach announcing that (Manchester United) will soon be recruiting tennis and hockey players as well, and enlarging the team to include all the spectators. From our standpoint it seems quite obvious, though, because, after all, most of us are those outsiders God was planning to bring in!

Now read today's Gospel, where Jesus is warning people not to assume they'll have automatic entry to eternal life just because of their Jewish genes, or because they've been to the synagogue regularly. In fact, he says, there is no automatic entry, and we can't work hard to earn our place in heaven, either. The whole thing seems to hinge on whether or not we are recognisable as friends of Jesus. If, by our motives, attitudes and actions, we can be recognised as such, then it's through Jesus opening the way to us that we walk freely in. And we need to remember that while people look on outward appearance, the Lord looks at the heart.

Finally read the passage from Hebrews. Having read that Gospel we begin to realise that we need some heart-training and we need it fast! The writer prepares us for what will happen if we are serious about wanting to grow more like Jesus. It may hurt, just as getting fit hurts. Sometimes we'll feel as if we're making real progress, and at other times God will seem to have distanced himself. All this is part of the training, and a sure sign that God loves us enough to bother with us.

Praying

O Jesus, I have promised
to serve thee to the end;
be thou for ever near me,
my Master and my friend:
I shall not fear the battle
if thou art by my side,
nor wander from the pathway
if thou wilt be my guide.

Activities

On the sheet there is a physical and spiritual fitness link, and they continue to explore what Jesus sees as of most importance for us, contrasting that with what we, both as individuals and as the Church, often see as important.

TWENTY-SECOND SUNDAY OF THE YEAR

Thought for the day

When we live God's way, both individually and as a community, we will be greatly blessed.

Reflection on the readings

Ecclesiasticus 3:17-20, 28-29
Psalm 67
Hebrews 12:18-19, 22-24
Luke 14:1, 7-14

Often when people are first converted, they are bursting to tell people about the God they have just discovered, and can't understand how anyone could not want what they have found, even though for years they themselves have also been struggling with leaking wells without realising the reality of God's alternative. The more Christians there are gossiping the good news among their own contacts in a regular, informal and friendly way, the more chance there is of people hearing about God's offer at the point when their hearts are ready to listen.

It was at a 'Sunday dinner' equivalent, as one of the guests, that Jesus brought the conversation round to what people needed to hear, spoken anecdotally and through the after-dinner stories. They described a way of thinking that was quite radical, turning accepted values upside-down and suggesting a way of living which could liberate people and transform them.

The reading from Ecclesiasticus provides us with some good, practical guidelines for living God's way, both as individuals and as a community. All the behaviour described is a natural result of loving one another as brothers and sisters – as 'family'. There is a great need for the importance of community, with the mutual care and respect that results from being bound together in love. Perhaps we need to recover some enthusiasm for community again, and recognise that in God's way of living, individuals have a calling and a responsibility to be members of a corporate unit of loving: the Church of God.

Discussion starters

1. Is it running counter-cultural to be humble, or are truly humble people respected?

2. Although we hear Jesus' teaching, does our list of friends show that we have taken it on board?

All-stage talk

Beforehand prepare two chunks of wood, which should be quite different from each other. From each cut a small chip.

First give out the two chips of wood and show everyone the blocks they came from. Ask a cluster of people round each chip to decide which block their chip came from. How can they tell? (Perhaps by the way it feels and looks and smells; by the colour and the grain.)

In our readings today we are hearing quite a bit about humility, and there's a good reason for this. We are made in the image of God, which means we should be like chips off the old block. People should be able to look at us and the way we think and feel and behave, and see that we are children of our heavenly Father. And one of the great hallmarks of God is *humility*.

Jesus, the Word or Expression of God, had been present when our universe first began. He knew all about the excitement of stars bursting into being, planets being formed and all the ideas of creation taking shape. But in order to put us right and give us life that doesn't end, he was quite prepared to put all that aside and become a human baby, starting at the weakest level. God was humble enough to become one of the creatures he had made.

Like these chips of wood, whatever kind of people we are on the inside will show in the way we behave on the outside. So rather than working on doing things we think will impress people (even humble things like taking the lowest place), God is inviting us to work with him on a transforming process from the inside. He can make us the kind of people who are naturally full of humility, simply because we are more and more like God himself.

All-age ideas

- Make some tiny posies of flowers which match up with the colours of the main flower arrangement. Have the children carrying these little arrangements at the offering of the gifts, so they are clustered around their 'parent' arrangement.

- As part of the Penitential rite, or following the Gospel, provide space for people to reflect on where they are in their spiritual growing, and where they need to recognise areas that require attention. This can either be silence, or a time with quiet music playing.

Prayer of the Faithful

Celebrant
Let us do the work of prayer
that God has asked of us.

Reader
As the body constantly breathes,
may the Church, the Body of Christ,
constantly pray,
breathing God's life
into all its members and activities.

Silence

The Lord is our helper:
we shall not be afraid.

As a new week begins in our world,
may wrong priorities be challenged and adjusted,
may our societies reflect God's concern
for righteousness, true justice and responsive love,
and may all leaders grow in humility,
attentive to the needs of those they serve.

Silence

The Lord is our helper:
we shall not be afraid.

As we call to mind our loved ones,
all who depend on us,
and those on whom we depend,
all with whom we laugh, cry, work or play,
cleanse and refresh our relationships
and give us greater love,
understanding and forgiveness.

Silence

The Lord is our helper:
we shall not be afraid.

We think of those who are in prison,
locked in cells or depression or dysfunctional bodies;
we think of those in hospital wards
and accident centres,
those unable to reach medical help
and those on long waiting-lists for operations;
as we think of them all, we pray for them all.

Silence

The Lord is our helper:
we shall not be afraid.

We remember the dying and those who love them;
we remember those whose earthly life
has come to an end,
and we commend them to God's undying love.

Silence

The Lord is our helper:
we shall not be afraid.

Mindful of Mary's quiet
and prayerful acceptance of God's will,
we join our prayers with hers:
Hail, Mary . . .

In silence, we pray for our own intentions
to God, our loving Father.

Silence

Celebrant
Lord God, giver of all good gifts,
we ask you to hear these prayers.
Through Christ our Lord.
Amen.

TREASURE SEEKERS

Aim: To know the story of the guests choosing the most important seats.

Starter

While the music plays, pass round a grand hat or a crown. Whenever the music stops, whoever is wearing the hat or crown stands up, and all the others bow and curtsey to them, saying, 'Yes, your majesty; no, your majesty!'

Teaching

You can either use puppets to tell the story today, or an assortment of character toys, some of which are very new and posh, while others are well loved, old and tatty. Lay a low table with a cloth and plates of drawn food, and arrange all the chairs around it. One by one the characters come in, talking to themselves about the party, and admiring the food.

One of the new, posh ones looks to see which the most important seat is, and decides to sit there because they are *so important*.

One of the old and tatty well-loved ones comes and looks for the lowest, least important seat, because they are conscious of being old and worn, and not very grand.

When the host comes in they go to the old, worn one and give him a big hug, really pleased that he has been able to come to the party. They ask him to come up and sit with them at the top of the table, as he's so important, having been such a good friend for years. When they get to the top of the table the hosts find the posh guest sitting there and ask them to move down so their special guest can sit there instead. The posh guest voices her embarrassment as she moves down and the old worn one takes his place at the top of the table.

This story teaches us not to think we're far more important than anyone else and deserve better than anyone else. Instead of rushing for the best place, or the biggest cake, or the first go, sometimes we need to enjoy giving the best to other people.

Praying

Big and small,
short and tall,
you made us all,
you love us all!

Activities

On the worksheet the children are drawing in the guests in the right places, and the food on the plates. Also, they can paint or model some food on a paper plate to remind them of the story. Today's prayer can be written out on the back of the plate.

PEARL DIVERS

Aim: To look at the implications of Jesus' teaching about hospitality.

Starter

In pairs feed one another with spoonfuls of water. Provide clothing protection!

Teaching

Beforehand prepare two children to act out the guests at the party who are taking the top and bottom seats, and have to swap round when the host wants the lower one up at the top.

Talk about the way we usually feed ourselves when we're hungry, and give ourselves drinks when we're thirsty. When we were feeding one another we got an idea of what it's like to look after someone else, checking that they have caught the spoonful, and don't have drips down their chin.

Thinking of other people's needs is an important part of the Christian way of living. One day Jesus was invited out to lunch, and he noticed the pushy way some of the guests were making sure they had the best seats, nearest the food and drink and near the hosts, so sitting there would make them look important. Jesus didn't like what he saw. It made him sad that people were pushy like this, wanting to be more important than anyone else, and not thinking of other people's feelings. So he told them this story to help them understand a better way of living.

Now ask the children to perform the sketch they have prepared, with the rest of the children being the rest of the guests. Draw out the point Jesus was making about wrong values – being thought of as important shouldn't matter to us nearly as much as it often does. As Christians we are not to think, 'What's in this for me?' all the time.

Praying

Jesus, teach me to give
and not to count the cost,
to toil and not to seek for rest,
to work and not to ask for any reward
except the reward of knowing
I am doing your will. Amen.

Activities

The worksheet encourages the children to look at the second part of today's teaching, dealing with our hospitality with no strings attached. There are also recipes and suggestions for staging a party, with an invitation format, so that they can put the teaching straight into practice as part of your parish outreach programme.

GOLD PANNERS

Aim: To look at what true humility is.

Starter

If you have access to a remote-control vehicle, bring it along and give everyone turns at controlling it. Otherwise provide some other 'controlling' experience, such as taking it in turns to design the group into a sculpture.

Teaching

Start by reading the passage from Ecclesiasticus, discussing their reaction to this as a piece of valuable advice from a father to his son. Is it still true? How does it fit in with our society's advice to young people?

Next look at the Gospel, taking parts and moving seats as appropriate. Look at how Jesus' guidelines for hospitality fit in with how we usually decide who to invite to parties. Try to identify the kind of people Jesus might be hoping we would invite. Is his advice still relevant today? Look too at the way people go straight for the most important seats. What has this to say in our age of valuing self-esteem and 'go for it'?

What is this humility which Jesus is suggesting we have swapped for our sense of self-importance and privilege? Read the passage from Hebrews to put us in God's perspective, so that we can see the truth about ourselves, and our need to keep this in mind in all our thinking, speaking and doing.

Praying

Lord, may I show my love for you
in the way I treat other people.

Teach me your ways
and encourage me to stick with them.
Help me get my motives right
so I'm doing right things for the right reasons.

Activities

There is a short sketch on the sheet to try out either among yourselves or to perform in church. The worksheet also suggests planning an outreach event either separate from the Pearl Divers event or alongside it.

TWENTY-THIRD SUNDAY OF THE YEAR

Thought for the day

Following Jesus is expensive – it costs everything, but it's worth it.

Reflection on the readings

Wisdom 9:13-18
Psalm 89
Philemon 9-10, 12-17
Luke 14:25-33

No sooner have you missed paying a credit card bill than invitations to get further into borrowing start crashing through your letter box. We live in an age of plastic or electronic money where the planning of our finances is pressurised to include living beyond our means, and many discover, too late, that they have over-reached themselves and are heavily, and dangerously, in debt. Jesus' words from today's Gospel hit home to us very powerfully. It is so easy to start enthusiastically committing yourself financially to a new bathroom, car or double-glazing, and regret your decision once the 'pay later' date has arrived in the present.

Although Jesus' words sound very strict and demanding, they badly need to be taken on board. It is essential that no one is given the impression that following Jesus is all easy and happy, with no real cost involved. Part of spreading the good news is ensuring that people are properly informed of the small print. In fact Jesus would not have it in small print, but large letters, so there is no doubt about what is required in the way of commitment. God wants us to make a well-informed, well-considered decision; becoming a Christian, like undertaking marriage, should never be done lightly or carelessly.

Placing God at the very centre of our lives means deliberately placing him at the centre of our thinking and working, our emotions and feelings, our energy and ambitions and in the centre of every relationship, and every decision. Just as when you look at the world through a coloured filter, everything is coloured, so when we take the decision to follow Jesus, everything is coloured by that commitment.

So far, so demanding! Of course, the wonderful good news is that when we take this step we can trust God to lead us into the very best, most fulfilling life possible. Never will he demand of us less than we can, in his strength, give. Never will he push us too fast or overload us too quickly. In partnership with Jesus we can look forward to a lifetime of growing, blossoming and fruiting, in an environment of total security, warm affection and the knowledge of being precious and valuable.

Discussion starters

1. How would you justify the costliness of following Jesus?

2. What does it mean when Paul refers to 'all we have in common'?

All-stage talk

Bring along some catalogues with items which would appeal to the different ages and cultures of those likely to be present. Read out several of the items on offer, and ask people to raise their hands if they think each is a good offer. The more varied and unusual, the better. You might try, for instance, the latest sports car, an electronic game, a lawn mower and a Disneyland holiday. Would the items still be good bargains if you had to give up eating, hobbies or driving in order to pay for them? Establish that if something is important enough, we are prepared to give things up for it. If we're not prepared to change our habits to pay for it, we won't be able to have it.

We are called to follow Jesus. We are offered a fulfilling and rewarding life, inner peace and joy, and life that lasts for ever, even beyond our bodily death. That's quite an offer. But what does it cost? What would we have to give up to pay for it?

Have a long and a short piece of card, or two sticks, and show the long vertical one on its own. This looks like the word 'I'. Place the shorter piece across it. Following Jesus costs us the cross – it means deciding to give up the 'I want' way of living, and putting the sign of God's love (the cross) right at the centre of our lives. (Hold the cross you have made against your own body.)

That means that following Jesus is going to cost us quite a lot. It isn't a cheap, throwaway thing like a paper cup. We need to think very carefully about it before we decide to go for it. Is it worth it?

Yes, it certainly is! God made us, so his way is exactly right for us. No one but God can give us the lasting peace and happiness and complete forgiveness we long for. With God we can become more and more our true selves, selves we can face in the mirror and love. With God we can reach out to other people, and be brave enough to stand up for what is right and loving. Although our life as Christians may lead us into some difficult or dangerous situations, we will always have our friend Jesus with us, and that makes it all possible and all worthwhile.

All-age ideas

- Incorporate in a display or flower arrangement some money and a personal finance planner, or some flyers advertising financial advice. The text reads: 'If you wanted to build a tower, you would first sit down and decide how much it would cost . . . In the same way, you must give up everything you have to follow me.' Luke 14:28, 33.

- The passage from Wisdom can be read chorally with the questions read by a single voice.

Prayer of the Faithful

Celebrant
Let us pray to the God who has watched our growing throughout our lives, and loves us.

Reader
There is nothing hidden from the Lord.
All our thoughts and plans and secret fears
are open to him, even when we try to hide them.
May he give us the courage and strength
to deal with the doubts and misgivings
and fears of his Church,
with the love and mercy
which are part of his nature.

Silence

Gracious God:
in you we can trust.

The Lord feels for the oppressed and the forgotten;
understands the damage which can lead to violence,
the insecurity which can lead to defensiveness,
and the neglect which can lead to lack of control.
We pray that he may heal the nations,
restore what has been lost,
and turn our hearts to discern his will.

Silence

Gracious God:
in you we can trust.

The Lord knows the love inside our hearts
for one another
that sings and dances and aches and worries.
We pray that the Spirit may work on us now
in the depth of our being,
and bless our loved ones with a sense of joy.

Silence

Gracious God:
in you we can trust.

The Lord suffers with those who suffer
and weeps with those who weep;
we, too, stand alongside them now
in whatever pain, distress or sorrow
is engulfing them,
and we pray that they may be comforted.

Silence

Gracious God:
in you we can trust.

The Lord's death and resurrection
proclaim the message of hope
amongst the tears of our grieving
for those who have died.
May they be welcomed
into the eternal light of the kingdom.

Silence

Gracious God:
in you we can trust.

We join our prayers with those of Mary,
who spent her life in God's service:
Hail, Mary . . .

In silence, we make our own petitions
to God, who loves us as his own.

Silence

Celebrant
Father, accept our prayers;
all that we are,
and all we are capable of becoming,
we pledge to your service.
Through Christ our Lord.
Amen.

TREASURE SEEKERS

Aim: To know that it is worth the cost to follow Jesus.

Starter

Play shops, with play money, boxes and cartons,
cut-out fruit and some paper bags.

Teaching

Talk about going shopping, and what they like
buying and what they don't like buying. Talk about
how we sometimes see things we would like, but
we can't have them because they cost too much.

Tell the story, with the aid of a few appropriate
props, of a child who sees a toy she really loves and
would like for her birthday. Her mum tells her that
she won't be able to have it as it costs too much
money. The child keeps thinking about the toy, and
decides she wants it so much that she doesn't mind
not having any other presents, and no birthday
treat, if that means she can have it. Her mum and
dad talk it over with her. They don't want her to
choose to do without those things and then be upset
when she has only got one toy. The child is certain
that this toy is worth it, so her mum and dad
arrange for her to have the toy she wants so much.
And the child is so happy with this one thing that
she doesn't mind having no other presents and no
birthday treat.

Following Jesus is really wonderful. It's wonderful having Jesus as our friend and knowing he
loves us all the way through our life and wherever
we travel to. But when we follow Jesus, we choose
to do without some things.

We choose to do without being selfish, even when
we want to be. We choose to do without being
unkind, even when we feel grumpy. We choose to
do without wanting things all the time, even if we
like them.

But it's worth doing without these nasty things,
because being with Jesus makes us so happy.

Praying

Jesus, I love you
and I will live like you,
even when it is easier not to.

Activities

On the worksheet there is a picture to colour of
Jesus with the children, and the children can draw
themselves in the picture.

PEARL DIVERS

Aim: To look at what it costs to follow Jesus.

Starter

Tower building. Collect lots of boxes and cartons,
and sort them into sizes with price tags on them. Use
Monopoly money and make the prices of the 'bricks'
very high, so the children are dealing in hundreds
of pounds. Issue each small group with a set

amount of money and have a leader in charge of the brickyard. The members of the teams have to decide which bricks to buy with their money to stack up their tower. (No sticky tape allowed!)

Teaching

Use two leaders or a leader and a child to tell the story as a conversation, something like this:

Miriam is sweeping the floor when Alex comes bursting in.

Alex   Miriam! Miriam! Where are you? Oh, there you are!

Miriam Now, mind where you put the dust from those sandals, Alex. I've just swept over there!

Alex   Oh, yes . . . sorry, dear. But listen, I've had a *really* good idea.

Miriam Not another one already! I was cleaning up after your last good idea for days.

Alex   Ah, the olive tree shaker, you mean. Well, I wasn't to know the olives and insects would all shake off into your bowl of flour, was I! Anyway, this idea is different, and it's *really good*.

Miriam OK, dear, I'm listening. You do have some very good ideas, I know. You just need someone like me to stop you getting carried away, sometimes. Tell me your idea.

Alex   A tower.

Miriam A tower? What do you mean, a tower?

Alex   I'm going to build one! It'll be very high, so you'll be able to climb up the tower and check on all the sheep and lambs without having to go all the way to the fields! There, what do you think?

Miriam Mmm, it sounds like a good time-saver. I could sit at the top of your tower and sunbathe in between looking at the sheep, couldn't I?

Alex   Yes, Miriam, you could.

Miriam There's one rather big problem though.

Alex   Oh, really? What's that, Miriam?

Miriam Money. Bricks cost money, and we haven't got any spare money that I know of. How are you going to pay for it?

Alex   Well, I've got enough bricks to build the first bit, Miriam.

Miriam Oh, Alex, you'll look a prize idiot if you build the first bit and then can't finish it off! All the neighbours would tease you about it for years.

Alex   Yes, I suppose you're right. Perhaps I'll

go and sit under the olive tree before supper and work out a few sums.

Miriam It's chicken soup and matzos, and I'll need some help!

Then read Luke 14:28-30, 33. If we decide to join Cubs or Brownies, or start a new sport or learn to play the flute, we know we are committing ourselves. We know our choice will take up time, and we won't be able to do some other things.

Following Jesus is a commitment, too. We have to be prepared to work at telling the truth, or getting on with people we find hard, or standing up for what is right even when we get teased for it. We can't follow Jesus and go on winding everyone up and cheating and lying as if nothing has changed. We have to be prepared to put down those bad habits we have got into and Jesus will help us in that. We have to be ready to go wherever Jesus leads us; and that could be anywhere.

Praying

Lord, even before I say a word,
you already know what I am going to say.
You are all around me – in front and at the back.
You have put your hand on me.
Your knowledge is amazing to me.
It is more than I can understand.

(From Psalm 138)

Activities

There is a cost-counting puzzle on the worksheet, and the instructions for making a reversible cross which looks at the cost and the benefits of following Christ.

GOLD PANNERS

Aim: To explore the implications of the high level of commitment Jesus speaks about.

Starter

Skills which require lots of concentration. Give out a balloon each, and work at keeping it in the air, using only knees and feet. Try juggling, either with the proper balls or with rolled socks or bean bags.

Teaching

Those skills demanded a lot of concentration. Today we are looking at what Jesus told his followers about the level of commitment needed to live God's way.

First read the Luke passage, using either the New Century version (both the *International Children's Bible* and the *Youth Bible* have this) or *The Message*.

The translation is important because this passage can be easily misinterpreted and these versions are quite helpful. Draw attention to the sensible, practical way Jesus has of ensuring that we all know what we are taking on. He doesn't want us to have any illusions. We need to know that following him means being prepared to 'let go' of plans, possessions and people, so we have a different attitude to life, and travel light.

That doesn't mean that Jesus wants us all to rush off and leave our families and friends. Our God is a God of love, and those kinds of demands are not in his agenda at all. But he is talking about changed priorities being part of our decision to follow Jesus. We are placing God at the very centre of our life, and that will affect our very closest relationships and our dearest ambitions. Even these dearest things and people need to be valued in the context of our love for God, and must not become alternatives or substitutes for God.

Our walk with God is a two-way relationship. As we come to each choice, each problem and each stage of life, God will help us and work in us so that we keep on the right path – the path which is marked out by the 'Love God and love one another' signs. That path may well take us through some exciting and dangerous terrain, and it will not always be comfortable; it's more like back-packing than a holiday cruise. It's a great adventure, and one we need to take seriously, and prepare for, so we're not caught unawares by the first storm or rock-face.

Praying

You made my whole being.
You formed me in my mother's body.
I praise you because you made me
in an amazing and wonderful way.

(From Psalm 138)

Activities

The worksheet includes an activity to weigh up the cost and the reward of following Jesus, so they are helped to take on board what discipleship involves. The resulting work can be displayed in church to help the rest of the congregation.

TWENTY-FOURTH SUNDAY OF THE YEAR

Thought for the day

Jesus does not avoid the company of sinners but befriends them.

Reflection on the readings

Exodus 32:7-11, 13-14
Psalm 50
1 Timothy 1:12-17
Luke 15:1-32 *

* For those who wish to focus on the Gospel story of the prodigal son, there is a full treatment of that parable under the Fourth Sunday of Lent (C).

Today's readings take us on a journey from near despair to strong hope. We begin with the Exodus passage, where we look the human condition full in the face and recognise the human capacity for making wrong, self-centred choices, excelling at mastering the skills of evil, and sidling away from the responsibility of godly living, preferring to indulge in the pursuit of personal comfort and the easy life. Ancient Israel could equally be the world in the twenty-first century.

How does a totally good and loving God cope? In Jesus we find out: God comes to the rescue, in person, searching out the lost, untangling them from the messy situations they have got themselves into, and carrying them safely home. The whole of heaven rejoices over each and every one.

In his letter to Timothy, Paul cites himself as living proof that God is indeed merciful and ready to forgive sinners, wherever they are coming from. He, after all, was actively persecuting the followers of Jesus when God alerted him to the truth and transformed his life. Many of us know the same truth in our own lives – I used to be a passionate atheist and now here I am writing this book! The Lord is an excellent shepherd and can find any bedraggled sheep, no matter where they have wandered off to, or how muddy and unsavoury they have become.

God will always search for us because he loves us, and doesn't want any of us to be lost. But it is still up to us whether or not we agree to be rescued.

Discussion starters

1. How do these readings trace a developing understanding of God's nature?

2. Do we, as the body of Christ, have a responsibility towards those who have wandered off from the

flock? Or should we wait for them to find their own way back?

All-stage talk

Gather a mixed group of 'sheep', and appoint a shepherd who is given a crook. Talk about the way the shepherd looks after sheep, finding fresh water and fresh grass, and protecting them from the dangers of wolves and bears. Sometimes a sheep will wander off on its own. (Send one of the sheep to go off and hide somewhere in the church, ensuring that enthusiastic sheep are prevented from going right outside.)

Jesus thought the way we wander off from living good lives was rather like sheep wandering off and getting lost. He loves all of us, and doesn't want any of us to be lost, so, like a good shepherd, he checks that all the rest of the people in the church are OK. (Are they?) Then he sets off to search for the one who has wandered off.

As the shepherd searches for the lost sheep (tell him/her to wait with the sheep when it is found), give some examples of what makes us wander off from God. Perhaps other things crowd God out and take over our life; perhaps we want to disobey God's rules and please ourselves; perhaps some tragedy in our life shakes our faith, and we think God has caused the pain instead of realising that he is weeping with us. Whatever it is, once we realise we are a long way from God, we feel very lost and alone. Sometimes we have got ourselves trapped in habits we can't break out of on our own.

Thankfully Jesus, our good shepherd, is out looking for us, and he will search and search until he finds us. We can help by bleating – which is praying, calling out to God from where we are.

It is very good to be found. As the shepherd brings the wandering sheep, hand in hand, back to the flock, talk about how wonderful it is to know that we are forgiven, and that God loves us enough to forgive us even when we ran away from him. When the sheep comes back to the flock everyone can clap, as, with all the angels of heaven, we celebrate the truth that our God is such an excellent rescuer, full of understanding and mercy, and willing to give up his life to get us back home again.

All-age ideas

- Have an arrangement of model sheep, or a picture or poster of sheep on a hillside.

- If possible, have a pictorial display and explanation of a Middle Eastern marital head-dress, and other examples of something of similar value from other parts of the world – for example, wedding rings.

Prayer of the Faithful

Celebrant
Let us pray to the God who longs for all to be rescued.

Reader
We pray for our bishops, priests and deacons,
and all who are called
to the different ministries in the Church.
May they be blessed
as they work in the service of the Lord.

Silence

God our shepherd:
all our needs are known to you.

We pray for all peace initiatives
and every genuine attempt at negotiation
in conflict resolution.
May those who govern
be governed by the Father's love;
may those who lead be led by the Spirit's directing;
may the whole world come to know
its need of Christ.

Silence

God our shepherd:
all our needs are known to you.

We pray for our families and friends,
for those we meet each day and those we seldom see;
may all our loved ones be drawn closer to the Lord.
May he search out those whose faith
is fragile or fragmented.

Silence

God our shepherd:
all our needs are known to you.

As we recall the needs
of those who are sad or lonely,
lost, or afraid of what they have become,
we pray for the knowledge of the Father's love
to wrap warmly around them,
and his living presence
to bring them to a place of safety and hope.

Silence

God our shepherd:
all our needs are known to you.

We pray for those who have recently died;
may they enjoy the eternal life of heaven,
where there is no more pain, sorrow or weariness,
and every tear shall be wiped away.

Silence

God our shepherd:
all our needs are known to you.

We join our prayers with those of Mary,
Mother of our forgiving Lord:
Hail, Mary . . .

Together in silence,
we name those known to us
who especially need our prayer.

Silence

Celebrant
Merciful Father, accept these prayers,
through Christ our Lord.
Amen.

TREASURE SEEKERS

Aim: To know the story of the good shepherd and
the lost sheep.

Starter

Hide and seek, using a model sheep.

Teaching

Let the children help make a landscape from
upturned bowls draped with a green sheet or towel.
Use model sheep, either plastic ones or home-made
from thin card and cotton wool. Bushes and shrubs
can be small house plants in pots, such as spider
plants and money trees.

When the landscape is set up, tell the story,
moving the sheep around as you talk about the
normal daily routine for the shepherd caring for his
flock, and the lost sheep being found and brought
safely home.

Praying

Good shepherd,
thank you for looking after us.
Help us to look after each other. Amen.

Activities

The children can make sheep masks using the
instructions on the worksheet, and search for lost
sheep in a picture which can then be coloured in.

PEARL DIVERS

Aim: To explore the meaning of the lost sheep and
the lost coin.

Starter

Hunt the coins. For larger groups, have several coins
on the go at the same time.

Teaching

Share your stories of losing something really
important and then finding it again after searching
everywhere for it. (Or you could pretend to have
lost something and get everyone searching for it.
When it is found you can draw attention to the relief
and happiness.)

Jesus knew what this was like. Perhaps it was
his mum or auntie who had once lost one of those
coins from a marriage necklace, and he remembered
the way they had all searched and celebrated.

Show the children a picture of such a necklace,
or, if possible, a real example borrowed from your
local Resource centre, and tell the story of the
woman losing one of the coins. Use a real broom as
you describe the sweeping of the whole house.

Explain that whenever one of us gets 'lost' – cut
off from God – he too is really sad, and keeps
searching and searching until he finds us again.

Praying

We pray for those
who have made wrong choices
and cut themselves off from God.
We pray for all those
who are living evil lives.
May all the lost be found again. Amen.

Activities

There are instructions on the worksheet for making
a marriage necklace and a sheep, and a puzzle to
reinforce the two stories of the sheep and the coin.

GOLD PANNERS

Aim: To see the mercy of God shown in Jesus compared with the Old Testament view of God.

Starter

Mount a good poster-sized picture on card, and cut
it into squares. Put dice numbers on the back of
each piece and arrange the whole picture face down
on the floor so that only the numbers show. The
dice is thrown by everyone in turn, and a piece with
that number on is turned over, so that the picture is
gradually revealed.

Teaching

Point out how we gradually understood more and
more about the full picture as we saw more and
more of it. It was the same with the people of Israel
gradually getting to understand more and more
about the nature of God. Read the Exodus passage,

and talk about what it shows us about their under-standing of God, as well as God's actual character. Then read the Psalm.

When Jesus came to earth in person, it was like seeing the whole picture. Read the passage from Luke about the lost sheep and coin, and talk about what these stories are telling us about the nature of God. Compare this passage with the Exodus reading, looking at any similarities or differences.

There is still the same deep longing for people to be saved. Jesus shows us the willingness of God to get totally involved in the rescue in a personal way: 'Emmanuel' means 'God with us'.

The reading from Paul's letter to Timothy shows God's mercy and love in action in the way Paul himself is forgiven and given a fresh start.

Praying

Oh God, in your kindness have mercy on me
and in your compassion blot out my offence.
Wash me and wash me from all of my guilt
and cleanse me from all of my sin.

(From Psalm 50)

Activities

On the worksheet there are instructions for making a gradually revealed picture of God's nature through Bible references, and space to record a dis-cussion about why 'sheep and coins' get lost and need finding.

TWENTY-FIFTH SUNDAY OF THE YEAR

Thought for the day

If you cannot be trusted with worldly riches, or even small amounts of money, then you will not be trusted with spiritual riches either.

Reflection on the readings

Amos 8:4-7
Psalm 112
1 Timothy 2:1-8
Luke 16:1-13

Today's readings remind us that the way we deal with worldly finances and possessions should be scrupulously honest, fair and wise. It should be directly affected by our spiritual values, and reflect our beliefs completely.

The story of the cheating manager and his cun-ning way of avoiding trouble has the rich man praising him for his cleverness. This does not mean that Jesus is advising us all to follow the manager's example, of course, but it certainly highlights the zeal given to worldly affairs compared with the laid-back attitude so often given to eternal and spiritual matters. If we were to take the same trouble over our spiritual journey as criminals invest in embezzlement, the results would be dynamic in the extreme.

Jesus also picks up on our need to be responsible with our worldly affairs. It is no good excusing ourselves from such responsibilities on the grounds that we are only interested in spiritual things. Jesus is always práctical, and realises that the way we manage our weekly budget, our expenses and our life-decisions is important. If we can't manage these honestly and sensibly, we are likely to be irre-sponsible about the important things of life as well.

Amos was deeply saddened by his own people using their privileged position as a cover for ungodly behaviour. The closer we get to God's way of think-ing, the more saddened we will be by the lack of integrity we see around us. We are bound to start noticing people's misdirected 'worth-ship' and longing for a change of direction. This sadness and yearning is all part of walking in step with the God who loves us and desires that sinners should turn and live.

Discussion starters

1. Is it possible to live as a Christian in the world of business and competition?

2. How can we make sure we take seriously our responsibility to support our leaders in prayer?

All-stage talk

You will need to prepare this talk with another adult. The two of you will be bosses, standing at either end of the church.

Begin by asking for a volunteer who doesn't mind doing a few jobs. This person stands halfway down the church, and you introduce them to the two bosses they are to work for this morning. They are to serve both people as well as they can.

First one boss gives an order, such as to put three chairs out in a line in the middle of the church. As soon as this is done, the other boss gets annoyed that the chairs are arranged like this and tells the servant to put only two chairs out, facing different ways. The first boss tells the servant to put a hymn book on each chair. The other boss tells the servant to put the hymn books away and put a kneeler on each chair. Continue the orders so that the poor servant is running about the church pleasing no one.

Thank the volunteer, and explain how Jesus said in today's Gospel that it is impossible to serve two bosses like that. Either you end up loving the first and hating the second, or hating the first and loving the second. It is the same with trying to serve God while we are still bound up with materialism, money and possessions. (Have two signs: 'God' and 'Worldly Riches'. These can include appropriate symbols, such as a cross and some money.) It simply can't be done. While God is whispering to your conscience to live simply and generously, Worldly Riches is insisting that you get the latest fashion in clothes or music. While God is expecting you to commit time to prayer and Bible reading, Worldly Riches is expecting you to commit that time to reading the latest magazines and watching the latest videos.

If we choose to serve God (display the 'God' sign) we have to choose not to serve Worldly Riches. (Tear up the 'Worldly Riches' sign.)

All-age ideas

- The Gospel works well with several different voices.

- Instead of the usual collection plate today, invite people to get out of their seats and bring their offering to a plate which is placed before the altar.

Prayer of the Faithful

Celebrant
As God has taught us, let us pray
for the coming of the kingdom in every situation.

Reader
We pray for the Church to be pure and holy,
alight with God's love and compassion,
and free from behaviour which is unworthy
of God's chosen people.

Silence

God our Father:
let your kingdom come.

We pray for the nations to be wisely governed,
with just laws and a sense of vision
which reflects the best of human nature.
We pray for peace and mutual respect
in each community throughout the world.

Silence

God our Father:
let your kingdom come.

We pray for our homes to be filled with God's love,
so we are happy to put ourselves out for others,
to listen with full attention, and to value one another.
We pray for the strength
to clear away anything in our life-style
which competes with God for our commitment.

Silence

God our Father:
let your kingdom come.

We pray for those who feel neglected
or rejected by society,
that they may know God's love
and acceptance of them.
We pray for all those in pain and distress,
that they may be comforted and relieved.

Silence

God our Father:
let your kingdom come.

We pray that the dying may recognise
their need of God and his power to save;
that those who have died may be judged with mercy
and rest in God's peace.

Silence

God our Father:
let your kingdom come.

We pray with Mary, Mother of Jesus:
Hail, Mary . . .

In silence, now,
we pour out to God our Father
any needs and burdens known to us personally.

Silence

Celebrant
Lord God of all creation,
accept these prayers,
through Christ our Lord.
Amen.

TREASURE SEEKERS

Aim: To learn that we are to be good 'caretakers' and look after things as well as people.

Starter

A potato and spoon game. For each small group of children (2-4 in a group), place a bowl at each end of the room. In one of the bowls there is a potato and a spoon. The first person carries the potato in the spoon from one bowl to the other. The next carries it back to the first bowl, and so on. They can all have two turns. This can either be competitive or simply an activity which several groups happen to be playing at the same time, depending on the age of the children.

Teaching

Talk about how careful they all had to be to walk along holding the potato in the spoon without it falling off. Think how careful we have to be carrying a bowl of cereal, or a drink of juice. We have to really think about what we are doing. If we start thinking about something else, we can end up spilling it all over the floor!

Jesus told his friends that God takes great care making us and looking after us, and he wants us to take great care of things as well. Show a picture of different age groups working or playing together. He wants us to look after one another. (How?) Show a globe. He wants us to look after our world. (How?) Show a toy and a jacket. And he wants us to look after any things we are given to use or play with. (How?)

Praying

Dear God,
thank you for all the things I have been given
to use and to play with.
Help me to look after them well
and be ready to share them with others. Amen.

Activities

There is space on the sheet for the children to draw the things to use and to play with that they like most, and some pictures of things being looked after well and badly, so they can develop their understanding of what good stewardship means.

PEARL DIVERS

Aim: To get to know the story of the clever manager, and explore its meaning.

Starter

Who's in charge? One person goes outside the room. The others decide on a leader. Everyone stands in a circle and copies the leader's actions, while the person who was outside tries to guess who the leader is.

Teaching

Today we are going to hear a story Jesus told about someone who was put in charge, and got into a spot of bother.

If possible, use a few costume items, such as a suit jacket for the manager, Hawaiian shirt and shades for the rich man, a large accounts book, a plastic bottle of olive oil, and a bag of flour. First the rich man interviews the manager and gives him the job. They shake hands and the rich man leaves the manager to sort out the accounts. The manager thinks aloud, casually helping himself to the petty cash, and writing it in as expenses. He makes a careful job of forging the rich man's signature on large cheques, pleased that his cheating is going so well, and priding himself on all his skill and hard work at making money like this.

Then the rich man comes in, waving a cheque and saying his bank manager has just shown it to him. He demands a full report and fires the manager. On his own again, the manager makes his plans to ensure he'll be well looked after once he is without a job. He can go to different children and ask them what they owe, looking in his book and saying, 'Now let's see – you owe 3,000 litres of olive oil/ 36,000 litres of flour, I believe?'

The rich man can be creeping behind him, watching what he is doing, and amazed at his cheek. As the manager turns round after the last transaction, he bumps into the rich man, and starts pretending he's been checking up on this person's old mother (or some other con story). The rich man stops him and says he's seen everything. He shakes his hand and laughs, saying something like, 'Well, you're a terrible rogue, and I wouldn't trust you as far as I can jump, but you certainly work hard at it!'

When Jesus told this story, he said that we all know crooks work really hard cadging money from people to get rich; it's a pity that we don't work as hard at getting rich with God's treasures! If we put as much energy into our caring love as that crooked manager put into his cheating, the world would be a much more loving place.

Praying

Dear God,
help us to work hard
at good things
like loving and sharing,
and not to work hard
at bad things
like lying and cheating. Amen.

Activities

On the worksheet there is a blotted page of the accounts book for them to put right, and a checklist of the things in life they work hardest at. They are encouraged to look at the way they spend their pocket money, and to think about giving some away each week to help someone else. Organisations like CAFOD have children's packs with suggestions for co-operative giving which you could consider.

GOLD PANNERS

Aim: To look at the implications of the dishonest manager story in our spending of time and money.

Starter

Wink murder. One person is chosen to be the detective and goes outside, while the others stand in a circle and a murderer is chosen. The detective returns and has to work out who the murderer is. Every time the murderer winks at someone, they die in dramatic fashion.

Teaching

That was a game of deceit and cunning. The manager in Jesus' story was well practised at such skills. Read or tell the story of the manager (Luke 16:1-8), using different people to act out the parts. Bring out the rather comic 'rogue' nature of the manager; they need to see the funny side of Jesus teaching the lesson of working at our spiritual life using an out-and-out scoundrel!

Then read the passage from Amos, picking up on his sadness at the double dealing and dishonesty of the people of God. In common with many Christians today, Amos feels quite lonely in his faith, since he is surrounded by people with widely different values and standards from his own. And, since they are his own people, he longs for them to realise what they are doing, and turn around to face God again. When we love God deeply, we will naturally share his sadness at the wrong direction chosen by so many people.

What can we do about it? Read the passage from 1 Timothy to learn from Paul's advice to the young Christian leader, just setting out in ministry. Make a note of the recommendation to pray for all our leaders, and write their names (in the parish, the country and the world) on pieces of card.

Praying

Lord, we pray for our leaders
in the church (name them),
in our country (name them),
and in the world (name them).
Guide them in their decisions,
keep them listening to the needs,
and bless the good they do.

Activities

On the worksheet they can follow up the teaching with an interview of the dishonest manager and his boss. Have some recent newspapers, a loose-leaf file and some clear plastic wallets, and create a prayer book to keep in church, so that the congregation is encouraged to pray for the leaders on a more regular basis.

TWENTY-SIXTH SUNDAY OF THE YEAR

Thought for the day

Wealth can make us complacent so that we fail to notice the needs of those around us.

Reflection on the readings

Amos 6:1a, 4-7
Psalm 145
1 Timothy 6:11-16
Luke 16:19-31

Amos underlines for us the danger of being comfortably well off; the very comfort can cushion us from feeling for the poor and needy until we barely notice their suffering. So often this goes along with a sense of well-being which lulls us into thinking life is like this for everyone else too. We can become so cut off from the real world that we actually believe the needs are not there. It is this blindness, and the injustice of the situation, which angers the God of love and compassion. He feels for the ones who get despised and ignored, simply because they possess less.

Paul has more good advice for young Timothy. He, too, recognises that many sins can get traced back to the 'love of money' rootstock, and advises Timothy to stay well away from it, pursuing instead the kind of riches that are good and eternal. God is by far the better bargain!

The parable of the rich man and Lazarus focuses our minds on the seriousness and urgency of this whole question. We are not to know when our opportunities for living thoughtfully and generously will run out; it would be sensible to sort it all out now, while we still have the chance. As we take stock of how we are living, we can hold in front of us the picture of this wealthy man who did nothing particularly evil, but neglected to notice the needs of those he probably saw every day.

Discussion starters

1. Why does God sometimes ask us to do things which, in the world's terms, are madness?

2. Is it wealth itself which is wrong, or the way it cushions us from reality? Can real Christians be wealthy?

All-stage talk

Arrange for the following items to be in church today, giving different people responsibility for them, so that they will emerge from various people all over the congregation: a pair of sunglasses, some well-known expensive brand of sun cream (the bottle can be empty), a luxurious, squashy cushion, a bottle of champagne (or a champagne bottle) in an ice bucket, and a tape/CD player with some easy-listening music in it ready to play. You will need one of those comfortable sun-loungers. Arrange for another person to walk quietly to the middle of the aisle with a begging bowl and sit down there.

Get the sun-lounger out and invite someone to be cosseted and pampered for a few minutes of the morning. They can lie on the lounger, and various people from all over the church bring them all their comforts. Enthuse about each item as you make the volunteer really comfortable. Leave them snoozing in luxury as you pose the question: 'Is there anything wrong with living in wealth and luxury, and pampering ourselves?'

In itself, no, there isn't. Of course it is good to have times of rest and relaxation, and it is fine to enjoy the good things of life. But if we use wealth to cushion ourselves from the real world, shield our eyes from the harsh glare of suffering, protect ourselves from feeling people's pain, block out the sound of people's crying, and deaden our sense of duty, then we run the danger of rejecting all the needs, and not feeling we have any responsibility to do anything about them anyway. (Hold a 'speech bubble' of card over the volunteer, which says, 'What problems?')

In Jesus' story, the rich man was probably a nice guy, and there is no mention of him doing anything really evil. But he simply hadn't noticed the beggar who sat at his own front gate every day. Point out that all the time we've been enjoying indulging ourselves up here, there has been someone begging down there.

It's all too easy for us to ignore the needs. Jesus reminds us to check that our lack of poverty doesn't prevent us from doing the practical caring love we are called to.

All-age ideas

- Use different voices in the reading of the Luke passage.

- Involve the congregation in this, printing it on the handout or showing it on the OHP.

A	Being wealthy is having a meal every day.
B	Being wealthy is having a bicycle.
C	Being wealthy is owning a house.
D	Being wealthy is having lots of exotic holidays.
E	Being wealthy is not having to work, and collecting Rolls Royces.
All	Being wealthy is all relative. Being poor is all relative. Having needs is part of being human.

Prayer of the Faithful

Celebrant
All our needs are God's concerns.
Let us pray to him now.

Reader
May we be a listening Church,
welcoming to the hesitant,
encouraging to the young,
sensitive to the differences and attentive to the needs.

Silence

God, in mercy:
hear us as we pray.

May we be a caring world,
wise in government,
honest in promises,
far-sighted in the management of resources,
and open-hearted in charitable giving.

Silence

God, in mercy:
hear us as we pray.

May we be a responsible community,
supporting our neighbours and friends,
sharing one another's sorrows and joys,
and opening our homes to the presence of the Lord.

Silence

God, in mercy:
hear us as we pray.

As we remember those
who have asked for our prayers,
we ask that the Lord may take their needs
and provide for them,
take their wounds and heal them,
take their suffering and comfort them.

Silence

God, in mercy:
hear us as we pray.

As we call to mind those who have died,
may they know the welcoming of God's love
into eternal joy.

Silence

God, in mercy:
hear us as we pray.

We make our prayer with Mary,
whose generous heart
was so open to God's will:
Hail, Mary . . .

In silence, let us commend
our own particular needs and thankfulness
to the God of power and mercy.

Silence

Celebrant
Heavenly Father, hear these prayers,
through your Son, Jesus Christ.
Amen.

TREASURE SEEKERS

Aim: To know that we are to notice one another's needs.

Starter

Spot the difference. The children hide their eyes while you change something (you might take a shoe off, or swap your watch to the other wrist) and then they have to guess what is different.

Teaching

Tell a story about a child noticing someone's need. Here is one possibility:

Emily and her dad were doing the shopping. It was the big weekly shop in the supermarket to get things like toothpaste, Sugar Puffs, toilet paper and bread. Emily had got the list, and Dad was pushing the trolley.

The shop was full of people, some of them filling plastic bags with apples and potatoes, and others trying to work out the cheapest way to buy cheese. They were so busy with what they were choosing to buy that no one noticed a sticky white line on the floor by the cat food.

At least, nearly no one noticed. Emily saw it and wondered what it was. As she went to find the rabbit and chicken flavour (her cat's favourite) she followed the sticky white trail, and smelt the smell of concentrated washing liquid. So that's what it was! Emily could see the trail disappearing round the corner into the lemonade and coke part of the shop.

'Dad!' said Emily. 'Look!'
Dad looked.
'Mmm, well spotted, Emily,' he said. 'We had better follow that trail and find out why it's there.'
'It's concentrated washing liquid I think,' said Emily.
'I think you could well be right,' said Dad.
They pushed their trolley round the corner. There, just between the large bottles of lime and lemon and the small bottles of blackcurrant and apple was a woman pushing a trolley. And on the front of the trolley was a refill of concentrated washing liquid, leaking white sticky stuff along the floor as the trolley went along. Anyone could slip over on it and hurt themselves.

Emily and her dad showed the woman the white sticky trail.

'Oh good heavens, fancy that!' said the woman. 'Fancy me not noticing! What a good thing you noticed it before anyone hurt themselves.'

Dad and Emily smiled at each other.

The woman and Emily and her dad told the shop assistants and helped them mop up the mess with paper towels. The manager put down some orange cones saying 'Wet floor' on them, so people would know it wasn't safe to walk there yet.

Talk about how good it was that Emily noticed, and share any stories the children want to tell about times they have noticed when people need help.

God wants us to notice things and be ready to come to the rescue.

Praying

Dear God,
use our eyes
to see the needs around us
and use our hands to help. Amen.

Activities

On the sheet there is a picture on which to spot various needs, and a pair of glasses to make.

PEARL DIVERS

Aim: To get to know the story of the rich man and Lazarus.

Starter

During a song, arrange for one of the leaders to come in wearing a hat and carrying a trowel, walk across the room and go out again. Don't draw attention to this; ignore it. After the song, ask the children if they noticed anyone coming in during the song, and what they looked like. The person comes in again, and explains that today we are going to hear about someone who didn't take any notice of the needs of someone he saw every day.

Teaching

Use the children to be Lazarus and the rich man, the dogs, the angels and Abraham, as you narrate the story, either directly from the Bible (the New Century Children's International Bible is excellent) or in your own words. If you have a spare leader you can go for voice-overs as well.

After the story, talk about what the rich man had done wrong, and how his wealth had made him so comfortable that he didn't notice the needs of others staring him in the face. The children may have some ideas of how the rich man could have done it better.

Praying

Lord, we pray for the poor
and those who don't have enough to eat.
We give you ourselves
for you to use
in helping them. Amen.

Activities

On the sheet they can confirm their commitment to put their faith into practice by drawing someone they can help, and how they plan to do it.

GOLD PANNERS

Aim: To explore the dangers of wealth and complacency.

Starter

A protection racket. Each small group is given an egg, some bubble wrap, newspaper, tape and string. They have to wrap their egg protectively so that it won't break when dropped. Then drop the packages from a height on to a hard surface, and see how well they survived. Today we are going to look at how people can use wealth to protect themselves against feeling for those in need.

Teaching

When eggs are not protected and you drop them, they crack and break up. Deciding to go through life in God's loving way is also a bit risky because, like the egg, you can get hurt when you love and care for people. Many of us use wealth to buy a kind of protection against the suffering of the world, like the man in the Gospel today.

Read the passage together, with different voices as appropriate, and talk about how the rich man's lifestyle shielded him from the needs of Lazarus. All the separation of strong walls and class structure effectively gave him permission to ignore the needs and get on with his own comfortable life. Does this still happen? Where?

Read Paul's advice to Timothy. Do you agree with Paul about the dangers of wealth? Do we think of ourselves as wealthy – within our local area . . . compared with people in some other countries?

Finally look at the indignation of Amos in verses 4-7. Is he just jealous of these people's lives, or is there a deeper reason for his anger? Is there any way that we, as the rich of the world, can make sure our wealth doesn't lull us into irresponsible complacency?

Praying

Take me, Lord, and train me.
Let me not trust the protection of wealth
and risk becoming hardened
to the needs around me.
Instead, give me your protection
which keeps me eternally safe
but allows me to feel and suffer
with the suffering world,
and work to relieve it. Amen.

Activities

Look at some of the possible ways to help the very poor, using material from CAFOD, or one of the other large charities, and make some practical plans.

TWENTY-SEVENTH SUNDAY OF THE YEAR

Thought for the day

God hears our distress and our crying, and feels it with us.

Reflection on the readings

Habakkuk 1:2-3; 2:2-4
Psalm 94
2 Timothy 1:6-8, 13-14
Luke 17:5-10

Today's readings are full of laments and heartbroken crying. Our faith is not a fair-weather faith, but speaks into our pain as well as our joy, into our darkest valleys as well as our hilltop experiences. It is both crucifixion and resurrection. God never does nothing when we pray; he may not come charging into the situation and sort it in the way we would like, but in his time, which is the best time, he will redeem it for good, and while we are waiting he will provide all the courage, inner peace and hope we need.

The important thing for us to establish as we cry is God's position in the suffering. So often when there are national tragedies we hear people crying, 'How could a loving God let this happen?' as if God were there orchestrating the evil or, even worse, watching it with his arms folded. This is a terrible distortion of the truth, for the real God of compassion is neither tyrannical, nor aloof and unconcerned. Nor is he well-intentioned but ineffectual. He is actually there suffering alongside the broken-hearted, sharing their grief and distress and ready to comfort them by being there. The costly gift of free will is matched by the costly gift of loving redemption.

At the same time, as today's Gospel reminds us, there is no room for spiritual self-pity. We have no built-in rights for everything in our lives to run smoothly and easily, and Jesus is forthright in talking of the servant who simply accepts the work and weariness as part of his duty, without expecting any special payment or privileges. If following Christ brings us hardship and suffering, that is no more than we were told to expect, and we are asked to accept it as such, always on the understanding and conviction that we will be provided with whatever grace and strength we need to cope and triumph over the difficulties.

Discussion starters

1. Has the message of the media – that it is normal and our right to be happy, wealthy and healthy – given us false assumptions and expectations in this age?

2. What benefits does God manage to harvest from suffering, provided we allow him to work his redeeming love in the situation?

All-stage talk

Bring along a football, a musical instrument, a cross and a Bible. Choose someone to come out and give them the football, telling them that you are letting them borrow this so that you can watch them on television, this week, playing in the next (Liverpool) game. Give someone else the musical instrument and say you'll be looking forward to hearing them on Classic FM tomorrow morning, then.

Are these things really possible? Why not? Obviously it doesn't really happen like that. Just having a football doesn't mean you can get out there and land the goals against fierce opposition. For that you need lots of training and lots of skills. Just having a musical instrument doesn't mean that you can join a top orchestra and get all the notes and phrasing right. For that you need years of training and practice, and a musical gift.

We know about this in football and music, but we sometimes forget it when it comes to our faith, even though it's still true. Give someone the cross and the Bible. Just because they now have these things doesn't mean that they have arrived as a Christian, and can now make all the right decisions, and be perfect in every way. Living Christ's way will take us a lifetime of training and practice, and we are bound to make mistakes and get into scrapes along the route.

So when the going gets hard work, and we find it's a challenge and a struggle to live by God's rule of love, we mustn't get discouraged. Jesus never promised us it would be easy all the time. All training, whether it's in tackling or goal defence, vibrato on the violin or overcoming the break on the clarinet, forgiving wholeheartedly or conquering self-indulgence – all these things are difficult to learn and require dedication and perseverance.

When you are finding it's hard being a Christian, don't give up or decide it's too difficult; go to God and ask for some more help. Throughout your whole life he will provide all the training, practice and gifts you need for the work he asks you to do, whether that work is preaching to thousands, or helping your next-door neighbour.

All-age ideas

• The mood of sadness in the Old Testament reading can be expressed well in dance. Look into any dance contacts you may have with groups using the church hall, and consider inviting them. Some of the Scottish strathspey dances are very poignant, for instance, or the slow Greek dances. A local dancing school might welcome the challenge. Or, for a home-grown dance, while the choir sing or recorded music is played, a group of people from the congregation can move slowly up the centre aisle, hands at their sides, doing a slow *pas de basque* in formation, in the style of a folk dance. At the front they link hands and circle first left and then right, then move into the centre, raising their arms, and back again. They all turn outwards and sway from one foot to the other, before moving back down the aisle again. Keep the steps simple and controlled.

- Ask the flower-arranging team to create an arrangement expressing grief and sadness, with a centre of bright hope, perhaps using purple and dark red colours and cascading foliage.

Prayer of the Faithful

Celebrant
Knowing that God hears our prayers,
let us share our concerns with him
for the Church and for the world.

Reader
We pray for all in lay and ordained ministry,
as they labour for the growth
of God's kingdom on earth;
may he keep them strong in the faith,
provide them with the energy
and resources they need,
and inspire them daily with his love.

Silence

Lord, you are our hope:
you are our strength.

We pray for all meetings, conventions,
and conferences,
for all policy making and planning;
may delicate negotiations be sensitively led,
and painful decisions bravely and wisely taken.

Silence

Lord, you are our hope:
you are our strength.

We pray for those we have upset or angered,
and those who have upset or angered us;
we pray for those who worry us,
and those we love but seldom manage to see.

Silence

Lord, you are our hope:
you are our strength.

We pray for those who are far from home
and those for whom it is too dangerous
to return home;
we pray for the lonely, the unhappy,
those in pain and those convalescing.

Silence

Lord, you are our hope:
you are our strength.

We remember those who have come
to the end of their earthly life,
and for those whose lives feel bleak
and empty without them.
We pray for mercy and peace and comfort.

Silence

Lord, you are our hope:
you are our strength.

We pray with Mary,
whose faith was unfaltering:
Hail, Mary . . .

Trustingly we pray in silence
to our loving God for our own needs and cares.

Silence

Celebrant
Father, as we dedicate ourselves afresh
to serving you,
accept these prayers,
through Christ our Lord.
Amen.

TREASURE SEEKERS

Aim: To learn about perseverance.

Starter

Have some buckets and beanbags, so the children can try throwing the beanbags into the buckets.

Teaching

Make up an obstacle course which a soft toy, such as a bear, could negotiate with a bit of help from his friends. This might include something high to balance along, a dark tunnel he must hurry through on his own, and something to climb up.

Make a bear walk the obstacle course, talking to himself in a growly voice as he goes along. He is sometimes scared and anxious by the height, sometimes frightened and sad about being alone in the dark, and sometimes finding it all an uphill struggle. There are also parts of his journey with fun and excitement and good views. Through all the difficult parts the bear bravely perseveres. The children can applaud him when he eventually reaches the end of the course.

Talk about how the bear kept on going, even when he was scared or tired. That's what God wants us to do in life.

Praying

Make a ring of string which everyone holds and passes through their hands as they pray:
Lord, help me to keep trying
again and again and again!
Lord, help me to keep loving
on and on and on.

Activities

On the worksheet there is an obstacle course for the children to make their fingers walk along, and a 'keeping on and on' game to make, for which they will need string.

PEARL DIVERS

Aim: To get to know the parable of the servant doing his duty.

Starter

Put on some music, and do a challenging fitness workout, including, perhaps, running on the spot, stepping, skipping, bunny jumps, stretching, and touching toes. Praise them for the way they kept going and kept trying, even when it was hard or tiring.

Teaching

Like our fitness training session, life can sometimes be hard work – such as when we feel jealous of a brother or sister, or when we are finding it difficult to do the work at school, or when there are arguments and rows at home. Collect their ideas and experiences.

How does our God help us at these times, and what tips has Jesus got for coping?

Use simple puppets to act out the story that Jesus told about the servant, doing it the first time with the servant coming in and putting his feet up, and the master protesting that he can't behave like that because he's a servant, not the master. Then make a 'take two' sign and act the situation out with the servant being praised at the end for doing all the jobs. The servant can then protest that he was only doing his duty.

What does the story mean? Jesus says that we are not to expect life to be easy and perfect all the time because it isn't. We can expect there to be sad and difficult times as well as all the happy and easy times. And when they happen, we are to just carry on doing what we know is right, without grumbling too much. God will be there with us in all the difficult times, so we won't be left alone, and he will give us the strength we need to carry on.

Praying

Set out a train layout, with a tunnel (which can be a shoe box with holes at the ends), a gradient and some points. Start the train round the track as you pray:

When life seems an uphill struggle, Lord,
All: keep me on track with you, Jesus.

When we go through dark and lonely times,
All: keep me on track with you, Jesus.

When we have to make choices about how to behave,
All: keep me on track with you, Jesus. Amen.

Activities

There are instructions on the worksheet for making a spinner to remind them of the need to persevere when times are hard, and there is a Bible study activity for which they will need Bibles.

GOLD PANNERS

Aim: To explore the way God gives us the strength to suffer for the Gospel.

Starter

Ping. You will need some empty Smartie tubes, complete with lids. This may necessitate bringing full Smartie tubes and eating the contents! Mark a line on the floor to stand behind and measure how far everyone can ping the lid, by holding the tube and thumping it with their fist. (This is a game my daughter and her student friends devised one evening, from an upstairs room in their hall of residence.)

Teaching

Work out the physics behind the 'ping' game. The lid is propelled forward by the sudden rush of air behind it. It wouldn't be able to move any distance at all on its own.

We need the power of God's Spirit to urge us forward and move us into action; it is God who provides us with the strength and courage to suffer for the Gospel. Without that power and encouragement we could easily become downhearted and discouraged. Read Paul's letter to Timothy, where Paul has found that God's power makes him quite happy to accept the dangers and difficulties that go with the job of working for the spreading of the kingdom.

Then look at the servant who is expected simply to do his duty, and think about how our work as Christians may well mean that we run into some hard or even dangerous situations. What is Jesus saying we ought to do when the going is rough?

Look at some examples of Christians who have persevered in difficult times or jobs.

Praying

Lord, remember my suffering
and how I have no home.
Remember the misery and the suffering.
I remember them well and I am very sad.

But I have hope when I think of this:
The Lord's love never ends. His mercies never stop.
They are new every morning.

(From Lamentations)

Activities

Try out the role-play on the sheet, based on the Gospel, and fill in the chart about the things which make us feel sad and downhearted, and the strategies for learning perseverance.

TWENTY-EIGHTH SUNDAY OF THE YEAR

Thought for the day

God can always use even seemingly hopeless situations for good.

Reflection on the readings

2 Kings 5:14-17
Psalm 97
2 Timothy 2:8-13
Luke 17:11-19

We have probably all known at some time the misery of being rejected and isolated. Whether we are in that condition through our own fault or through circumstances beyond our control, it is still a bleak and painful place to be.

Some of us will have known the haunting suspicion that we could infect others, either physically or emotionally; most of us can only guess at the terrible sense of chronic isolation and terror experienced by those with leprosy, like Naaman, or the lepers of Jesus' time.

Jesus meets the ten lepers in their community of isolation, outside one of the villages, and all their years of suffering pour out poignantly as they plead for pity from their contamination zone. Jesus, ever practical, tells them not that they are healed, but that they are to go and do what healed lepers have to do by law – show themselves to the priest. It is typical of godly direction to use the existing framework so as to bless as many people as possible.

Paul, writing to Timothy, is actually chained up in prison, but quite content to be there as anywhere else, because he knows that although he is chained, the good news is not, and can bring anyone blessing, wherever you happen to spread it.

This is rather heartening, because it means that all of us can blossom with God's love where we are planted; we don't have to wait until we are in a 'better' situation, or get discouraged because we only meet those in the office or on the bus each day. The wholesome goodness of the Gospel can be brought to those we meet – by us!

Discussion starters

1. Is it acceptable for Christians to be sad and downhearted, or should their new life in Christ mean that they are always happy and rejoicing?

2. How would you answer someone who was complaining that their prayers for healing had not been answered? (Is it just an answer that would be needed in the circumstances?)

All-stage talk

Ask for ten volunteers and dish out 'bandages' for them to wear on arms, legs and head. Explain that they are lepers and, because the disease is thought to be very catching, they can't stay with everyone else here but must go and sit somewhere else. Direct them to a place separate from the rest of the congregation. As they go, tell everyone how the lepers of Jesus' day had to leave their homes and live right away from the villages and towns, and look after themselves. How must they have felt? Lonely? Left out? Guilty? Unacceptable? Frightened?

We may not have the disease of leprosy, but there are lots of people in our world, in our country and in our town – perhaps even in our church – who feel lonely, left out, guilty, unacceptable and frightened, like the lepers. People cry themselves to sleep and wake up feeling sad about the day ahead. People who have lost contact with friends, or whose loved ones have died, try hard to be cheerful when they have a big ache of sadness inside them. Lots of people are hurting, and longing for their life to be different.

That's how these ten lepers felt that morning when they saw Jesus walking along the road on his way to a village. They couldn't come too close to him, but they came as close as they could, and shouted to him, 'Jesus, Master, have pity on us!' (This can be written on a sign so the ten 'lepers' can shout it out.) People still cry out to God in their hearts like this. Does God hear?

He certainly does! Jesus shows us what God is like, and what Jesus did was to tell the lepers to go and show themselves to the priest. Why ever did he tell them that? Because if you were a leper and you were healed, you had to show yourself to a priest, so he could check you over and pronounce you fit and well.

Send your lepers off to 'the priest', who has ten cards saying, 'I declare this leper is now CLEAN. Signed: Fr (John Hayward).' Tell them that when they have their certificate of health they are free to join the other people in the congregation.

If any of the volunteers decides to come and say 'thank you' you can of course use this and praise it. However, since they haven't actually been healed of anything, they will probably all sit down in their places. Tell everyone how one leper (choose one) came back to Jesus to say 'thank you'. All the others had been keen to talk to Jesus when they needed something, but they forgot him once he had sorted them out.

Let's make sure that when God answers our prayers, we don't forget to say thank you – even if his answer is not the answer we expect.

All-age ideas

- Give out small pieces of bandage (cut from old sheeting) to people as they come in. At the Penitential Rite ask them to hold their bandage and wrap it round their hand. Just as the lepers were cut off from their community, so our sin cuts us off from God. Ask them to bring to mind the sins that they need God to heal them of, so that their relationship with him can be restored. At the words of forgiveness they can unwind the bandages and throw them away.

- Involve both sides of the congregation in these responses taken from 2 Timothy 2:

   A   If we died with him,
   B   then we shall live with him.
   A   If we hold firm,
   B   then we shall reign with him.
   A   If we disown him,
   B   then he will disown us.
   A   We may be unfaithful,
   All   but he is always faithful,
         for he cannot disown his own self.

Prayer of the Faithful

Celebrant
God has proclaimed his love for us.
We can trust him with all our cares and concerns.

Reader
We pray that the Church may be healed
of all its splits and divisions,
and grow towards unity.

Silence

Have pity on us, Lord:
you alone can save us.

May our society be mindful of those
who have particular difficulties;
may our laws testify to our sense of justice,
honour and integrity;
may the world's leaders be wisely advised
and honestly motivated.

Silence

Have pity on us, Lord:
you alone can save us.

May the Lord walk in our homes
with gifts of peace, patience, forgiveness and joy;
may he help us through the disappointments
and tragedies,
and celebrate with us in all our festivities,
as our most honoured guest.

Silence

Have pity on us, Lord:
you alone can save us.

We pray for all suffering from leprosy
and other infectious and life-threatening diseases;
may the Lord give courage
to the long-term and chronically ill,
and respite to those who are at their wits' end.

Silence

Have pity on us, Lord:
you alone can save us.

We remember those who have died,
and we think of their loved ones, who miss them.
May this earthly death be a birth
into the eternal joy of heaven.

Silence

Have pity on us, Lord:
you alone can save us.

We make our prayer with Mary,
whose heart was full of thanks and praise:
Hail, Mary . . .

Confident in God's welcoming love,
we pray in silence, now,
for any needs known to us personally.

Silence

Celebrant
Heavenly Father, to whom all glory belongs,
accept our prayers, through Christ our Lord.
Amen.

TREASURE SEEKERS

Aim: To know that Jesus healed the ten lepers and one said 'thank you'.

Starter

Provide a selection of sorting-out games and toys, such as building something from a jumble of bricks or boxes, putting shapes in the right holes, and jigsaw puzzles. Today we are going to look at the way Jesus sorted out ten problems all at once!

Teaching

Using the carpet tiles surface, tell the story of today's Gospel. You will need cut-outs of the lepers, a distant village, some trees, Jesus, the priest, and the leper who said 'thank you'. You can base them on the pictures below. The road to the village can either be a cloth, or strip of paper.

Praying

When we are sad *(chin in hands)*,
you cheer us up *(trace big smile with finger)*.
When we cry *(fists in eyes)*,
you brush our tears away *(brush face with hands)*.
When we feel weak *(go droopy)*,
you make us strong *(show muscles)*
and we say THANK YOU! *(shout)*

Activities

There is a picture of the lepers throwing off their bandages happily when they are healed which the children can colour, after they have counted the lepers and various other things.

PEARL DIVERS

Aim: To look at the healing of the lepers and the significance of the one who said 'thank you'.

Starter

Musical chairs, or a similar game, where there is always an odd one out when the music stops. Today we are going to think about ten odd ones out, and one odd one out.

Teaching

Two mothers, dressed up in head cloths, are in a village with their pots, collecting water from the village well. They pass the time of day, and then catch sight of the ten lepers in the distance, wondering who they are shouting to. One of the lepers, Jonas, is the son of one of the women and they talk about how sad they are that he can't live at home any more, and how badly he is missed, and how they have never stopped praying for him to be healed. They see that Jesus, the healer and teacher, is coming towards their village, and has stopped to listen to the lepers.

They wonder if Jesus could possibly be making the lepers better. They watch the lepers running away from Jesus and suddenly realise they are heading for the priest's house and are throwing off their bandages as they run. The women get very excited and soon they see some of the lepers running into their own houses in the village. They must be healed! The women start praising God, and are looking forward to Jonas coming back when they see him running all on his own back up the road to Jesus. What on earth is he doing? Then they see Jonas kneel down in front of Jesus. He is pouring out his thanks to Jesus, who is smiling and sharing Jonas's delight. The two women pick up their pots of water and go off to join them.

Praying

Put up all ten fingers and lower the fingers one by one as you say the first ten words. As you say 'Thank you!' you make a thumbs-up sign with one thumb, representing the thankful leper.

You always make us feel better.
Help us to say, 'Thank you!'

Activities

The worksheet gives instructions for making a pop-up thank-you card. There is also a puzzle for which they will need access to a Bible. This reinforces the week's teaching.

GOLD PANNERS

Aim: To look at the nature of God which is always ready to hear the cries of the world.

Starter

Scrambled messages. Half the group sit at one end of the room and shout a message to their partners who are sitting at the other end of the room. They are all shouting different messages, so the hearers have to listen carefully and unscramble their message from the general noise.

Teaching

There is so much suffering in our world, and so many people all crying to God at any one time, from all over the place. Happily God doesn't have our problem of unscrambling all the messages. He is able to attend to all of us at once, without even putting us in a stacking system.

Read the passage from 2 Timothy which shows that God is always true to his own nature – God cannot not be God – a God of healing, love and compassion.

The story of the ten lepers shows us God's compassion for those who feel that they are outcasts. Jesus hears their cry for pity, and responds to it with all the practical care of the God of love.

Praying

Collect some pictures and information about leprosy and AIDS, and lay them down in front of a cross, with flowers and candles among them, as you sing *O Lord, hear my prayer* (Taizé) and say these words from Psalm 65:

God, you have tested us.
You have purified us like silver.
You let us be trapped,
you laid a heavy load on us.
You let our enemies walk on our heads.
We went through fire and flood.
But you brought us to a place with good things.
You did not hold back your love from me.

Activities

Make the pictures into a poster or banner for display in church, mounted on a length of strong wallpaper, with the text from Psalm 65 on it.

TWENTY-NINTH SUNDAY OF THE YEAR

Thought for the day

Don't get side-tracked; always pray and don't give up.

Reflection on the readings

Exodus 17:8-13
Psalm 120
2 Timothy 3:14-4:2
Luke 18:1-8

I have a half-finished tapestry somewhere in the back of a cupboard, which has been in that state for years. Whenever I rediscover it, I make the decision to keep it, as one day I may have the time to finish it. Even as I put it back in the cupboard I know this is unlikely; the commitment simply isn't there, as my tapestry doesn't rank high enough in my order of priorities.

For many people, faith in God is similarly packed away, and brought out and looked at from time to time. Their prayer-life is haphazard and irregular, with long gaps of inattentiveness punctuated with occasional attempts to open up the communication channels. For whatever reasons, building a deep relationship with God is simply not a high priority at present. If it were, the commitment would show in a regular and more persistent prayer pattern.

Whereas my tapestry remains much the same sitting in the cupboard, relationships are dynamic and do not store well without attention. It is always rather sad when a close friendship subsides into the printed Christmas letter category. Although this can be a valiant effort to avoid losing touch completely, it is a poor substitute for the daily contact and shared lives. And so often our prayer-life and Bible-reading, if similarly rare and impersonal, result in a very stilted relationship with God, which is such a poor substitute for the rich, vibrant companionship he has in mind for us.

We live in a rather fragmented and disjointed culture, which doesn't help. Many young children are now entering school with a marked increase in poor listening and concentration skills. Persistence in anything, whatever it is, does not come easily. But prayer, like our heartbeat, needs to be regular and constant, a quiet rhythm pulsing faithfully under all our other activities. We also have a responsibility to keep up our study of the Bible so that we, like Timothy, are thoroughly equipped for every work.

Discussion starters

1. Do we have God's word in our minds and written on our hearts? What can we put in place to improve our present situation?

2. If God knows our needs before we ask, why does Jesus advise us to be persistent in prayer?

All-stage talk

Bring along (or ask someone else in the congregation to bring) something which you have made or are making, which requires lots of persistence and perseverance (such as a garment or model, diary or recipe). Talk about the struggle you have had keeping going with it. Use parts of the church building, particularly if it is an ancient one, and draw everyone's attention to some piece of stained glass or carving, and all the persistence and hard work that went into making it. Emphasise the value of doing these things, even though they are difficult.

Jesus tells us to keep going with our prayer, and never give up. Suggest a pattern of praying when you wake up, before you eat a meal, and before you go to sleep at night, showing large posters of logos for these (as below). Or they can be shown on an OHP. If we get into a prayer habit like this, we will be deepening our friendship with God, and getting to know him better.

There is another good habit we need to have as well as praying, and that is reading the Bible every day. There are lots of books and schemes to help us, and we can choose one which suits our age, interests and experience. Show a few of these and draw attention to the display suggested in the All-age ideas. If we don't know much about the Bible there are people in the parish to talk it over with.

However we read it, it's important to pray and read God's word in Scripture so that we really can have God's law of love remembered in our minds and written on our hearts. That way we will be ready for any jobs God asks us to do, and we will be better able to hear him speaking into our lives.

All-age ideas

- Have a display of Bible study aids for all ages and characters, and also a selection of different Bible translations, with recommendations.

- In a flower arrangement have an open Bible and a picture or model of 'praying hands', with the arrangement titled 'Daily prayer, daily Scripture reading'.

- Use this short sketch to reinforce the Gospel reading, or prepare people for it:

Woman Knock, knock.

Judge Who's there?

Woman Winnie.

Judge Winnie who?

Woman Winnie you going to do something about that money I was cheated of?

Judge Oh don't worry, that case will be coming up very soon. Now if you don't mind, it's my day off and I'm going to play golf.

(Sign held up saying 'Next day')

Woman Knock, knock.

Judge Who's there?

Woman Winnie.

Judge Winnie who?

Woman Winnie you going to do something about . . .

Judge OK, you don't have to say all that again. I remember. I'll deal with it, madam. Leave it to me. *(Aside)* But not yet because I'd rather watch telly and have a snooze.

Woman Knock, knock.

Judge *(Sounding sleepy)* Who's there?

Woman Winnie.

Judge Winnie who? *(Aside)* Oh, hang on, I won't ask! I don't know, there's no rest for the wicked. Wretched woman, I'd better do what she asks or I'll never get any peace! *(Shouts)* All right, Winnie, you win. I'll come with you and sort it out *now*!

Prayer of the Faithful

Celebrant
Our help comes from the Lord.
Let us pray to him now.

Reader
We pray for those who teach prayer
and open the Scriptures to others
at schools and colleges, retreat houses,
and conferences,
and in churches and homes all over the world.
We pray that many will find in Scripture
words speaking into their situation
and providing the guidance they need.

Silence

Lord, we love your ways:
our help comes from you.

We pray for those picking their way
through situations of potential conflict and danger;
for law makers and keepers
and all who are oppressed unjustly;
for the leaders of the nations and their people.

Silence

Lord, we love your ways:
our help comes from you.

We pray for the grace to listen to one another
and respond to one another's needs;
we pray for a spirit of co-operation and generosity
in our homes and neighbourhoods.

Silence

Lord, we love your ways:
our help comes from you.

We pray for those who are wrestling with problems
which seem too big to cope with;
for those who have recently received news
that has stunned or appalled them,
and are still in a state of shock.

Silence

Lord, we love your ways:
our help comes from you.

We pray for those who have gone through death,
that they may be judged with mercy
and brought safely into the eternal life of heaven.

Silence

Lord, we love your ways:
our help comes from you.

Encouraged by Mary's prayerful example,
we join our prayer with hers:
Hail, Mary . . .

We pray in silence our own petitions
to God our Father,
who knows all our needs.

Silence

Celebrant
God, our heavenly Father,
bless our lives to your service,
and accept our prayers,
through Christ our Lord.
Amen.

TREASURE SEEKERS

Aim: To look at the value of regular prayer.

Starter

Here we go round the mulberry bush. With one of the regular morning jobs being: 'This is the way we pray to God on a cold and frosty morning'.

Teaching

Bring a large circle of card split into the four seasons, and a circular band of paper showing the regular events of a day, based on the pictures below.

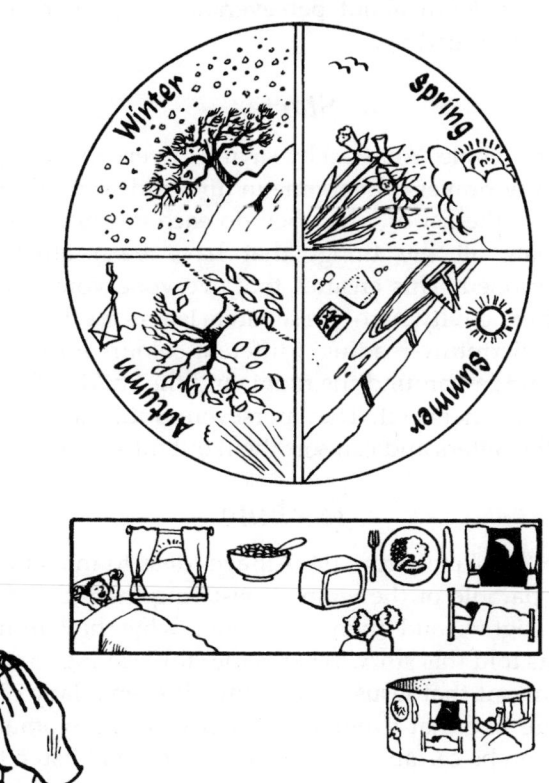

Turn the chart round like a wheel, and talk about the seasons and the way the same thing happens every year. Then point out that the days all have a pattern as well. Move the band round so that they can see the same pictures coming up day after day. There are some things we do every day.

Jesus tells us that we should make praying part of our daily pattern too. Have the praying picture, and stick it on the band in the morning, before eating, and before sleeping. Then turn the whole thing round a few times so they get the idea of the ongoing pattern.

Praying

When I wake up I say:
Good morning, Jesus!
Help me live your way today.

When I sit down to eat I say:
Thank you for this food.
Before I go to sleep I say:
Goodnight, Jesus.
Thank you for looking after me.

Activities

The worksheet helps them make their own day's band to use, and there is some pictorial teaching on how to pray.

PEARL DIVERS

Aim: To learn about perseverance in prayer and Scripture-reading.

Starter

Sit in a circle. You start by saying, 'Every morning I say my prayers.' Everyone in turn adds something else to the list of what they do each morning, and repeats all the things that have been already mentioned. This ensures that everyone voices the prayer activity. Also, the separate letters for 'Prayer' and 'Scripture-reading' (different colours for each) are hidden around the room, and the children sent to hunt them out. They persevere until they have all the letters and can sort them out into the words.

Teaching

Use the sketch from the All-age Ideas to introduce the parable of the woman pestering the judge for her rights, and then talk about why they think Jesus told this story. What is the story saying to us? Point out that Jesus was saying, 'If even a lazy old judge like that eventually listened to the woman, we can be certain that our loving God will listen to us straight away every time, and answer our prayer.' Sometimes his answer might be that we have to wait, or that what we are asking for wouldn't help us forward as much as we think it would.

Have an alarm clock, a knife and fork and spoon, a musical box lullaby, and a toothbrush and toothpaste.

Set them down and talk about these as being the times to remember to pray, so that we are sure to be praying at least at these times. It doesn't have to take hours, but we do need to make contact with God several times each day. Put a praying logo next to all of the items, and an open Bible in front of them, asking them to think of the best time for them to do this.

Show them some suitable daily Scripture-reading aids and invite parents to look at some Bible translations you recommend. (See page 11 for those I have found useful.)

Praying

Use the symbols from the teaching.

Lord God, I want to keep in touch with you
all through the day.
Help me to remember that in the morning
    (ring the alarm)
before I eat
    (clash the knife and fork)
and before I go to sleep
    (play the lullaby or brush teeth)
I can talk to you and know you are listening.

Activities

The worksheet helps them make a week's chart to set them off on the praying and Scripture-reading habit, for which they can be rewarded next week.

GOLD PANNERS

Aim: To learn the importance of Scripture-reading and prayer in growing as Christians.

Starter

Around the room have some Bible references displayed, and in other places the appropriate verses written out, without references. Number the references and letter-name the verses. Everyone is given paper, pen and Bible, so they can discover which verses and references go together. Recap on how to look references up in the Bible if necessary. Choose for the references some they are very familiar with and some from recent weeks' teaching.

Teaching

Check the Bible reference answers and point out how they are now able to find their way around their Bibles well enough to do that activity, which is excellent. Paul would be proud of them!

Read today's excerpt from Paul's letter to Timothy, so they can see that they are all following Paul's advice in learning from the Scriptures and getting to know them well. List the reasons given for Scripture-reading being beneficial.

God's Spirit enables us to grow as Christians, with daily prayer and Scripture-reading to help us.

Show a school timetable, and talk about why we organise our day with Maths and PE nearly always at the same time every week. Bring out the value of regular structure and routine in developing skills. It's just the same with prayer. We need to be persistent in our prayer. Jesus told one of his stories to make the point. Read the passage from Luke, or use the sketch from the All-age ideas.

Praying

Lord, you have taught us to pray
every day and in every situation.
You have taught us to read the word of God
and learn from it.
Help us to give more time
to these important things
so that we get to know and love you more
day by day throughout our lifetime. Amen.

Activities

Have a selection of daily Scripture-reading schemes available to look at and discuss, together with various different Bible translations they may find helpful. There is space on the worksheet to record the chosen times to set aside for Scripture-reading and daily prayer.

THIRTIETH SUNDAY OF THE YEAR

Thought for the day

When we recognise our dependence on God we will approach him with true humility and accept his gifts with joy.

Reflection on the readings

Ecclesiasticus 35:12-14, 16-17
Psalm 33
2 Timothy 4:6-8, 16-18
Luke 18:9-14

We all want to be independent, and any parent can remember the battles which mark the route! One of the hardest things for the ageing is having to gradually relinquish their independence, and many struggle on with great difficulty rather than asking for help. This kind of pride in our independence as humans is good and healthy. The danger comes when we lose touch with where we have come from, and forget that as created beings we are fundamentally dependent on our creator and sustainer, God himself.

The readings today express the praise and thanksgiving which result from recognising God's lavish showering of gifts on his people. There is so much to be thankful for, and the whole pattern of seasonal rain and growth work as a visible sign of God's Spirit drenching and soaking us as it is poured out over us in life-giving abundance.

To receive such a drenching we need to be like the earth, open and vulnerable, and ready to accept a soaking. It isn't any coincidence that the word 'humility' means 'earthiness'. And we simply can't be earthy if we are working on the principle that we have no need of God, or of anyone's help, and can manage perfectly well on our own, thank you.

While the Pharisee in today's Gospel is going through the motions of communicating with God, he is really affirming his own independent worth and has no concept of his deep need of God at all. It's like insisting on protecting our earth from rain; and if we do that, nothing can grow. In contrast the tax collector, complete with questionable morals and principles, at least recognises his basic dependence on God, and his need of God's mercy. It is this honesty before God that Jesus recommends.

Discussion starters

1. What kind of things in life remind us of our need of God, and what kind of things give us a false sense of superiority and independence of him?

2. What is your hope in God based on?

All-stage talk

Involve a couple of children in constructing a tower, using building blocks or large packing case cartons. When it is really high, suggest that now they won't need the big block at the bottom any more. Take it away, and of course the whole lot falls down. Be surprised, and protest that you only took one brick away! Then point out that it was the important brick you took – the foundation stone – and everything else depends on that.

Our whole lives depend on God. It's God who gives us life for a start, and provides our planet with what we need to live on. It is God's rain, sunshine and earth which we use to grow our wheat for bread and pizzas. We might sometimes forget to think about God, but he never ever forgets to think about us. He looks after us through our whole lives as we grow up and get old.

We heard another of Jesus' stories this morning, with some more cartoon-type characters. There's Pharisee Ferdinand and Tax Collector Ted.

Both of them have gone to pray. Let's look again at how Pharisee Ferdinand prays. (Display the picture, while a pompous voice reads the part. He needs to sound really smug.) Let people give their ideas of what's wrong with his prayer.

Let's listen in on Tax Collector Ted. (Show the picture, and have someone saying his prayer. This should sound quite genuine.) Comment on the way this person knows he needs God's mercy. And it was this person, Jesus said, who went away right with God, rather than Pharisee Ferdinand who did lots of good things but didn't have any idea of how much he depended on God, thinking that doing good things could earn him a special place in God's kingdom all by himself.

We owe our whole life to God. Let's not kid ourselves that we don't need him.

All-age ideas

- Act out today's Gospel, or use different people for the different voices.

- Have a display or a banner with words taken from Psalm 33: 'The humble shall hear and be glad'; or from the Gospel: 'For everyone who exalts himself will be humbled and everyone who humbles himself will be exalted'.

Prayer of the Faithful

Celebrant
Let us pray to the God who made us and sustains us.

Reader
We pray for the Church,
with all our faults and failings,
missed opportunities and misunderstandings;
may we be guided
to be truly the Body of Christ on earth.

Silence

God of our making:
have mercy on us.

We lay before the Lord the political issues,
the moral dilemmas and the dreams of peace
that concern our world,
and all who share its resources.
Where we can see no clear way forward
we pray for vision to enable us
to be good stewards of all God provides.

Silence

God of our making:
have mercy on us.

We pray that the Lord may take all our relationships
and drench them in his transforming love,

so that we appreciate one another more,
and value what each has to offer.

Silence

God of our making:
have mercy on us.

We pray for those who feel spiritually dried-up
or emotionally drained;
may the Lord heal and mend
broken bodies and broken hearts,
and provide clear pools of water for those
who are walking the valley of misery and depression.

Silence

God of our making:
have mercy on us.

We pray for those who have run the race
and fought the good fight;
may the Lord have mercy
on all who are at the point of death,
and receive them into his kingdom.

Silence

God of our making:
have mercy on us.

May we learn from the humility of Mary,
as we pray with her to the God of heaven:
Hail, Mary . . .

In silence now,
we make our private petitions to God,
who always hears our prayers of faith.

Silence

Celebrant
Lord God, accept these prayers,
through Christ our Lord.
Amen.

TREASURE SEEKERS

Aim: To know that we are to let God into our life as the earth lets in water.

Starter

Play with water and have lots of sponges, so they can try transferring water from one container to another using the sponges' soaking and water-holding quality.

Teaching

Have a tray of dry earth, and point out how nothing will grow in it if it stays as dry as this all the time, because things need water to grow. We can't grow any goodness in our lives if we don't get showered with God's love.

But that's all right, because God is always there showering us with his love. As you talk, shower the earth with a watering can. He gives us a beautiful world to live in, fruits and vegetables and animals and families to enjoy and look after. He gives us life, and minds to think with, and bodies to move around with.

All the time we keep ourselves open to God like this earth is open to the water, he can fill our lives with his love and we will grow more and more loving and truthful and good.

Praying

Thank you God
for the rain that falls.
(*make fingers into falling rain*)
Thank you for trees
that grow so tall.
(*stretch up*)
Thank you for this life
you have given us all!
(*move and dance about*)

Activities

Use the wet earth to plant some bulbs to be ready in the spring. The worksheet has a picture to colour and add the raindrops. Provide raindrops cut from shiny blue and silver wrapping paper for this.

PEARL DIVERS

Aim: To get to know the parable from Luke 18:9-14 and learn about being right with God.

Starter

A 'getting it right' game, such as sticking the tail on the donkey, blindfold, or using some conkers to roll on to a board with numbered squares on it. Where your conker lands is your score.

Teaching

Explain that Jesus found some people he was with were always looking down on others, and making out they were much better than everyone else. They seemed to have forgotten that they owed their whole life to God. Jesus didn't like to see that, and it made him sad. So he told them this story to show them how they were behaving, hoping it would make them realise what they were doing and try to change.

Use simple puppets, made out of wooden

spoons or spatulas, to tell the story. The pictures below will help you with the expressions. Then talk about which one of the two went home right with God, and why. Reinforce that we all depend on God for our life, and everything comes from him.

Praying

You know us, Lord,
so we can't pretend with you.
You shower us with blessings
like a shower of rain;
you give us your power
to make us grow more loving
all through our lives.

Activities

Using the sheet the children can make their own puppets. With these they can use the script provided, which reinforces our need to be in a right position with God, knowing our dependence on him.

GOLD PANNERS

Aim: To look at God's gifts poured out on us when we are right with him.

Starter

A *'correct alignment' challenge*. Place a marble on a chair, and a tray on the floor about one metre away. Provide an assortment of tubes. The challenge is to get the marble from the chair to the tray, using the tubes. This will only work if they get the tubes lined up correctly.

Teaching

Point out how the marble wouldn't have arrived at the tray unless they had got the tubes right. God pours out the blessings of his Spirit on us, but if we are not right with him we can't access them in the same way. Read the passage from Ecclesiasticus, showing how the person who is wholeheartedly working with God will be heard.

We need to be aware of all God gives us. Make a

group list of the ways in which God hears different people and responds to them. Obviously, having the right attitude to God is important.

Read the Gospel for today, where Jesus is drawing attention to wrong attitudes to God and one another in our praying. Have different people reading the different parts, and discuss the reason why Jesus said that the tax collector went home right with God rather than the Pharisee, even though the tax collector was obviously not a paragon of virtue. What does this say to us about our prayer life? Record some guidelines for a good and valuable prayer life which you can pick up from the story. (Examples might be being honest with God, telling him how we really feel, recognising his power in our lives, valuing his love and help, asking him for insight to see what needs changing and help in doing something about it.)

Finally read Paul's letter to Timothy to hear Paul's thankfulness at God's constant friendship and help right through his life.

Praying

I will bless the Lord at all times,
his praise always on my lips;
in the Lord my soul shall make its boast.
The humble shall hear and be glad.

(From Psalm 33)

Activities

Along the pieces of tube write: 'Line yourself up with God's values and receive his blessing!' Then line them up again and send lots of marbles sliding down the tubes and into the tray. The worksheet helps them record the main points of the discussion and the prayer life hints.

THIRTY-FIRST SUNDAY OF THE YEAR

Thought for the day

Jesus came to search out the lost and save them. Through him we come to our senses and make our lives clean.

Reflection on the readings

Wisdom 11:22-12:2
Psalm 144
2 Thessalonians 1:11-2:2
Luke 19:1-10

With all the hurt of a parent who expects honesty from a child he loves and finds instead that he is living a lie, God's indignation burns. Perhaps we too have felt the pain of discovering that someone, who has been speaking pleasantly to our faces, has been ridiculing or insulting us behind our backs. The deceit hurts as much as the actual offence.

God cannot bear hypocrisy. All through the Bible, both in the Old and the New Testament, we find this loathing of falsehood and pretence; we get the impression that he would prefer an honest sinner any day to the mealy-mouthed obsequiousness described so well in Dickens' Uriah Heap. In Jesus' day it was the hypocrisy of the Pharisees which most often drew his harshest words.

The reading from Wisdom shows that God rides way above human hypocrisy or fickleness. He is a God of mercy and compassion to whom everyone can turn to find a better way of living.

Psalm 144 beautifully expresses that wonderful feeling of freedom and lightness that comes when we finally get round to accepting the forgiveness and healing compassion that God gives to us.

Perhaps Zacchaeus had spent considerable time and effort persuading himself of all kinds of good reasons for living the life he did, but there was always the deep-down nagging suspicion that there was a better way. Certainly he made quite an effort to see Jesus once he knew he would be in the area, and Jesus, always in touch with his Father's viewpoint, noticed the first tentative reaching out and responded to it.

So it is with us. As soon as we make the first tentative move to desire honesty and cleansed thoughts, God will pick up our longing and run with it, bringing us into contact with help and encouragement or challenge, just as we need it. Real and expensive sacrifices may well need to be made, but we will find we are making them out of choice, without resentment, and over the years God will keep his promise to restore the years the locusts have eaten.

Discussion starters

1. Are we sometimes put off from making big, radical changes to our lifestyle or our giving in case we won't be able to cope? What does Zacchaeus' story say to us about such fears?

2. In what ways would we like God to 'make us worthy of his call'?

All-stage talk

Bring along some wallpaper, paste and brush, and some foundation make-up. Introduce these items, talking about what a difference they can make to the look of a room or a face, and how we carefully choose and apply them.

Point out that much as we may want to make our faces and rooms beautiful with what shows, like wallpaper and make-up, we always have to start on the hidden hard work. We need to make sure our faces are completely clean before we go on making them even more beautiful; we have to make sure our walls are properly repaired and strong before applying the wallpaper.

In our spiritual lives it is just the same, and in our first reading we heard how God patiently and lovingly helps us with the whole process. He understands the way we want to rush, or miss out the boring but necessary bits, and gently he trains us to be better at this. He knows that if we don't attack the root problems of sin in our lives it will be like using nice wallpaper to cover a crumbling wall, or make-up to cover a spot. It certainly doesn't help the problem and may well make it worse.

Zacchaeus knew something was wrong in his life. When Jesus came to his house, he helped him to sort out the problem properly, instead of just covering it over and hoping it would go away. Sin never goes away unless we deal with it properly. It isn't any good trying to make it look pretty or covering it over with excuses. Like Zacchaeus we need to invite Jesus in and deal with it.

All-age ideas

- Have a group of people to read the Wisdom passage, some lines with a single voice, others with two or three voices together. Work through the reading and try out different voice group-ings to bring out the meaning and the gentle mercy of it.

- Act out the Gospel, using a narrator and other people reading the different parts.

Prayer of the Faithful

Celebrant
Let us still ourselves in our Father's presence
and tell him what is on our hearts.

Reader
We pray that the Lord may look into us and teach us
to know ourselves more honestly,
to recognise the areas which need cleansing,
and inspire us to live more faithfully and fruitfully
as the people of God.

Silence

Lord, may our lives:
express our love for you.

We pray that parliaments
and all places of government
throughout the world may be filled
with a desire for integrity and a determination
to stamp out corruption and deceit.

Silence

Lord, may our lives:
express our love for you.

May the Lord speak his peace and reconciliation
into all family disputes
and hurtful misunderstandings;
and may a spirit of loving community
be nurtured in our neighbourhood,
heightening our awareness of one another's needs.

Silence

Lord, may our lives:
express our love for you.

We pray that the Lord may bring
reassurance and practical help
to those who are close to despair
and those in long-term suffering;
may he use us as instruments of his healing love.

Silence

Lord, may our lives:
express our love for you.

We pray for those
who have faithfully lived out their days;
as we miss their physical presence,
may they be brought into the peace
of God's kingdom.

Silence

Lord, may our lives:
express our love for you.

As we join our prayers with those of Mary,
may we learn from her responsive love:
Hail, Mary . . .

In silence, now,
we pour out to God our Father
any needs and burdens
known to us personally.

Silence

Celebrant
Heavenly Father,
trusting in your amazing love,
we ask you to accept these prayers.
Through Christ our Lord.
Amen.

TREASURE SEEKERS

Aim: To be introduced to the story of Zacchaeus.

Starter

Spot the birds. Fix a number of bird pictures high up around the room. Show the children an example of what they are looking for, and set them off hunting for the pictures, but don't tell them they will have to look up to see them. Let them discover that for themselves.

Teaching

Prepare the tree by fixing a card or thick paper tree outline to a chair, so that when Zacchaeus stands on the chair you can just see his face over the top of the tree. Give Jesus and Zacchaeus head-dresses to wear, and have all the other children standing at the side of the road as Jesus comes walking through their village. Let Zacchaeus lead Jesus and his friends across the room to his house (some chairs can make the walls) where they sit down to eat. Then they can come outside for Zacchaeus to announce to all the people waiting outside that he is changing his life. He's going to stop cheating people out of their money, and pay back all his debts four times over. All the people can give him three cheers and a round of applause.

Point out that although Zacchaeus was short, he wasn't too short to work with God. They may be short, but they are not too short or too young to work with God either.

Praying

Look, Lord,
I may be short
but I am not too short
to be your friend.
I want to be in your team
and work with you today.

Activities

They can all make a tall tree with Zacchaeus in it to remind them of the story. You will need a length of wallpaper for each child, cut into a trunk, and the tree's crown.

PEARL DIVERS

Aim: To learn about the fun of being forgiven and having a fresh start.

Starter

Bring a selection of chalkboards, chalk and dampened cloths, magic slates (which let you erase what you have written), white board, pens and cleaning cloth, and sand trays. Have a time of free play with these, so they can enjoy the satisfaction of drawing and erasing and starting again.

Teaching

Talk about what they have been doing, and the fun of being able to start again whenever you make a mistake. Sometimes we make mistakes and do things that are wrong, and we wish they could be rubbed out as well as our drawings today.

Well, with Jesus, they can! Today we are going to hear about someone who met Jesus and was able to make a completely fresh start.

Tell the story of Zacchaeus using cut-out pictures on a background of carpet tiles or towels. The children can help place the houses and trees, and the crowd of people. As you tell the story, get the children to imagine what the other people were thinking when Jesus noticed the cheating tax collector, what Zacchaeus was thinking when he was noticed, and how he felt when he made a fresh start.

Praying

Lord my God,
you and I both know
the mistakes I make in life.
Please rub them out for me,
and forgive me all my sins
so that I can make a fresh start,
starting today.

Activities

On the worksheet there are instructions for making a tree with Zacchaeus in it (using a flap), and a cartoon story to remind them of how good it feels to be forgiven and start afresh.

GOLD PANNERS

Aim: To see that Jesus enables us to make a fresh start when we have got our lives into a mess.

Starter

Play 'Twister', or make a long loop of string which everyone holds. When they have made themselves and the string loop into a muddle they sort themselves out, without letting go of the string.

Teaching

Today we are going to look at how God helps us sort out our lives when we have got them into a mess. Start with the Wisdom reading which tells how, because he loves us, God can overlook our sins so that we can repent.

Then read the story of Zacchaeus, giving a few background details of how tax-collectors were generally regarded and why. What might the people have been expecting Jesus to say to Zacchaeus in the tree? How would they have felt about his actual words, in view of his reputation? What do they think made Zacchaeus want to change his ways?

Do we take seriously enough the fact that God will judge us, or do we tend to assume he'll let us off? Knowing there will be some kind of judgement, what do we need to sort out and change?

Praying

When I kept things to myself,
I felt weak deep inside me.
I moaned all day long.
Day and night
you punished me.
My strength was gone
as in the summer heat.
Then I confessed my sins to you.
I didn't hide my guilt.
I said, 'I will confess my sins to the Lord.'
And you forgave my guilt.

(From Psalm 31)

Activities

Allow them to spend a little time on their own, thinking over their life with God, and looking for any areas they want to put right, and then come together in the shape of a cross, to offer these things silently to God and celebrate his forgiveness and the promise of a fresh start.

THIRTY-SECOND SUNDAY OF THE YEAR

Thought for the day

Life after death is not wishful thinking but a definite reality.

Reflection on the readings

Maccabees 7:1-2, 9-14
Psalm 16
2 Thessalonians 2:16-3:5
Luke 20:27-38

When you have a favourite author, it is disappointing to get to the end of the last available novel she has written; my mother, with considerable enforced reading time, felt quite lost after the Cadfael books ran out. On one occasion I read *War and Peace* straight through twice because I couldn't bear to finish it!

When we set off on the journey of discovery into friendship with God, there is no problem of getting to the end of him, or having to break our relationship with him simply because our physical body has stopped working. We can carry on enjoying his friendship, and an ever-deepening understanding of his nature throughout the whole of eternity. There is no end to God, and, through the redeeming work of Christ, there need be no end to us either, so we can look forward to life beyond death and enjoy the prospect of living in God's company for ever.

The Sadducees had decided that the idea of resurrection wasn't workable and therefore couldn't be true. As so often happens, they were judging God's ways by human limitations. They worked out this complicated problem to make Jesus realise how silly it is to think there can be life after death. Faced with this conundrum he will surely have to admit that they are sensible and right in their belief.

What Jesus does is to show them that they are asking the wrong question. Resurrection life is not a tangled continuation of the earthly order of things, but a new and different experience, just as real but with whole new dimensions of possibility.

It is rather like arguing that caterpillars couldn't possibly fly. In their present state and with their present limitations it is indeed impossible, but the freshly emerging butterfly proves that flying is a perfectly natural progression from leaf munching. Few of us would ever guess that a caterpillar could turn into a butterfly, and similarly we have little exact idea of what our resurrection life will be like. What we do know is that it will be fulfilling and rewarding, full of joy, peace and love.

In the meantime we are to stand firm and stick to the teachings we have been handed down faithfully through the generations in an unbroken line which can be traced back to Christ himself. That will enable us to discern the false rumours from the truth, and we will be ready to enter the glorious heritage of resurrection life in heaven.

Discussion starters

1. Why do you think many who would call themselves Christians find it difficult to accept the reality of life after death?

2. Pool any remembered references in the Bible that point to life after death being a reality, and look

up some others using a concordance. Using these, how would you help someone to understand more about heaven?

All-stage talk

Bring along some tasters of a particular cheese, tiny chunks such as those you find in most supermarkets from time to time. Bring also a block of the same cheese, labelled.

Show your tray of tasters for the cheese you have brought to recommend. Since these tasters came off the main block of cheese, you can guarantee that they will taste as good as the main block.

Although we haven't been to heaven, God gives us lots of little 'tasters' which help us find out what it is like. Whenever we sense Jesus giving us peace of mind or joy, or the lovely knowledge that God really loves and cares for us, we are getting a taster of life after death. Jesus lives in heaven so when he comes into us, he doesn't leave heaven behind but brings it with him. So the more we live in God's company and follow Jesus, the more of heaven we will have in our lives even before we die.

Explain that lots of people think Christians are crazy believing that there is life after death. Since they can't see beyond death, they don't think there can be anything like heaven. If I had never seen the yellow daffodil flowers in spring, I would probably think people were crazy burying dry bulbs in their earth at this time of year. But because I have seen what happens to those bulbs, I trust that they won't just rot in the ground. If I were a caterpillar, I would probably laugh at anyone suggesting that one day I would be flying about with colourful wings. It isn't true that the only real things are those we can see.

It is sometimes difficult to trust that what we can't see is still there, but we make the effort to do it whenever we drive in fog, walk along looking around instead of at the path under our feet, or wash our backs. So it is quite possible. And Jesus has told us that there really is life after death, and lots of people saw him alive after he had died. So we aren't crazy for believing there is life after death; we happen to know it's true, and we've already tasted little bits of how lovely it is.

All-age ideas

• Play a recording, or suggest the choir sing *I know that my Redeemer liveth*.

• Decorate the church with brightly coloured flowers and dried flowers, to make it all look bright and beautiful, even in November.

• Make a colourful 'Welcome!' for everyone to walk through as they come into church.

Prayer of the Faithful

Celebrant
Let us pray to the great God of heaven
who stands among us now.

Reader
We pray that we, the earthly part of the Church,
may always reflect
the living presence of Christ among us,
in our liturgy and in our daily living.

Silence

You are our God:
living for ever and ever.

We pray for guidance in our world
as we work out policies and target needs,
and misunderstand one another's cultures
and get carried away with excesses
and the taste of power.

Silence

You are our God:
living for ever and ever.

We pray that our waking, working, eating,
relaxing and sleeping
may become a pattern coloured and lit by God's love;
may our homes reflect it,
our places of work be energised by it,
and our relationships glow with it.

Silence

You are our God:
living for ever and ever.

To those who are losing heart
we pray that the Lord may give
his heavenly encouragement and patience;
to the young and vulnerable
give his heavenly protection;
to the ill and the damaged
give his heavenly healing and inner peace,
as he touches our lives.

Silence

You are our God:
living for ever and ever.

Knowing that physical death
is not the end of life,
but the beginning of a new dimension,
we recall our loved ones who have died
and commend them to God's eternal keeping.

Silence

You are our God:
living for ever and ever.

We pray now with Mary,
Mother of our risen Lord:
Hail, Mary . . .

God our Father loves us as his children;
together in silence,
we name our personal prayer burdens.

Silence

Celebrant
All-powerful God, accept these prayers,
through Christ our Lord.
Amen.

TREASURE SEEKERS

Aim: To know that Jesus told us life goes on after death.

Starter

Place some tiny cakes decorated with chocolate drops in a box or tin, and have an extra packet of chocolate drops with you. Tell the children that there is something nice in the tin. Can they see it, without taking off the lid? No. Do they trust you to tell them the truth? (I wonder!) Do they believe that there really is something nice in the tin?

Assure them that there really is something nice in it, and you are going to give them a little idea of what it is like. Now give each child a chocolate drop to enjoy. What do they think is in the tin? Well, it's certainly something to do with chocolate drops. Open the tin so they can all see. It's like chocolate drops but even better, because there's a whole cake, decorated with a chocolate drop for everyone. Now you can give them out one by one, so that everyone has one.

Teaching

When Jesus was walking about on our earth he told his friends that life goes on after our bodies wear out and die. He told them heaven was a nice place to be, and they would be very happy there. (As you say this, hold the closed tin.)

Can we trust Jesus to tell us the truth? Yes, we can.

So if Jesus said there is life after we die, and people are happy there, can we believe him? Yes, we can.

What will it be like? (Pick up the empty packet of chocolate drops.) Jesus gives his friends some clues, and he lets us feel the joy and happiness and peace and love of heaven sometimes. Heaven will be like that only much, much better!

Praying

Be near me, Lord Jesus, I ask thee to stay
close by me for ever and love me I pray.
Bless all the dear children in thy tender care
and fit us for heaven to live with thee there.

Activities

There is a dot-to-dot angel to complete, and then they can draw and paint heaven in their favourite colours. If you want to make this a collage picture, bring along an assortment of different colours and textures for them to use.

PEARL DIVERS

Aim: To stretch our minds to imagine things beyond our physical sight.

Starter

Put on some praise music on tape, and do lots of strenuous stretching exercises to the music, till their bodies are well and truly stretched.

Teaching

Explain that we have been stretching our bodies and now we are going to stretch our minds as well. (Don't rush this journey – shut your own eyes and actually imagine it as you direct them and that will get the timing right.) Get them to shut their eyes and imagine their town all around them . . . and beyond that all the countryside stretching out to the sea all around them . . . imagine the round world curving away from where they are sitting so they are riding on the ball-shaped planet earth through space, going slowly round the brilliant sun. Take them on a speeded-up reverse journey to end up back in (St Andrew's) hall, where they can open their eyes.

Even though we don't usually think about it or imagine it, we are actually doing that journey all the time! We really are perched on the outside of a planet, riding through space around the sun.

Jesus liked to get people to stretch their minds. There is so much that we can't see because it's too huge, or too minute, or simply invisible. We can't see heaven but Jesus told his friends that there definitely is life after death, and when we die we will know exactly what it is like.

For the moment, though, while we live bound by things like time and space, we can only imagine how wonderful and brilliant heaven will be.

Some people, both now and then, didn't believe in life after death. They came to Jesus and asked him a tricky question. (You can either use children or lego-type people for this.)

There was this woman (choose a girl to stand up) and she got married (choose a boy to stand). Then the husband died (boy falls down) so she married someone else (another boy stands up) . . . Carry on for seven husbands. Now at the resurrection (all the dead husbands stand up again), who is the woman going to be married to? (The girl pretends to look very puzzled.)

Let everyone sit down again. The people asking the question thought Jesus would have to agree that life after death was a silly idea. But he didn't. Jesus told them that they were expecting life in heaven to carry on in just the same way as life on earth, but it's not like that. In heaven there won't be things like who's married to whom, because we will be like angels, just happy to be God's children.

Praying

And our eyes at last shall see him
through his own redeeming love.
For that child, so dear and gentle,
is our Lord in heaven above.
And he leads his children on
to the place where he is gone.

Activities

On the sheet there are some examples of the 'tasters' of heaven we are given on earth, and space for them to include others. There are also some mind-stretching puzzles.

GOLD PANNERS

Aim: To explore the evidence for believing in life after death.

Starter

Beforehand collect a tape of fragments of pop music. Play this and see if they can work out which songs the snippets have come from. (Or do this with TV programmes – either the dialogue or music.)

Teaching

Like the little snippets of sound we've just heard, we are given little experiences of what heaven is like while we are still living on earth. Since life in heaven is life with God, we don't have to wait till we die to begin living our resurrection life of love and joy and inner peace; we can start now. When Jesus broke through death and took his humanity

into heaven, all kinds of possibilities were opened up for us.

The book of Maccabees was written long before Jesus' time, and yet in this curious story there is an amazing confidence in the reality of eternal life.

Next look at the Sadducees and their trick question for Jesus. Use pictures of men and a woman cut from a mail-order catalogue to accompany the complicated situation, and stop before finding out what Jesus said for their own ideas of a reply. Then read what Jesus said, trying to tease out the way he replied to their fears and misunderstandings, rather than the question itself.

Obviously this is an area where some false teaching could easily creep in. Read 2 Thessalonians 2:16-3:5 to see that Paul is determined about us standing firm and sticking to the teaching which goes directly back to when Jesus was walking about visibly in person.

Praying

I call to you, God, and you answer me.
Listen to me now; hear what I say.
Protect me as you would protect your own eye.
Protect me as a bird hides her young under her wings.

(From Psalm 16)

Activities

On the worksheet they can be lawyers on the case of 'Heaven?' and record their answers to various common questions and misunderstandings about life after death, using the suggested Bible references to help.

THIRTY-THIRD SUNDAY OF THE YEAR

Thought for the day

There will be dark and dangerous times as the end approaches, but by standing firm through it all we will gain life.

Reflection on the readings

Malachi 3:19-20
Psalm 97
2 Thessalonians 3:7-12
Luke 21:5-19

The Gospel for today makes terrifying reading. The seemingly solid beauty of the temple seems to have triggered in Jesus a vision of the world from outside time. Like a speeded-up film we scan the great cosmic cycles and seasons, natural disasters and human agonies, as the earth labours towards its time of accomplishment.

Amongst the terror, distress, upheavals and ructions are scattered the bright lights of individuals who are unperturbed and faithful; those who are not drawn into the panic but remain steadfast, strong as rocks in their perseverance.

We may well wonder how we could ever survive; what hope there could possibly be of us joining the number of those who will win eternal life by their endurance. Certainly Jesus is anxious to stress that it will not be an easy ride, nor a natural consequence of setting out with enthusiasm on the Christian journey. We can't take our salvation for granted and then sit back with our feet up.

We are warned of what to expect to enable us to be prepared, and the important truth is that we shall not be doing all this on our own or in our own strength. We will be yoked up with Jesus, sustained by his power and provided with the right words and the necessary courage. Only one second at a time will be expected of us!

There is no way church congregations or individual Christians will be able to shut their doors and hide away from the troubles and threats of the world. Our place is right in the centre of the action, getting involved, and standing up for what is right and just, whatever the personal consequences may be.

Discussion starters

1. What are the dangers of spiritual idleness, both personally and corporately, and how can we guard against it sidling into our lives?

2. What are the effects of opposition and persecution on people's faith?

All-stage talk

Prepare some large card road signs, and a cereal packet which is labelled 'The last age' on the front and has 'Warnings and advice' with a copy of today's Gospel stuck on the back. Bring these along, together with a packet of cigarettes, and something packed in a plastic bag with the warning of suffocation printed on it.

Begin by asking volunteers to hold the road signs at intervals down the aisle, and ask a couple of people to 'drive their car' among the signs. Talk them through, getting people to say what the signs mean as they come to them, and encouraging them to react appropriately. (If a roundabout sign is used, for instance, they can drive round an imaginary roundabout.) Point out how useful the signs are in warning us so that we are better prepared as we drive.

Show the cigarette packet and read out the warning on that, and on the plastic bag. Lots of things have warnings and good advice printed on them – hair colouring, pain-killers, frozen pies and skateboards – the manufacturer wants customers to be warned of any dangers and know how to avoid them.

Now pick up the prepared cereal packet, and show the 'product name'. Today's Gospel is doing the same thing. It's offering us some warnings and advice for living through this: the last age. We are in the middle of this at the moment. It's the time between Jesus dying on the cross and coming to life again and going to heaven (which has already happened) and the Day of Judgement, or the Second Coming, which will mark the end of things as we know them. (That hasn't happened yet.)

Jesus knew this would be a very difficult and dangerous age to live in, and he told his disciples to watch for the signs and be prepared. (Turn the packet of cereal round and show the warnings and advice.) Compulsive cereal packet readers will find it may put them off their breakfast. It's the section of Luke's Gospel that we've all just heard this morning.

Pick up on some of the phrases to remind people, and help them see that these things are indeed happening in places all over the world. The signs are there. So what are we to do about them?

Our job as Christians is to stand firm and not get fazed when these terrible things happen, but be in there helping, comforting and doing our best to show and proclaim God's love by our words and actions, even when we get laughed at, despised or persecuted in the process.

Perhaps you are thinking that sounds very hard. Well, you're right, it is very hard and we may feel like giving up. But God promises to be there with us through it all, and will make sure we have all the courage we need to do it. We are warned and prepared specially, because God wants us to be able to stay firm to the end and be saved.

All-age ideas

- As a reflection on the Gospel, try this mime. Play some music from Delirious? ('Sanctify' from *King of Fools* works really well) as a background, or if your parish has more traditional tastes, try some Taizé music, such as *O Lord, hear my prayer*; if tastes are classical try some Shostakovich. Have groups of people all over the church ready to jeer and buffet two or three people who are starting at the back of the church and trying to make their way through the persecution and terror of the last days. One of them gives up and stomps off to the back, but the others make it all the way to the front, reaching out to others along the way in love and comfort, in spite of their treatment. One or two of the jeerers are persuaded to join them. As they reach the front they raise their arms in praise and joy, and everyone in the congregation can applaud. Make the actions slow and deliberate.

- Read part of Psalm 97 in parts using the whole congregation, like this:

Men   Let the sea and all within it thunder,

Children the world and all its peoples.

Women   Let the rivers clap their hands *(all clap)*

Men   and the hills ring out their joy

Children at the presence of the Lord.

Women   For the Lord comes, he comes to rule the earth.

All   *(to one another)*
He will rule the world with justice
and the peoples with fairness.

Prayer of the Faithful

Celebrant
The Lord is always ready to listen;
let us pray to him now.

Reader
We pray particularly for those
whose faith is being battered
and those who no longer pray;
we pray that our faith
may be deepened and strengthened.

Silence

Lord, keep us faithful:
firm to the end.

We pray for those whose responsibility it is
to manage the world's economy,
and for those who have difficult
ethical decisions to make;
we pray for wisdom and courage to do what is right.

Silence

Lord, keep us faithful:
firm to the end.

We pray for the world our children will inherit
and ask blessings on all parents
and the responsibilities they face;
we ask for understanding, maturity,
and the gift of laughter.

Silence

Lord, keep us faithful:
firm to the end.

We pray for the victims of disasters,
famines, earthquakes and plagues;
for all who are crying
and those who have no tears left.
We pray for comfort, renewed strength,
and available friends.

Silence

Lord, keep us faithful:
firm to the end.

We pray for those who are nearing death
and those who have died;
especially we pray for those
who have died suddenly and unprepared.
We pray for mercy and forgiveness.

Silence

Lord, keep us faithful:
firm to the end.

We pray with Mary,
who followed her Son even to Calvary:
Hail, Mary . . .

In silence now,
we make our private petitions to God,
who knows what is in our hearts.

Silence

Celebrant
God our Father,
trusting in your constant care and protection,
we bring you these prayers.
Through Christ our Lord.
Amen.

TREASURE SEEKERS

Aim: To know that God is a fair judge.

Starter

Weighing and sorting games, using lots of different items, such as stones, vegetables, pasta, bricks, saucepans and feathers. Sort according to shape, use or colour. Use balance scales, or hang two baskets at either end of a broom handle and hold it in the middle. The children can try to balance the baskets.

Teaching

Using toys or puppets, act out several situations which are not fair. Tell the children to shout out

'That's not fair!' as soon as they spot something which isn't. Then talk about why it isn't fair, and act out the same situation, this time making it fair. Here are some ideas for situations:

- Three sweets are shared out between three toys with one toy having two sweets and one having none.

- It's clearing-up time and one toy is allowed to carry on reading while the others have to do all the tidying up on their own.

- The toys are playing 'catch' and one says he hasn't been caught when really he has.

Our God always judges justly, or fairly. He always knows both sides of the story, and he is always fair. So we can trust him.

God has made us able to tell what is fair, so that we can play fairly and grow wise, choosing to do what is right and just. God wants us to stand up for what is fair. He doesn't want people to treat each other badly and unfairly.

Praying

Dear God,
you are a good judge.
You are always fair.
Help me to be fair as well.

Activities

They can make their own set of balances to use at home. They will each need two yoghurt pots, wool, and half a pea stick. The worksheet gives instructions.

PEARL DIVERS

Aim: To know that standing firm to the end is hard but worthwhile.

Starter

No yes, no no. Try to answer everyone's questions without using the words 'yes' and 'no'.

Teaching

Look at some examples of signs that tell us about things that are going to happen, like posters to advertise plays and concerts, road signs, weather signs (such as 'red sky at night, shepherds' delight', and cloud formations) and illness signs (such as feeling hot and shaky, or having a rash).

Today we are going to hear about the signs which Jesus said would mark the coming of the last age before all things are completed at the end of time.

Have ready a large sheet titled: 'Signs of the last age', and pictures to represent the signs and events, which are fixed on to the sheet as they are mentioned. You can use the pictures below.

Point out that we are in the last age at the moment, as we live between the Resurrection and the Second Coming.

Jesus warned his friends that this would be a difficult and dangerous age to live in and stay faithful to God. And that is true. Since Jesus said these words, lots of his followers have been arrested and imprisoned.

At this point, have a leader bursting into the room with some plastic handcuffs, without smiling, and very officious. Is there a Thomas Godshill here? They have reason to believe that this man is a Christian and they've come to arrest him. The other leaders protest, in a frightened way, that there aren't any Christians here, but Thomas (forewarned and primed, of course) stands out and proclaims that yes, he is a Christian, and worships the living God! The police angrily grab and arrest him, putting him in prison, behind a row of chairs.

Hopefully this episode will take the children by surprise so that they get a sense of danger, but without being unduly scared.

Jesus promised that though being his followers may involve getting teased or even imprisoned and tortured, we will always have Jesus' companionship, and 'by standing firm, you will gain life'.

Praying

O Jesus, I have promised
to serve thee to the end;
be thou for ever near me,
my Master and my friend;
I shall not fear the battle
if thou art by my side,
nor wander from the pathway
if thou wilt be my guide.

Activities

Make a group banner or poster to express the darkness and dangers, with candle flames of light to represent people living out good Christian lives in the middle of it. These form a winding path through the turmoil to a burst of light at the top of the picture.

GOLD PANNERS

Aim: To recognise the dangers that Christians are willing to face as they stand firm to the end during the last age.

Starter

Any kind of team game where you are playing against an opposition team, and aiming to get through the difficulties to a goal – for example, football, netball, basketball.

Teaching

Read the passage from Malachi first, with one person reading the destruction part in verse 19, and another the verses of hope in verse 20. These are shown on the worksheet in the form of a pair of scales to help them see the sense of God's justice.

Explain that people of Israel had been told about the coming of 'the terrible day of the Lord', or the day of God's judgement, all through their history, by one prophet after another. When Jesus was getting close to the end of his earthly ministry, he too taught them, urging them to look for the signs of its coming.

Now read today's Gospel from Luke 21:5-19. You may prefer to use *The Message* version for this passage with this age group. Make a note of what the signs are, what made Jesus foretell these things, and what he warned his followers about during the last age. Discuss the signs with reference to the history of the Church, and our own day.

Praying

Gracious Lord,
your Son came to bring us good news

and power to transform our lives;
grant that when he comes again as judge
we may be ready to meet him with joy;
through Jesus Christ our Lord. Amen.

(From the South African Prayer Book)

Activities

Copy some case histories of prisoners of conscience in various parts of the world, available from Amnesty International or from the Diocesan Justice and Peace Commission, together with their recommendations for letter-writing. Work out letters to ask for their release, write these on aerogrammes, pray for the people and the authorities, and have the letters sent.

CHRIST THE KING

Thought for the day

This Jesus, dying by crucifixion between criminals, is the anointed King of all creation in whom all things are reconciled.

Reflection on the readings

2 Samuel 5:1-3
Psalm 121
Colossians 1:11-20
Luke 23:35-43

The idea of a Shepherd King touches a deep chord in us; there is a rightness of balance, a wholesome combination of authority and practical caring, which rings true and speaks of safety and security. The tradition is already there in David, the shepherd boy anointed king, and now it is given even more powerful meaning.

God's great rescue plan is extraordinarily focused at the crossing of two rough pieces of wood, designed for use in Roman executions. Yet it is as if those two pieces of wood, which form the cross on which the Shepherd King hangs dying, extend onwards and outwards across the whole of human experience, the depth of human suffering and the height of human joy. They stretch out to unite our deepest needs with the most complete fulfilment; they draw together all things from all generations and cultures, into that point of reconciliation at the point of complete love.

The cross becomes a throne, where the kingdom of forgiving love is seen in action; costly forgiveness serenaded with insults and sneers. The attendants, finding the innocent Jesus beside them, sharing their hours of deserved agony, are representative of us all. Wherever our wanderings have taken us we need only turn our head to see him there suffering with us. We too can react either in disgust at this terrible vulnerability of God's love, or we can allow the acceptance and forgiveness to work its healing in us, long before we can understand the full implications.

Today we look back over the unfolded story of God's redeeming love that we have explored during the past year, and the journey brings us firmly back to the cross, which fixes and anchors everything. Being a cross, it also points us to look forward, to a deepening understanding of the Incarnation as we approach Advent and Christmas once again.

Discussion starters

1. Why didn't Jesus come down from the cross?

2. If the throne of the King we worship is a cross, how does that challenge our values and expectations of success in life?

All-stage talk

Beforehand prepare a flock of large card sheep. Numbers will depend on your congregation; there need to be at least six.

Begin by talking about the way sheep get easily scared, and will scuttle away a few metres and then stop and eat, and then scuttle away again and eat again. That's why they can easily get lost, because they don't realise how far they have scuttled! Children with little experience of sheep may have noticed a similar 'scuttle, eat, scuttle' pattern in rabbits, who also get scared very easily.

Introduce your flock of sheep, with a volunteer holding each one. Those who are holding them can give them names, or they can be given the names of the children. All through the Bible we read that people are rather like sheep. We get scared (though we usually try to hide that and pretend we aren't scared at all) and we follow one another into all sorts of rather silly and dangerous places and ideas, and we tend to wander off and get lost. (Send the sheep to do that now.)

God promised that he would be sending his people a king – a good king, whose kingdom would last for ever. Ask for a volunteer and place a crown on their head. But he also knew that his people were like sheep, so this king would not be the kind of king who bosses everybody around and makes them give him all their money so he can be the richest person in the world. God decided that this king would be a shepherd. (Give the king a crook.)

And he would go and search for all the lost sheep and bring them safely back to their pasture again. (Send the shepherd king off to do that.)

When the shepherd king has brought all the sheep back, explain that Jesus, the Christ, is our King, and he is the sort of king who knows us each by name, and searches for us when we are lost, and looks after us when he has found us.

In the Gospel today we heard that even when Jesus was dying on the cross he was still searching for lost sheep, right up to the moment he died. Two criminals were being executed with him that day, and one of them, only hours before he died, turned to him and asked for help. Straight away Jesus assured him of forgiveness; he had just brought another sheep back home to its pasture.

Ask the shepherd king to stretch out his arms. Point out that when Jesus, our King, was on the cross, his arms were stretched out like this, so he was in the shape of a cross, and this is the shape of welcoming love.

All-age ideas

- Lay the card sheep from the all-stage talk on the floor around the altar or some other place where everyone can see them.

- Focus attention on the cross today, surrounding it with flowers, and hanging a crown around it. Or have an arrangement of flowers which expresses the idea of a Shepherd King, with a crown and a crook.

Prayer of the Faithful

Celebrant
Through Jesus, our King,
let us pray to God the Father.

Reader
As we celebrate Jesus, the head of the Church body,
we pray for all the members
with their various gifts and ministries;
we pray that even our weaknesses
can be used for the glory of God
and for the good of the world.

Silence

Christ is the image:
of the invisible God we worship.

May all monarchs and heads of state
be led in ways of truth and righteousness,
and recognise with humility
that they are called to serve.
We pray for all shepherds,
rescue teams and trouble-shooters;
for all who work to recover the lost.

Silence

Christ is the image:
of the invisible God we worship.

May we reach out to one another
with greater love and better understanding;
we pray for our homes, our relatives,
our neighbours and our friends,
particularly those who do not yet realise
the extent of God's love for them.

Silence

Christ is the image:
of the invisible God we worship.

May those who have been scattered
far from their homes and loved ones
be enabled to live again in peace and happiness;
may the bitter and resentful find hope again
and the confused find new direction.

Silence

Christ is the image:
of the invisible God we worship.

May the dying know the closeness of God,
and those who mourn their loved ones
know for certain that God's kingdom
stretches across both sides of death.

Silence

Christ is the image:
of the invisible God we worship.

We pray with Mary,
Mother of Christ the King:
Hail, Mary . . .

In the warmth of God's love,
we pray in silence now
for our own particular concerns.

Silence

Celebrant
God our Father,
we ask you to accept our prayers,
through Christ our Lord.
Amen.

TREASURE SEEKERS

Aim: To know and celebrate that Jesus is our King.

Starter

Scatter different coloured and named circles all over the floor, one for each person. Everyone starts by standing on their own circle. When the music starts, everyone moves and dances around. When the music stops, they go and stand on their spot. A matching set of named circles (small ones) are in a basket, and one is drawn and that person is given a crown to wear. When the music starts this time, everyone follows what the King or Queen does. The crown is changed each time the music stops, and you can easily give everyone a go by removing their name from the basket once it has been chosen.

Teaching

Hold the crown and talk about what kings are often like in fairy stories, establishing that they are usually the most important person in the kingdom, with lots of power and lots of money.

As Christians, we belong to a kingdom. It's a kingdom of love and joy and peace and goodness and forgiveness. Anyone in any country can be part of this kingdom, if they ask to be. It's a kingdom which grows bigger and bigger as more people get to meet with God. And our King is someone who was born in a stable, and died on a cross, and came back to life again. Do you know his name? Yes, it's Jesus. And if we are part of the family of God, which we are, that means we are princes and princesses in the kingdom of God!

Praying

Dear Jesus,
you are my friend
and yet you are a King!
I am glad I live
in your kingdom.

Activities

The worksheet can be decorated and turned into a crown, which the children can wear as they sing some songs to celebrate, such as:

* *Who's the king of the jungle?*
* *I rejoice in making Jesus happy*
* *I'm H - A - P - P - Y*
* *If you're happy and you know it*

PEARL DIVERS

Aim: To explore the kind of King Jesus is.

Starter

What/who am I? Someone thinks of a person or thing, and the others ask questions to discover who or what it is. Only yes and no answers are allowed.

Teaching

In that game we were finding out more and more about the person or object until we were sure we knew who or what it was. Write up the name 'Jesus' in large letters in the middle of a sheet of paper and write around it all the things we have discovered about Jesus in our lives so far. Already we know quite a bit about him, and we are getting to know him in person as well. Encourage them to keep on their praying every day, and see if any of them have still got a prayer habit, and are using their prayer corner that they made this year. If we've got a bit slack, let's get that going again.

Today we are celebrating Jesus Christ as King. What kind of a King is Jesus?

On another sheet, with a crown with Jesus' name on it in the middle, collect their ideas about this, prompting them if necessary with suggestions of things Jesus isn't, like bossy, proud, or greedy. Then draw a cross going through the crown; the cross is a better sign for our King because all the things we've written are to do with love, which he showed by dying for us on the cross.

Read them today's Gospel to remind ourselves of just how loving and forgiving our King is.

Praying

When I survey the wondrous cross
on which the Prince of Glory died,
my richest gain I count but loss,
and pour contempt on all my pride.

Were the whole realm of nature mine
that were an offering far too small;
love so amazing, so divine,
demands my soul, my life, my all.

Activities

On the worksheet there are instructions for making a jigsaw in which the central piece which holds the rest together is in the shape of a cross.

GOLD PANNERS

Aim: To see how in Jesus all things are reconciled.

Starter

Make a fruit salad with everyone adding a particular ingredient until the whole thing is assembled. This can be spooned into disposable dishes for them to eat at the end of the service or session, or covered with clingfilm and taken home to eat or give away.

Teaching

Our fruit salad was made by bringing lots of different things together, and today, as we celebrate the feast of Christ the King at the end of the Church Year, we remember the way all things are brought together in Christ. The cross he died on is like a central hub of everything, reconciling humans to their maker, and reaching out to all times and places with the sign of God's love.

Give everyone two pieces of wood (such as spent matches) and a piece of wire with which to make a simple cross shape. They hold these while you all read the passage from Colossians.

Now read the Gospel, again holding the crosses, listening out for any 'reconciling' which is going on. Apart from the great act of giving his life for us so that we can live, notice the forgiveness and the reaching out to the thief beside him. For Jesus, his King's crown is a plait of thorns, and his throne is a cross of execution. Through him God and sinners are reconciled.

Praying

I rejoiced when I heard them say:
'Let us go to God's house.'
And now our feet are standing
within your gates, O Jerusalem.
Jerusalem is built as a city
strongly compact.
It is there that the tribes go up,
the tribes of the Lord.
For Israel's law it is,
there to praise the Lord's name.
There were set the thrones of judgement
of the house of David.

(From Psalm 121)

Activities

Hold the crosses as you bring to mind someone who you long to be reconciled to God through Christ. Construct one or two flags from lengths of fabric and canes, so that these can be waved during the hymns when you go into church. Instructions are on the sheet.

APPENDIX

Waiting for your Spirit
(Sixth Sunday of Easter)

Text: Mick Gisbey
Music: Mick Gisbey, arr. Noel Rawsthorne

Come, Spirit, come, prise open my heart
(Eighth Sunday of the Year)

2. Come, Spirit, come, take charge of my mind.
   Show me the darkness that you find.
   Help me to trust you, even with my shame,
   till I freely acknowledge where I am to blame.

3. Come, Spirit, come, bring life to my soul.
   Your forgiveness makes me whole.
   Then from the pain and stress of sin set free
   I am dazed by the awesome love you have for me.

Text: Susan Sayers
Music: Susan Sayers, arr. Donald Thomson
© Copyright 1997 Kevin Mayhew Ltd.